HALF Taste of Home homemade

TASTE OF HOME BOOKS • RDA ENTHUSIAST BRANDS, LLC • MILWAUKEE, WI

© 2019 RDA Enthusiast Brands, LLC.
1610 N. 2nd St., Suite 102,
Milwaukee WI 53212-3906

Title Banner: pa3x/Shutterstock
Title Lettering: Very_Very/Shutterstock

Visit us at **tasteofhome.com** for other Taste of Home books and products.

International Standard Book Number:
978-1-61765-837-2 (Paperback)
978-1-61765-974-4 (Hard Cover)

Library of Congress Control Number:
2018957773

Deputy Editor: Mark Hagen
Senior Art Director: Raeann Thompson
Editor: Amy Glander
Designer: Jazmin Delgado
Copy Editor: Ann Walter

Cover Photographer: Dan Roberts
Cover Food Stylist: Lauren Knoelke
Cover Set Stylist: Dee Dee Schaefer

Pictured on front cover: Easy Cheddar Chicken Potpie, p. 258
Pictured on spine: Herbed Bread Twists, p. 123
Pictured on back cover (clockwise from top): Slow-Cooker Spicy Pork Chili, p. 125; Easy Nutella Cheesecake, p. 314; Southwestern Fish Tacos, p. 235; Easy Irish Cream, p. 106; Cranberry Salad, p. 212; Ham & Cheese Biscuit Stacks, p. 62

Printed in China
5 7 9 10 8 6 (Paperback)
1 3 5 7 9 10 8 6 4 2 (Hard Cover)

155

LIKE US
facebook.com/tasteofhome

TWEET US
twitter.com/tasteofhome

FOLLOW US
@ tasteofhome

PIN US
pinterest.com/taste_of_home

SHOP WITH US shoptasteofhome.com

SHARE A RECIPE tasteofhome.com/submit

CONTENTS

Beautiful
Brunch Dishes.............................6

Party-Time
Classics 58

Shortcut
Soups & Breads 110

Scrumptious
Salads & Sides 162

Easy Meals.............................. 214

Sweet &
Simple Finales 266

Index.................................318

AT-A-GLANCE ICONS:

FAST FIX | 5 INGREDIENTS | SLOW COOKER | FREEZE IT

To make finding the ideal recipes easy,
refer to the four handy icons as you
flip though the pages of this book.

Here's to All Your Mealtime Faves
that are (almost) homemade!

Time-pressed cooks, rejoice! With *Taste of Home Half Homemade*, see just how easy it is to combine from-scratch flavor with time-saving convenience!

It's crunch time. Between work, school, chores, errands, holidays, birthdays and other special events, planning a delicious homemade meal can sometimes seem impossible. So what's a busy cook to do?

A beat-the-clock strategy to cooking smarter, not harder, is already in your hands. Introducing *Taste of Home Half Homemade*, the only cookbook that helps you serve satisfying family favorites packed with authentic cooked-all-day flavor in less time by combining fresh ingredients with shortcut, at-the-ready convenience items.

These are the recipes great home cooks love to share—and you will, too. From saucy Ravioli Lasagna (p. 245) to creamy Banana Cream Pie with Cake Mix Crust (p. 312) and everything in between, you can make any day

memorable with a heartwarming dish that takes less time to prep, uses fewer ingredients and delivers foolproof results.

You'll also find enticing brunch specialties, comforting soups, bubbly casseroles, popular appetizers, classic salads and sides, tempting desserts and other keeper recipes you'll be proud to include in your repertoire.

With 337 incredible dishes that come together in no time, getting a home-cooked meal on the table has never been easier!

98

"This is an amazing recipe. Very tasty and quick to make. We serve it often, either as an appetizer or beside a soup for supper. I usually do about 1½ times the cheese mixture, as we like a lot of the gooey, bubbly, warm topping." — DABAKER55126

289

112

"I made this for a group of friends and they said it was the best artichoke dip they've ever had! And then they asked for the recipe. Delicious!"

—COUNTRY-GIRL99

"This was quick, easy and refreshing in the hot summertime. I used vanilla ice cream and blueberries, and everybody loved it."

—MATTELIZ

EGG BASKETS BENEDICT,
PAGE 39

CHAPTER 1

Beautiful Brunch Dishes

Good mornings are guaranteed thanks to luscious sweet rolls, elegant breakfasts and coffeehouse specialties—all made easy!

FAST FIX

VERY VANILLA FRENCH TOAST

These French toast slices have creamy vanilla flavor from convenient pudding mix, plus a hint of cinnamon. We like to top them with fresh berries.

—Linda Bernhagen, Plainfield, IL

Takes: 10 min. • **Makes:** 4 servings

- 1 cup whole milk
- 1 pkg. (3 oz.) cook-and-serve vanilla pudding mix
- 1 large egg
- ½ tsp. ground cinnamon
- 8 slices Texas toast
- 2 tsp. butter

1. In a large bowl, whisk the milk, pudding mix, egg and cinnamon until well blended, about 2 minutes. Dip the toast in pudding mixture, coating both sides.

2. In a large cast-iron or other heavy skillet, melt butter over medium heat. Cook bread on both sides until golden brown.

2 slices: 336 cal., 8g fat (3g sat. fat), 65mg chol., 562mg sod., 57g carb. (21g sugars, 2g fiber), 9g pro.

CHILE RELLENOS SOUFFLE

After we spent the night at our friends' house in Arizona, we awoke to the tantalizing aroma of an egg souffle. When I make it now, it brings back wonderful memories.
—*Pat Coyne, Las Vegas, NV*

- -

Prep: 15 min. • **Bake:** 45 min.
Makes: 8 servings

    2   cans (4 oz. each) chopped
        green chilies
    ¼   cup sliced ripe olives
    ¼   cup finely chopped onion
    2   cups sharp shredded cheddar cheese
    4   large eggs
    1½ cups biscuit/baking mix
    2   cups 2% milk
    ¼   tsp. pepper
    1   cup 4% small-curd cottage cheese
        Salsa and sour cream, optional

1. Preheat oven to 350°. Spread green chilies in a greased 11x7-in. baking dish; sprinkle with the olives, onion and cheese. In a large bowl, whisk eggs, biscuit mix, milk and pepper until blended. Stir in cottage cheese; pour mixture over top.

2. Bake, uncovered, until golden brown, 45-50 minutes, puffed and a knife inserted in the center comes out clean. Let stand 5-10 minutes before serving. If desired, serve with salsa and sour cream.

Make Ahead: Refrigerate unbaked souffle, covered, several hours or overnight. To use, preheat oven to 350°. Remove souffle from refrigerator while oven heats. Bake, as directed, increasing the time as necessary until golden, puffed and a knife inserted in the center comes out clean. Let souffle stand for 5-10 minutes before serving.

1 piece: 305 cal., 17g fat (8g sat. fat), 128mg chol., 708mg sod., 23g carb. (5g sugars, 1g fiber), 16g pro.

TEX-MEX BREAKFAST HAYSTACKS

I love hash brown haystacks and wanted to make a fun Tex-Mex version for my family. Adding panko crumbs and Mexican cheese to the potatoes before cooking gives them a golden brown color and crisp texture. These are also delicious for dinner.
—*Donna Ryan, Topsfield, MA*

- -

Prep: 25 min. • **Cook:** 15 min.
Makes: 6 servings

- ⅔ cup sour cream
- 3 thinly sliced green onions
- 2 Tbsp. oil-packed sun-dried tomatoes, chopped
- 2 Tbsp. minced fresh cilantro
- 2½ tsp. Tex-Mex seasoning, divided
- 1 pkg. (3½ cups) refrigerated shredded hash brown potatoes
- ½ cup panko (Japanese) bread crumbs
- ⅓ cup shredded Mexican cheese blend
- ¼ tsp. salt

- 5 Tbsp. canola oil, divided
- 6 large eggs
- ½ cup salsa
- 4 cooked bacon strips, coarsely chopped
  Finely chopped green onions, optional

1. Combine sour cream, green onions, sun-dried tomatoes, cilantro, and ½ tsp. Tex-Mex seasoning; set aside.

2. Squeeze hash brown potatoes dry with paper towel to remove excess liquid. In a large bowl, combine the potatoes, bread crumbs, Mexican cheese, salt and the remaining Tex-Mex seasoning.

3. On an electric griddle, heat 3 Tbsp. oil over medium-high heat. Drop potato mixture by ⅔ cupfuls into oil; press to flatten slightly. Fry, adding oil as needed, until crisp and golden brown, 5-7 minutes. Drain on paper towels; keep warm.

4. On same griddle, heat remaining oil over medium heat. Break eggs, one at a time, onto griddle. Reduce heat; cook until whites are set and yolks have begun to thicken. Flip eggs if desired; cook to desired doneness.

5. To assemble, top each potato patty with an egg, salsa, bacon and sour cream mixture. If desired, sprinkle with green onions.

1 serving: 399 cal., 27g fat (8g sat. fat), 205mg chol., 688mg sod., 25g carb. (3g sugars, 2g fiber), 14g pro.

TEST KITCHEN TIP

Make extra sour cream mixture and use it as a chip or veggie dip.

HAWAIIAN HAM STRATA

I came up with this sweet and savory recipe because I love Hawaiian pizza and wanted a casserole I could make ahead and pop in the oven at the last minute. This is a perfect main dish to take to a potluck.

—Lisa Renshaw, Kansas City, MO

- -

Prep: 20 min. • **Cook:** 35 min. + standing
Makes: 8 servings

8	English muffins, cut into eighths and toasted
3	cups cubed fully cooked ham
1	can (20 oz.) pineapple tidbits, drained
4	green onions, chopped
1	jar (4 oz.) diced pimientos, drained
1½	cups shredded cheddar cheese
¼	cup grated Parmesan cheese
1	jar (15 oz.) Alfredo sauce
1½	cups evaporated milk
4	large eggs, lightly beaten
½	tsp. salt
¼	tsp. cayenne pepper

1. Combine the first five ingredients. Transfer to a 13x9-in. baking dish; top with cheeses.
2. Whisk together the remaining ingredients. Pour the sauce over layers, pushing down, if necessary, with the back of a spoon to ensure muffins absorb liquid. Refrigerate, covered, 1 hour or overnight.
3. Preheat the oven to 350°. Remove strata from refrigerator while oven heats. Bake, uncovered, until the strata is golden and bubbly, 30-40 minutes. Let stand 10 minutes before serving.

1 piece: 515 cal., 22g fat (12g sat. fat), 177mg chol., 1512mg sod., 48g carb. (16g sugars, 3g fiber), 31g pro.

BRUNCH PIZZA SQUARES

I love using convenience items like the crescent rolls in these easy squares. Guests always ask me for the recipe. To hurry along the preparation of this dish, I frequently brown a few pounds of sausage ahead of time and keep it in the freezer.
—LaChelle Olivet, Pace, FL

- -

Takes: 30 min. • **Makes:** 8 servings

- 1 lb. bulk pork sausage
- 1 tube (8 oz.) refrigerated crescent rolls
- 4 large eggs
- 2 Tbsp. 2% milk
- ⅛ tsp. pepper
- ¾ cup shredded cheddar cheese

1. In a large skillet, crumble sausage and cook over medium heat until no longer pink; drain. Unroll crescent dough onto the bottom and ½ in. up the sides of a lightly greased 13x9-in. baking pan; seal seams. Sprinkle with sausage.
2. In a large bowl, beat the eggs, milk and pepper; pour over sausage. Sprinkle with cheddar cheese.
3. Bake, uncovered, at 400° until a knife inserted in the center comes out clean, about 15 minutes.
1 piece: 320 cal., 23g fat (7g sat. fat), 134mg chol., 664mg sod., 14g carb. (3g sugars, 0 fiber), 14g pro.

BANANA CHIP PANCAKES

Perfect for weekends or a special birthday-morning treat, these fluffy pancakes can be customized to your heart's content! One of my kids eats the plain banana pancakes, another likes just chocolate chips added, and a third one goes for the works.
—Christeen Kelley, Newark, CA

- -

Takes: 30 min. • **Makes:** 12 pancakes

- 2 cups biscuit/baking mix
- 1 large egg
- 1 cup whole milk
- 1 cup mashed ripe bananas
- ¾ cup swirled milk chocolate and peanut butter chips
  Maple syrup and additional swirled milk chocolate and peanut butter chips, optional

1. Place biscuit mix in a large bowl. Whisk the egg, milk and bananas; stir into biscuit mix just until moistened. Stir in chips.
2. Pour batter by ¼ cupfuls onto a greased hot griddle; turn when bubbles form on top. Cook until the second side is golden brown. Serve with maple syrup and additional chips if desired.
3 pancakes: 589 cal., 25g fat (16g sat. fat), 59mg chol., 903mg sod., 74g carb. (29g sugars, 3g fiber), 17g pro.

SAUSAGE BACON BITES

These tasty morsels are perfect with almost any egg dish or as finger foods that party guests can pop into their mouths.

—*Pat Waymire, Yellow Springs, OH*

- -

Prep: 20 min. + chilling • **Bake:** 35 min.
Makes: about 3½ dozen

- ¾ lb. sliced bacon
- 2 pkg. (8 oz. each) frozen fully cooked breakfast sausage links, thawed
- ½ cup plus 2 Tbsp. packed brown sugar, divided

1. Preheat oven to 350°. Cut bacon strips widthwise in half; cut sausage links in half. Wrap a piece of bacon around each piece of sausage. Place ½ cup brown sugar in a shallow bowl; roll sausages in sugar. Secure each with a toothpick. Place in a foil-lined 15x10x1-in. baking pan. Cover and refrigerate 4 hours or overnight.

2. Sprinkle with 1 Tbsp. brown sugar. Bake until bacon is crisp, 35-40 minutes, turning once. Sprinkle with remaining brown sugar.

1 piece: 51 cal., 4g fat (1g sat. fat), 6mg chol., 100mg sod., 4g carb. (4g sugars, 0 fiber), 2g pro.

CHILI & CHEESE CRUSTLESS QUICHE

This filling Tex-Mex egg casserole is perfect for breakfast or any meal of the day. I add a salad and dinner is on!

—*Gail Watkins, Norwalk, CA*

- -

Prep: 15 min. • **Cook:** 3 hours + standing
Makes: 6 servings

- 3 corn tortillas (6 in.)
- 2 cans (4 oz. each) whole green chilies
- 1 can (15 oz.) chili con carne
- 1½ cups shredded cheddar cheese, divided
- 4 large eggs
- 1½ cups 2% milk
- 1 cup biscuit/baking mix
- ¼ tsp. salt
- ¼ tsp. pepper
- 1 tsp. hot pepper sauce, optional
- 1 can (4 oz.) chopped green chilies
- 2 medium tomatoes, sliced
  Sour cream, optional

1. In a greased 4- or 5-qt. slow cooker, layer tortillas, whole green chilies, chili con carne and 1 cup cheese.
2. In a small bowl, whisk the eggs, milk, biscuit mix, salt, pepper and, if desired, pepper sauce until blended; pour into slow cooker. Top with chopped green chilies and tomatoes.
3. Cook, covered, on low 3-4 hours or until a thermometer reads 160°, sprinkling with remaining cheese during the last 30 minutes of cooking. Turn off slow cooker; remove insert. Let stand 15 minutes before serving. If desired, top with sour cream.
1 serving: 420 cal., 24g fat (11g sat. fat), 182mg chol., 1034mg sod., 32g carb. (7g sugars, 4g fiber), 20g pro.

GRANDMOTHER'S TOAD IN A HOLE

I have fond memories of Grandma's Yorkshire pudding wrapped around mini sausages, a puffy pancake dish my kids called "the boat." We slather it with butter and maple syrup for a meal that's out of this world.

—*Susan Kieboam, Amherstburg, ON*

- -

Prep: 10 min. + standing • **Bake:** 25 min.
Makes: 6 servings

- 3 large eggs
- 1 cup 2% milk
- ½ tsp. salt
- 1 cup all-purpose flour
- 1 pkg. (12 oz.) uncooked maple breakfast sausage links
- 3 Tbsp. olive oil
  Butter and maple syrup, optional

1. Preheat oven to 400°. In a small bowl, whisk eggs, milk and salt. Whisk flour into the egg mixture until blended. Let stand 30 minutes. Meanwhile, cook the sausage according to the package directions; cut each sausage into three pieces.
2. Place oil in a 12-in. nonstick ovenproof skillet. Place in oven until hot, 3-4 minutes. Stir batter and pour into prepared skillet; top with sausage. Bake until golden brown and puffed, 20-25 minutes. Remove from the skillet; cut into wedges. If desired, serve with butter and syrup.
1 wedge: 336 cal., 22g fat (6g sat. fat), 126mg chol., 783mg sod., 20g carb. (2g sugars, 1g fiber), 14g pro.

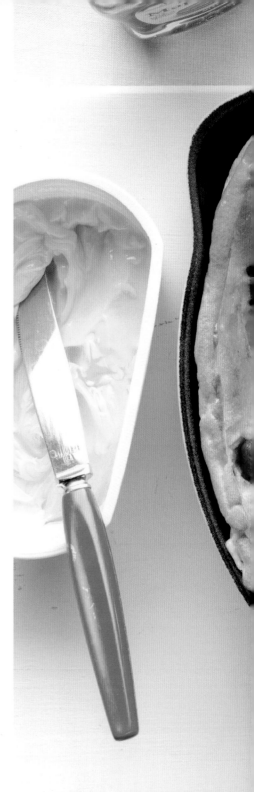

BLUEBERRY OATMEAL

We love homemade oatmeal, and this recipe topped with blueberries is a delightful choice. It's so delicious it could be eaten for dessert.
—*Lesley Robeson, Casper, WY*

Takes: 10 min. • **Makes:** 2 servings

- 1¾ **cups 2% milk**
- 1 **cup quick-cooking oats**
- ⅛ **tsp. salt**
- ⅓ **cup packed brown sugar**
- ½ **tsp. ground cinnamon**
- ¾ **cup fresh or frozen unsweetened blueberries, thawed**

In a small saucepan, bring milk to a boil. Stir in the oats and salt. Cook mixture over medium heat until the oatmeal is thickened, stirring occasionally, 1-2 minutes. Stir in the brown sugar and cinnamon. Divide between two serving bowls; top with blueberries.

1 cup: 455 cal., 7g fat (3g sat. fat), 16mg chol., 271mg sod., 89g carb. (57g sugars, 7g fiber), 13g pro.

SPINACH FETA STRATA

A friend shared this recipe with me. It was a new dish for me, but my family loved it the first time I made it, so it'll be a regular.
—*Pat Lane, Pullman, WA*

- -

Prep: 10 min. + chilling • **Bake:** 40 min.
Makes: 12 servings

- 10 slices French bread (1 in. thick) or 6 croissants, split
- 6 large eggs, lightly beaten
- 1½ cups 2% milk
- 1 pkg. (10 oz.) frozen chopped spinach, thawed and squeezed dry
- ½ tsp. salt
- ¼ tsp. ground nutmeg
- ¼ tsp. pepper
- 1½ cups shredded Monterey Jack cheese
- 1 cup crumbled feta cheese

1. In a greased 3-qt. or 13x9-in. baking dish, arrange French bread or croissant halves with sides overlapping.
2. In a large bowl, combine the eggs, milk, spinach, salt, nutmeg and pepper; pour over bread. Sprinkle with cheeses. Cover and refrigerate for 8 hours or overnight.
3. Remove from the refrigerator 30 minutes before baking. Bake, uncovered, at 350° until a knife inserted in the center comes out clean, 40-45 minutes. Let stand for 5 minutes before cutting. Serve warm.
1 serving: 190 cal., 10g fat (5g sat. fat), 128mg chol., 443mg sod., 13g carb. (2g sugars, 2g fiber), 12g pro.

---

5 INGREDIENTS | FAST FIX
FRUITY FRAPPE

Making a copycat of a restaurant drink is fun, but better yet, I know exactly what's in this one. My frappe gets its sweetness from berries, juice and honey.
—*Patty Crouse, Warren, PA*

- -

Takes: 10 min. • **Makes:** 4 servings

- 1 cup water
- 1 cup fat-free milk
- ⅔ cup thawed orange juice concentrate
- 3 Tbsp. honey
- ½ tsp. vanilla extract
- 1 cup ice cubes
- 1 cup frozen unsweetened mixed berries

Place all ingredients in a blender; cover and process until blended. Serve immediately.
1¼ cups: 166 cal., 0 fat (0 sat. fat), 1mg chol., 28mg sod., 39g carb. (37g sugars, 1g fiber), 3g pro.

PUFF PASTRY DANISHES

Even though they're simple, these jam-filled pastries are right at home in a holiday brunch spread. They were my dad's favorite, so the recipe will always be close to my heart.
—*Chellie Helmke, Jackson Center, OH*

Prep: 30 min. • **Bake:** 15 min.
Makes: 1½ dozen

- 1 pkg. (8 oz.) cream cheese, softened
- ¼ cup sugar
- 2 Tbsp. all-purpose flour
- ½ tsp. vanilla extract
- 2 large egg yolks
- 1 Tbsp. water
- 1 pkg. (17.3 oz.) frozen puff pastry, thawed
- ⅔ cup seedless raspberry jam or jam of choice

1. Preheat oven to 425°. Beat first four ingredients until smooth; beat in 1 egg yolk.
2. Mix water and remaining egg yolk. On a lightly floured surface, unfold each sheet of puff pastry; roll into a 12-in. square. Cut each into nine 4-in. squares; transfer the squares to parchment-lined baking sheets.
3. Top each pastry square with 1 Tbsp. cream cheese mixture and 1 rounded tsp. jam. Bring two opposite corners of pastry over filling, sealing with yolk mixture. Brush the tops with remaining yolk mixture.
4. Bake until golden brown, 14-16 minutes. Serve warm. Refrigerate leftovers.
1 pastry: 197 cal., 12g fat (4g sat. fat), 33mg chol., 130mg sod., 20g carb. (3g sugars, 2g fiber), 3g pro.

FAST FIX
BERRY BREAKFAST PARFAITS

Expecting brunch company, but short on time? Parfaits are the perfect solution. Feel free to mix and match with berries you have on hand.
—*Lisa Speer, Palm Beach, FL*

Takes: 20 min. • **Makes:** 8 servings

- 6½ cups frozen unsweetened raspberries
- ¼ cup packed brown sugar
- ¼ cup orange juice
- 2 Tbsp. cornstarch
- ½ tsp. grated orange zest
- 2 cups fresh blueberries
- 2 cups fresh blackberries
- 2 cups granola
- 4 cups vanilla Greek yogurt
  Additional brown sugar, optional

1. Place the raspberries and brown sugar in a blender; cover and process until pureed. Press through a sieve; discard seeds.
2. In a small saucepan, combine raspberry puree, orange juice, cornstarch and orange zest. Cook and stir over medium heat until thickened and bubbly. Reduce heat to low; cook and stir 2 minutes longer. Remove from the heat; cool.
3. In eight parfait glasses, layer half of the raspberry sauce, berries, granola and yogurt. Repeat layers. Sprinkle with additional brown sugar if desired. Serve immediately.
1 parfait: 304 cal., 4g fat (0 sat. fat), 0 chol., 64mg sod., 54g carb. (27g sugars, 9g fiber), 17g pro.

PRESSURE-COOKER HAM & CHEDDAR BREAKFAST CASSEROLE

This easy, cheesy casserole has made many appearances at holiday breakfasts, potlucks, and even my daughter's college apartment to feed her hungry roommates. It's my go-to recipe for action-packed mornings.
—*Patty Bernhard, Greenville, OH*

Prep: 20 min. • **Cook:** 35 min. + releasing
Makes: 6 servings

- 6 **large eggs**
- ½ **cup 2% milk**
- ½ **tsp. salt**
- ¼ **tsp. pepper**
- 4 **cups frozen shredded hash brown potatoes, thawed**
- 1 **cup cubed fully cooked ham**
- ½ **medium onion, chopped**
- 2 **cups shredded cheddar cheese**
- 1 **cup water**

1. Whisk together eggs, milk, salt and pepper. Combine potatoes, ham, onion and cheese; transfer to a greased 2-qt. souffle or round baking dish; pour egg mixture over top.

2. Pour water into a 6-qt. electric pressure cooker. Cover baking dish with foil. Place on a trivet with handles; lower into pressure cooker. Lock lid; make sure vent is closed.

3. Select manual setting; adjust pressure to high, and set time for 35 minutes. When finished cooking, allow pressure to naturally release for 10 minutes, then quick-release any remaining pressure according to the manufacturer's directions. Let casserole stand 10 minutes before serving.

1 serving: 304 cal., 19g fat (9g sat. fat), 239mg chol., 816mg sod., 12g carb. (2g sugars, 1g fiber), 22g pro.

TEST KITCHEN TIP

Other cooked breakfast meats, such as bacon crumbles, turkey sausage or pork sausage, will also work well in this recipe.

PUMPKIN-CHOCOLATE CHIP PANCAKES

Who can resist a sky-high stack of golden, fluffy pancakes? Pumpkin and chocolate chips take them over the top!
—*Elizabeth Godecke, Chicago, IL*

Prep: 15 min. • **Cook:** 5 min./batch
Makes: 15 pancakes

- 2⅓ cups pancake mix
- ½ tsp. ground cinnamon
- ¼ tsp. ground nutmeg
- ¼ tsp. ground cloves
- 2 large eggs
- 1¼ cups buttermilk
- ⅓ cup canned pumpkin
- ¼ cup butter, melted
- 1 Tbsp. honey
- ½ cup miniature semisweet chocolate chips
  Additional miniature semisweet chocolate chips and honey

1. In a large bowl, combine pancake mix, cinnamon, nutmeg and cloves. In a small bowl, whisk eggs, buttermilk, pumpkin, butter and honey; stir into the dry ingredients just until moistened. Fold in chocolate chips.
2. Lightly grease a griddle; heat over medium heat. Pour batter by ¼ cupfuls onto griddle. Cook until bubbles on top begin to pop and bottoms are golden brown. Turn; cook until second side is golden brown. Serve with additional chocolate chips and honey.
3 pancakes: 422 cal., 18g fat (10g sat. fat), 111mg chol., 844mg sod., 57g carb. (18g sugars, 5g fiber), 11g pro.

start WITH **PANCAKE MIX**

ANDOUILLE SAUSAGE HASH

I threw this hash together at the last minute for a church brunch. Folks liked it so much they asked me for the recipe, so I scrambled to write it down.

—*Paulette Heisler, Tampa, FL*

Prep: 20 min. • **Bake:** 30 min.
Makes: 8 servings

- 1 Tbsp. canola oil
- 1 lb. fully cooked andouille sausage links or smoked kielbasa, cut into ¼-in. slices
- 1 pkg. (28 oz.) frozen O'Brien potatoes
- 1 jar (16 oz.) double-cheddar cheese sauce
- 3 Tbsp. Louisiana-style hot sauce
- 2 cups shredded sharp cheddar cheese
  Thinly sliced green onions, optional

1. Preheat oven to 425°. In a large skillet, heat oil over medium heat. Add sausage; cook and stir until sausage is browned, 6-8 minutes; remove with a slotted spoon. In same pan, add potatoes. Cover and cook over medium heat until potatoes are tender, 6-8 minutes, stirring occasionally. In a greased 11x7-in. baking dish, layer sausage and potatoes.
2. In a small bowl, combine cheese sauce and hot sauce; pour over potatoes. Sprinkle with cheese. Bake, uncovered, until bubbly and the cheese is golden brown, 30-35 minutes. If desired, sprinkle with green onions. Let stand 10 minutes before serving.
Make Ahead: Refrigerate unbaked hash, covered, several hours or overnight. To use, preheat oven to 425°. Remove hash from refrigerator while oven heats. Bake as directed, increasing time as necessary until golden brown. Let stand 5-10 minutes before serving.
1 serving: 443 cal., 32g fat (12g sat. fat), 126mg chol., 1357mg sod., 21g carb. (2g sugars, 2g fiber), 21g pro.

SIMPLE ICED COFFEE

My husband came up with this recipe to replace the soda he was drinking every morning. It's a delicious and affordable alternative to coffee-house versions.

—*Sarah Lange, Watertown, WI*

Takes: 5 min. • **Makes:** 8 servings

- 2 cups water
- ¼ cup instant coffee granules
- ¼ to ½ cup sugar
- 4 cups 2% milk
- 2 cups half-and-half cream
- 2 tsp. vanilla extract or hazelnut flavoring syrup, optional

1. Microwave water 90 seconds. Stir in instant coffee. Add sugar.
2. Stir in milk, cream and, if desired, extract or flavoring until combined. Serve over ice.
1 cup: 174 cal., 8g fat (6g sat. fat), 40mg chol., 88mg sod., 15g carb. (14g sugars, 0 fiber), 6g pro.

SLOW-COOKER HAM & EGGS

This is good any time of the year, especially on holiday mornings. Once it's in the slow cooker, it requires little attention.

—*Andrea Schaak, Jordan, MN*

Prep: 15 min. • **Cook:** 3 hours
Makes: 6 servings

- 6 large eggs
- 1 cup biscuit/baking mix
- ⅔ cup 2% milk
- ⅓ cup sour cream
- 2 Tbsp. minced fresh parsley
- 2 garlic cloves, minced
- ½ tsp. salt
- ½ tsp. pepper
- 1 cup cubed fully cooked ham
- 1 cup shredded Swiss cheese
- 1 small onion, finely chopped
- ⅓ cup shredded Parmesan cheese

1. In a large bowl, whisk the first eight ingredients until blended; stir in remaining ingredients. Pour into a greased 3- or 4-qt. slow cooker.
2. Cook, covered, on low 3-4 hours or until eggs are set. Cut into wedges.
1 serving: 315 cal., 18g fat (9g sat. fat), 256mg chol., 942mg sod., 17g carb. (4g sugars, 1g fiber), 21g pro.

SAUSAGE SPINACH BAKE

A friend gave me this delicious recipe, which uses a packaged stuffing mix. It's so versatile, you can serve it at any meal. A fresh salad and bread of your choice is all you'll need to make it a full lunch or dinner.
—*Kathleen Grant, Swan Lake, MT*

Prep: 20 min. • **Bake:** 40 min.
Makes: 12 servings

- 1 pkg. (6 oz.) savory herb-flavored stuffing mix
- ½ lb. bulk pork sausage
- ¼ cup chopped green onions
- ½ tsp. minced garlic
- 1 pkg. (10 oz.) frozen chopped spinach, thawed and squeezed dry
- 1½ cups shredded Monterey Jack cheese
- 1½ cups half-and-half cream
- 3 large eggs
- 2 Tbsp. grated Parmesan cheese

1. Prepare stuffing according to package directions. Meanwhile, crumble sausage into a large skillet. Add onions; cook over medium heat until meat is no longer pink. Add garlic; cook 1 minute longer. Drain.

2. In a large bowl, combine the stuffing, sausage mixture and spinach. Transfer to a greased 11x7-in. baking dish; sprinkle with shredded Monterey Jack cheese. In a small bowl, combine cream and eggs; pour over sausage mixture.

3. Bake at 400° until a thermometer reads 160°, 35-40 minutes. Sprinkle with grated Parmesan cheese; bake until bubbly, about 5 minutes longer.

1 slice: 258 cal., 17g fat (9g sat. fat), 95mg chol., 494mg sod., 14g carb. (2g sugars, 2g fiber), 11g pro.

CORN CAKES WITH POACHED EGGS

These easy corn cakes are tender thanks to the creamed corn in the batter. Top them with poached eggs and fresh salsa, and you have one of my favorite breakfasts.

—Jamie Jones, Madison, GA

- -

Prep: 30 min. • **Cook:** 15 min.
Makes: 4 servings

SALSA
- 3 plum tomatoes, seeded and coarsely chopped
- ¼ cup finely chopped sweet onion
- ¼ cup chopped sweet red pepper
- ¼ cup chopped green pepper
- 1 Tbsp. minced fresh cilantro
- 1 Tbsp. lime juice
- 1½ tsp. honey
- ½ tsp. salt
- ⅛ to ¼ tsp. cayenne pepper
- ⅛ tsp. pepper

CORN CAKES
- 1 can (14¾ oz.) cream-style corn
- 1 pkg. (6½ oz.) cornbread/muffin mix
- ½ cup water

EGGS
- 1 Tbsp. white vinegar
- 4 large eggs

1. In a bowl, combine all salsa ingredients; let stand at room temperature while preparing corn cakes.

2. In a large bowl, mix corn, muffin mix and water. Lightly grease a griddle; heat over medium heat. Pour batter by ⅓ cupfuls onto griddle. Cook until bubbles on top begin to pop and bottoms are golden brown. Turn; cook until second side is golden brown.

3. Meanwhile, place 2-3 in. of water in a large saucepan or skillet with high sides; add white vinegar. Bring liquid to a boil; adjust heat to maintain a gentle simmer. Break cold eggs, one at a time, into a small bowl; holding bowl close to surface of water, slip egg into water.

4. Cook, uncovered, until whites are completely set and yolks begin to thicken but are not hard, 3-5 minutes Using a slotted spoon, lift eggs out of water. Serve with corn cakes and salsa.

2 corn cakes with 1 egg and ½ cup salsa: 366 cal., 11g fat (3g sat. fat), 187mg chol., 1019mg sod., 58g carb. (17g sugars, 5g fiber), 12g pro.

HASH BROWN PANCAKES WITH SMOKED SALMON & DILL CREAM

On weekends when I was growing up, pancakes, salmon and bagels were our brunch staples. I've combined the concepts and use whipped cream instead of cream cheese.
—*Arlene Erlbach, Morton Grove, IL*

Prep: 15 min. • **Cook:** 20 min.
Makes: 4 servings

- ⅓ cup heavy whipping cream
- 1⅛ tsp. dill weed, divided
- 4 cups frozen shredded hash brown potatoes, thawed
- 2 large eggs, beaten
- 2 Tbsp. minced chives
- ¼ tsp. salt
- 1 pkg. (3 to 4 oz.) smoked salmon or lox

1. Beat heavy whipping cream and 1 tsp. dill on high until stiff peaks form. Cover and refrigerate.

2. Preheat griddle over medium heat. Stir together the potatoes, eggs, chives and salt until well combined. Grease griddle. Drop potato mixture by heaping ½ cupfuls onto griddle; flatten to ½ in. thick. Cook until the bottoms are golden brown, about 10 minutes. Turn; cook until second sides are golden brown. Keep warm.

3. To serve, place salmon slices on pancakes. Top with whipped cream; sprinkle with remaining dill.

1 serving: 187 cal., 11g fat (6g sat. fat), 125mg chol., 350mg sod., 14g carb. (1g sugars, 1g fiber), 9g pro.

BIRTHDAY CAKE WAFFLES

Soft on the inside and crisp on the outside, these waffles taste just like cake! They make birthday mornings, or any day, feel special.
—*Andrea Fetting, Green Bay, WI*

Prep: 20 min. • **Cook:** 25 min.
Makes: 6 waffles

- 1 cup all-purpose flour
- 1 cup (about 5 oz.) confetti cake mix or flavor of choice
- 2 Tbsp. cornstarch
- 3 tsp. baking powder
- ¼ tsp. salt
- 2 Tbsp. rainbow sprinkles, optional
- 2 large eggs
- 1¾ cups 2% milk
- ¾ to 1 cup plain Greek yogurt
- ½ tsp. vanilla extract
- ½ tsp. almond extract

CREAM CHEESE FROSTING
- 4 oz. softened cream cheese or reduced-fat cream cheese
- ¼ cup butter, softened
- 1½ to 2 cups confectioners' sugar
- ½ tsp. vanilla extract
- 1 to 3 Tbsp. 2% milk

1. Preheat oven to 300°. Combine the first five ingredients and, if desired, rainbow sprinkles. In another bowl, whisk eggs, milk, yogurt and extracts. Add yogurt mixture to flour mixture; mix until smooth.

2. Preheat waffle maker coated with cooking spray. Pour batter and bake waffles according to the manufacturer's directions until golden brown. Transfer cooked waffles to oven until ready to serve.

3. For frosting, beat cream cheese and butter on high until light and fluffy, 2-3 minutes. Gradually beat in confectioners' sugar, ½ cup at a time, until smooth. Beat in vanilla. Add enough milk to reach desired consistency. Spread over warm waffles. For a cakelike look, cut waffles into fourths and stack them; decorate with birthday candles.

1 waffle: 528 cal., 22g fat (13g sat. fat), 115mg chol., 695mg sod., 72g carb. (45g sugars, 1g fiber), 10g pro.

LOADED TATER TOT BAKE

I keep frozen Tater Tots on hand for dishes like this yummy casserole. It's a super brunch, breakfast or side dish that everyone loves.
—*Nancy Heishman, Las Vegas, NV*

Prep: 15 min. • **Bake:** 35 min.
Makes: 6 servings

- 1 Tbsp. canola oil
- 1 medium onion, finely chopped
- 6 oz. Canadian bacon, cut into ½-in. strips
- 4 cups frozen Tater Tots, thawed
- 6 large eggs, lightly beaten
- ½ cup reduced-fat sour cream
- ½ cup half-and-half cream
- 1 Tbsp. dried parsley flakes
- ¾ tsp. garlic powder
- ½ tsp. pepper
- 1½ cups shredded cheddar cheese

1. Preheat oven to 350°. In a large skillet, heat oil over medium heat. Add onion; cook and stir until tender, 2-3 minutes. Add Canadian bacon; cook until bacon is lightly browned, 1-2 minutes, stirring occasionally. Remove from heat.

2. Line bottom of a greased 11x7-in. baking dish with Tater Tots; top with Canadian bacon mixture. In a large bowl, whisk the eggs, sour cream, cream and seasonings until blended. Stir in cheese; pour over top of Tater Tots and bacon. Bake, uncovered, until golden brown, 35-40 minutes.

1 piece: 443 cal., 29g fat (12g sat. fat), 243mg chol., 917mg sod., 23g

SPINACH-EGG BREAKFAST PIZZAS

I like my food to look pretty, and these sunny breakfast pizzas are eye-popping. Bring them to the table with a bowl of berries or grapes and coffee.
—*Lily Julow, Lawrenceville, GA*

Prep: 20 min. • **Bake:** 15 min.
Makes: 4 pizzas

Cornmeal
1   loaf (1 lb.) frozen pizza
    dough, thawed
1   Tbsp. plus additional extra
    virgin olive oil, divided
5   to 6 oz. fresh baby spinach
⅓   cup plus additional grated
    Parmesan cheese, divided
3   Tbsp. sour cream
1   small garlic clove, minced
¼   tsp. sea salt
⅛   tsp. plus additional coarsely
    ground pepper, divided
4   large eggs

1. Preheat oven to 500°. Line two 15x10x1-in. baking pans with parchment; sprinkle lightly with cornmeal. Cut dough into four pieces; stretch and shape into 6- to 7-in. circles and place in pans.
2. Meanwhile, in a large skillet, heat 1 Tbsp. olive oil over medium-high heat. Add spinach; cook and stir just until spinach starts to wilt, 1-2 minutes. Combine spinach with next five ingredients; spread spinach mixture over each pizza. Leave a slight border of raised dough along edge. Bake on a lower oven rack about 5 minutes.
3. Remove from oven; break an egg into center of each pizza. Return to lower oven rack, baking until egg whites are set but yolks are still runny, 6-10 minutes. Drizzle olive oil over pizzas; top with additional Parmesan and pepper. Serve immediately.
1 pizza: 433 cal., 14g fat (4g sat. fat), 199mg chol., 865mg sod., 55g carb. (3g sugars, 1g fiber), 16g pro.

start WITH
CREAM CHEESE

ORANGE DREAM PULL-APART BREAD

My therapy is to bake treats for friends and co-workers. This pull-apart bread makes everyone smile as they face a busy day.
—*Vickie Friday Martin, Scroggins, TX*

Prep: 25 min. • **Bake:** 35 min.
Makes: 10 servings

- 1 pkg. (8 oz.) cream cheese
- 2 tubes (7½ oz. each) small refrigerated buttermilk biscuits (10 count)
- 1 cup packed brown sugar
- 1 cup chopped pecans
- 4 tsp. grated orange zest
- ½ cup butter, melted

1. Preheat oven to 375°. Cut the cream cheese into 20 pieces. Using a small knife, cut a horizontal pocket into the side of each biscuit; fill each with a piece of cream cheese. Pinch opening to seal.
2. In a shallow bowl, mix brown sugar, pecans and orange zest. Dip the biscuits in melted butter; roll in brown sugar mixture. Stand biscuits on their side in a greased 10-in. fluted tube pan.
3. Bake until golden brown, 35-40 minutes. Cool in pan 5 minutes before inverting onto a serving plate. Serve warm.
2 filled biscuits: 444 cal., 30g fat (12g sat. fat), 49mg chol., 612mg sod., 42g carb. (25g sugars, 1g fiber), 5g pro.

5 INGREDIENTS | FAST FIX

SAUSAGE CHEESE BISCUITS

These biscuits are a brunch-time favorite. I love that they don't require any special ingredients.
—*Marlene Neideigh, Myrtle Point, OR*

Takes: 30 min. • **Makes:** 10 servings

- 1 tube (12 oz.) refrigerated buttermilk biscuits (10 count)
- 1 pkg. (8 oz.) frozen fully cooked breakfast sausage links, thawed
- 2 large eggs, beaten
- ½ cup shredded cheddar cheese
- 3 Tbsp. chopped green onions

1. Preheat oven to 400°. Roll out each biscuit into a 5-in. circle; place each in an ungreased muffin cup. Cut sausages into fourths; brown in a skillet. Drain. Divide the sausages among muffin cups.
2. In a small bowl, combine eggs, cheese and onions; spoon into cups. Bake until browned, 13-15 minutes.
1 biscuit: 227 cal., 16g fat (6g sat. fat), 57mg chol., 548mg sod., 16g carb. (3g sugars, 0 fiber), 8g pro.

CHEESY POTATO EGG BAKE

I whipped up this cozy egg bake with potato crowns for an easy breakfast-for-dinner—or "brinner," as I like to call it. Add in extras that suit your tastes such as sweet bell peppers, onions, broccoli or carrots.

—*Amy Lents, Grand Forks, ND*

Prep: 20 min. • **Bake:** 45 min.
Makes: 12 servings

1	lb. bulk lean turkey breakfast sausage
1¾	cups sliced baby portobello mushrooms, chopped
4	cups fresh spinach, coarsely chopped
6	large eggs
1	cup 2% milk
	Dash seasoned salt
2	cups shredded cheddar cheese
6	cups frozen potato crowns

1. Preheat oven to 375°. In a large skillet, cook sausage over medium heat until meat is no longer pink, 5-7 minutes, breaking into crumbles. Add mushrooms and spinach; cook until mushrooms are tender and spinach is wilted, 2-4 minutes longer.

2. Spoon sausage mixture into a greased 13x9-in. baking dish. In a large bowl, whisk eggs, milk and seasoned salt until blended; pour over the sausage mixture. Layer with cheese and potato crowns.

3. Bake, uncovered, until set and top is crisp, 45-50 minutes.

1 piece: 315 cal., 20g fat (7g sat. fat), 154mg chol., 910mg sod., 16g carb. (2g sugars, 2g fiber), 20g pro.

CHEESE & SAUSAGE BREAKFAST PIZZA

My unique breakfast pizza with salsa and sausage is a crowd-pleaser at church events. Try a piece with a dash of sweet and spicy Tiger Sauce.

—*Kelly Buckley, Norton, KS*

Prep: 25 min. • **Bake:** 25 min.
Makes: 12 servings

- 1 lb. bulk pork sausage
- 1 medium onion, finely chopped
- ¼ cup salsa
- ½ tsp. onion powder
- ½ tsp. ground coriander
- ½ tsp. ground cumin
- 2 tubes (8 oz. each) refrigerated crescent rolls
- 2 cups shredded cheddar cheese
- 8 large eggs
- ¼ cup grated Parmesan cheese
- ¼ cup 2% milk
- ¼ tsp. salt
- ¼ tsp. pepper
  Tiger Sauce, optional

1. Preheat oven to 350°. In a large skillet, cook sausage and onion over medium heat until sausage is no longer pink, 5-7 minutes, breaking up sausage into crumbles; drain. Stir in salsa and seasonings. Remove from heat.

2. Unroll both tubes of crescent dough and press onto the bottom and up sides of an ungreased 15x10x1-in. baking pan. Press perforations to seal. Top with sausage mixture and cheddar cheese. In a bowl, whisk eggs, Parmesan cheese, milk, salt and pepper until blended; pour over sausage and cheese.

3. Bake pizza on a lower oven rack until crust is lightly browned and egg mixture is set, 23-28 minutes. If desired, serve pizza with Tiger Sauce.

Note: This recipe was tested with TryMe brand Tiger Sauce, a sweet and mildly spicy sauce. Look for it in the condiments section.

1 piece: 380 cal., 26g fat (10g sat. fat), 165mg chol., 798mg sod., 18g carb. (4g sugars, 0 fiber), 16g pro.

MAKE-AHEAD BISCUITS & GRAVY BAKE

Biscuits and gravy are usually prepared separately but served together. I created an easy way to bake them all at once.

—*Nancy McInnis, Olympia, WA*

Prep: 20 min. + chilling. • **Bake:** 25 min.
Makes: 10 servings

1	lb. bulk pork sausage
¼	cup all-purpose flour
3	cups 2% milk
1½	tsp. pepper
1	tsp. paprika
¼	tsp. chili powder
2¼	cups biscuit/baking mix
½	cup sour cream
¼	cup butter, melted

1. In a large skillet, cook the sausage over medium heat until no longer pink, breaking into crumbles, 6-8 minutes. Remove with a slotted spoon; discard drippings, reserving ¼ cup in pan. Stir in flour until blended; cook and stir until golden brown (do not burn), 1-2 minutes. Gradually whisk in milk. Bring to a boil, stirring constantly; cook and stir until thickened, 2-3 minutes. Stir in the sausage, pepper, paprika and chili powder. Pour into a greased 13x9-in. baking dish. Cool mixture completely.

2. Meanwhile, in a large bowl, mix the baking mix, sour cream and melted butter until the ingredients are moistened. Turn onto a lightly floured surface; knead gently 8-10 times.

3. Pat or roll dough to ¾-in. thickness; cut with a floured 2½-in. biscuit cutter. Place biscuits over gravy. Refrigerate casserole, covered, overnight.

4. Preheat oven to 400°. Remove casserole from refrigerator while oven heats. Bake, uncovered, until gravy is heated through and the biscuits are golden brown, 22-25 minutes.

Freeze option: Cover and freeze unbaked biscuits and gravy. To use, partially thaw in the refrigerator overnight. Remove baking dish from refrigerator 30 minutes before baking. Preheat oven to 400°. Bake as directed, increasing time as needed until gravy is heated through and biscuits are golden brown.

1 serving: 373 cal., 26g fat (11g sat. fat), 50mg chol., 640mg sod., 26g carb. (5g sugars, 1g fiber), 10g pro.

MINI HAM QUICHES

These adorable quiches are delightful for an after-church brunch when you don't want to fuss. Replace the ham with bacon, sausage, chicken or shrimp, or substitute chopped onion, red pepper or zucchini for the olives if you'd like.
—*Marilou Robinson, Portland, OR*

Prep: 15 min. • **Bake:** 20 min.
Makes: 1 dozen

- ¾   cup diced fully cooked ham
- ½   cup shredded sharp cheddar cheese
- ½   cup chopped ripe olives
- 3   large eggs, lightly beaten
- 1   cup half-and-half cream
- ¼   cup butter, melted
- 3   drops hot pepper sauce
- ½   cup biscuit/baking mix
- 2   Tbsp. grated Parmesan cheese
- ½   tsp. ground mustard

1. In a large bowl, combine the ham, cheddar cheese and olives; divide among 12 greased muffin cups. In another bowl, combine the remaining ingredients just until blended.
2. Pour over the ham mixture. Bake at 375° until a knife inserted in the center comes out clean, 20-25 minutes. Let stand for 5 minutes before serving.
1 serving: 141 cal., 11g fat (6g sat. fat), 84mg chol., 332mg sod., 5g carb. (1g sugars, 0 fiber), 6g pro.

READER RAVE

"I used sausage instead of ham, skipped the olives, put salsa in instead of hot pepper sauce, and it was still amazing!"
—JAVANZANDT, TASTEOFHOME.COM

CAMPER'S BREAKFAST HASH

I make this filling hash when we go camping. It's a favorite at home, too.
—*Linda Krivanek, Oak Creek, WI*

- -

Takes: 25 min. • **Makes:** 8 servings

¼ cup butter, cubed
2 pkg. (20 oz. each) refrigerated shredded hash brown potatoes
1 pkg. (7 oz.) frozen fully cooked breakfast sausage links, thawed and cut into ½-in. pieces
¼ cup chopped onion
¼ cup chopped green pepper
12 large eggs, lightly beaten
    Salt and pepper to taste
1 cup shredded cheddar cheese

1. In a deep 12-in. cast-iron or other heavy skillet, melt butter. Add potatoes, sausage, onion and green pepper. Cook, uncovered, over medium heat until potatoes are lightly browned, 15-20 minutes, turning once.

2. Push potato mixture to the sides of pan. Pour eggs into center of pan. Cook and stir over medium heat until eggs are completely set. Season with salt and pepper. Reduce heat; stir eggs into potato mixture. Top with cheese; cover and cook until the cheese is melted, 1-2 minutes.

1 cup: 376 cal., 27g fat (12g sat. fat), 364mg chol., 520mg sod., 17g carb. (2g sugars, 1g fiber), 18g pro.

ORANGE MARMALADE BREAKFAST BAKE

When I host brunch, I make something that can be prepped a day ahead so I have plenty of time to make other recipes the next day. This citrusy bake is always a winner. Feel free to use your favorite flavor of marmalade.
—*Judy Wilson, Sun City West, AZ*

Prep: 25 min. + chilling • **Bake:** 40 min.
Makes: 12 servings (1½ cups syrup)

  3 Tbsp. butter, softened
24 slices French bread (½ in. thick)
  1 jar (12 oz.) orange marmalade
  6 large eggs
2¾ cups 2% milk
⅓ cup sugar
  1 tsp. vanilla extract
¼ tsp. ground nutmeg
⅓ cup finely chopped walnuts
SYRUP
1¼ cups maple syrup
⅓ cup orange juice
  2 tsp. grated orange zest

1. Spread butter over one side of each bread slice. Arrange half of the the bread slices overlapping in a greased 3-qt. or 13x9-in. baking dish, buttered side down. Spread marmalade over bread slices; top with remaining bread slices, buttered side up.
2. In a large bowl, whisk eggs, milk, sugar, vanilla and nutmeg until blended; pour over bread. Refrigerate, covered, several hours or overnight.
3. Preheat oven to 350°. Remove casserole from refrigerator while oven heats. Sprinkle with walnuts. Bake, uncovered, until golden brown and a knife inserted in the center comes out clean, 40-50 minutes.
4. Let stand 5-10 minutes before serving. In a small saucepan, combine maple syrup, orange juice and zest; heat through. Serve with casserole.
1 piece with 2 Tbsp. syrup: 356 cal., 9g fat (4g sat. fat), 105mg chol., 244mg sod., 63g carb. (49g sugars, 1g fiber), 8g pro.

SALMON & ARTICHOKE QUICHE SQUARES

Salmon, goat cheese and artichoke hearts make this quiche feel a little fancy and taste extra delicious. Baked in an 11x7-in. dish, it comes together in a snap and makes enough to serve a hungry brunch crowd.
—*Jeanne Holt, Mendota Heights, MN*

Prep: 15 min. • **Bake:** 40 min. + cooling
Makes: 15 servings

- 1 tube (8 oz.) refrigerated crescent rolls
- ⅔ cup shredded Parmesan cheese, divided
- ½ cup crumbled goat cheese
- 1 cup thinly sliced smoked salmon fillets
- 1 cup water-packed artichoke hearts, drained
- ¼ cup chopped green onion (green portion only)
- 2 Tbsp. finely chopped fresh dill
- ¼ tsp. pepper
- 5 large eggs
- 1 cup heavy whipping cream

1. Preheat oven to 350°. Unroll dough into one long rectangle; place in an ungreased 11x7-in. baking dish. Press dough over the bottom and up the sides of dish, pressing perforations to seal.
2. Sprinkle with ⅓ cup Parmesan cheese. Top with goat cheese, salmon and artichoke hearts. Sprinkle with onion, chopped dill and pepper. Whisk eggs and cream; pour over salmon mixture. Sprinkle with remaining Parmesan cheese.
3. Bake until a knife inserted in center comes out clean, 40-45 minutes (loosely cover with foil if edges are getting too dark). Cool for 20 minutes. Cut into squares.
1 square: 179 cal., 13g fat (7g sat. fat), 89mg chol., 330mg sod., 8g carb. (2g sugars, 0 fiber), 8g pro.

5 INGREDIENTS | FAST FIX
EGG BASKETS BENEDICT

A little puff pastry turns Canadian bacon and eggs into a tasty update on eggs Benedict. I use a packaged hollandaise or cheese sauce for the finishing touch.
—*Sally Jackson, Fort Worth, TX*

Takes: 30 min.
Makes: 1 dozen (1 cup sauce)

- 1 sheet frozen puff pastry, thawed
- 12 large eggs
- 6 slices Canadian bacon, finely chopped
- 1 envelope hollandaise sauce mix

1. Preheat oven to 400°. On a lightly floured surface, unfold puff pastry. Roll into a 16x12-in. rectangle; cut into twelve 4-in. squares. Place in greased muffin cups, pressing gently onto bottoms and up sides, allowing corners to point up.

2. Break and slip an egg into center of each pastry cup; sprinkle with Canadian bacon. Bake until pastry is golden brown, egg whites are completely set, and yolks begin to thicken but are not hard, 10-12 minutes. Meanwhile, prepare the hollandaise sauce according to package directions.
3. Remove pastry cups to wire racks. Serve warm with hollandaise sauce.
1 pastry cup with about 1 Tbsp. sauce: 237 cal., 15g fat (6g sat. fat), 201mg chol., 355mg sod., 14g carb. (1g sugars, 2g fiber), 10g pro.

TEST KITCHEN TIP

Frozen puff pastry dough is available in sheets or individual shells. It has dozens of paper-thin layers of dough separated by butter. As it bakes, steam created from water in the dough makes the layers rise up and pull apart, resulting in a crisp, flaky pastry.

RED VELVET CINNAMON ROLLS

Turn a convenient box of red velvet cake mix into these easy breakfast rolls. The icing tastes just like the kind on Cinnabon treats.
—*Erin Wright, Wallace, KS*

Prep: 20 min. + rising • **Bake:** 15 min.
Makes: 12 servings

- 1 pkg. red velvet cake mix (regular size)
- 2½ to 3 cups all-purpose flour
- 1 pkg. (¼ oz.) active dry yeast
- 1¼ cups warm water (120° to 130°)
- ½ cup packed brown sugar
- 1 tsp. ground cinnamon
- ¼ cup butter, melted

ICING

- 2 cups confectioners' sugar
- 2 Tbsp. butter, softened
- 1 tsp. vanilla extract
- 3 to 5 Tbsp. 2% milk

1. Combine cake mix, 1 cup flour and yeast. Add water; beat on medium speed 2 minutes. Stir in enough remaining flour to form a soft dough (dough will be sticky). Turn onto a lightly floured surface; knead dough gently 6-8 times. Place in a greased bowl, turning once to grease the top. Cover dough and let rise in a warm place until doubled, about 2 hours. Meanwhile, in another bowl, mix brown sugar and cinnamon.
2. Punch down dough. Turn onto a lightly floured surface; roll dough into an 18x10-in. rectangle. Brush with melted butter to within ¼ in. of edges; sprinkle with sugar mixture.
3. Roll up jelly-roll style, starting with a long side; pinch seam to seal. Cut crosswise into 12 slices. Place in a greased 13x9-in. baking pan. Cover with a kitchen towel; let rise in a warm place until almost doubled, 1 hour.
4. Preheat oven to 350°. Bake until puffed and light brown, 15-20 minutes. Cool slightly.
5. Beat the confectioners' sugar, butter, vanilla and enough milk to reach a drizzling consistency. Drizzle icing over warm rolls.
1 roll: 429 cal., 10g fat (5g sat. fat), 16mg chol., 311mg sod., 81g carb. (48g sugars, 1g fiber), 5g pro.

FAST FIX
SAUSAGE, EGG & CHEDDAR FARMER'S BREAKFAST

This hearty combination of sausage, hash browns and eggs will warm you up on a cold winter morning.
—*Bonnie Roberts, Newaygo, MI*

Takes: 30 min. • **Makes:** 4 servings

- 6 large eggs
- ⅓ cup 2% milk
- ½ tsp. dried parsley flakes
- ¼ tsp. salt
- 6 oz. bulk pork sausage
- 1 Tbsp. butter
- 1½ cups frozen cubed hash brown potatoes, thawed
- ¼ cup chopped onion
- 1 cup shredded cheddar cheese

1. Whisk eggs, milk, parsley and salt; set aside. In a 9-in. cast-iron or other heavy skillet, cook sausage over medium heat until no longer pink; remove and drain. In same skillet, heat butter over medium heat. Add the potatoes and onion; cook and stir until tender, 5-7 minutes. Return sausage to pan.
2. Add egg mixture; cook and stir until almost set. Sprinkle with cheese. Cover and cook until cheese is melted, 1-2 minutes.
1 cup: 330 cal., 24g fat (11g sat. fat), 364mg chol., 612mg sod., 9g carb. (3g sugars, 1g fiber), 20g pro.

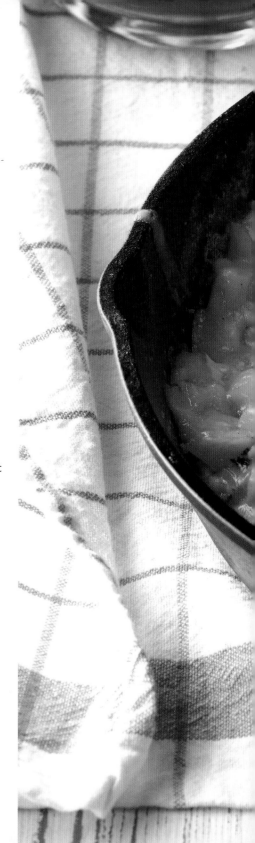

FRUITY CROISSANT PUFF

A good friend gave me this recipe. Sweet, tart, tender and light, it tastes like a danish.
—*Myra Almer, Tuttle, ND*

Prep: 10 min. + chilling • **Bake:** 45 min.
Makes: 6 servings

- 4 **large croissants, cut into 1-in. cubes (about 6 cups)**
- 1½ **cups mixed fresh berries**
- 1 **pkg. (8 oz.) cream cheese, softened**
- 1 **cup 2% milk**
- ½ **cup sugar**
- 2 **large eggs**
- 1 **tsp. vanilla extract**
  Maple syrup, optional

1. Place croissants and berries in a greased 8-in. square baking dish. In a medium bowl, beat cream cheese until smooth. Beat in milk, sugar, eggs and vanilla until blended; pour over croissants. Refrigerate, covered, for 8 hours or overnight.
2. Preheat oven to 350°. Remove casserole from refrigerator while oven heats.
3. Bake, covered, for 30 minutes. Remove the cover and bake until puffed and golden and a knife inserted in the center comes out clean, 15-20 minutes. Let stand 5-10 minutes before serving. If desired, serve with syrup.
1 serving: 429 cal., 24g fat (14g sat. fat), 132mg chol., 358mg sod., 44g carb. (27g sugars, 2g fiber), 9g pro.

start WITH LARGE CROISSANTS

FAST FIX

BREAKFAST SPUDS

Here's a dish that has it all—sweet potatoes, eggs, ham and cheese—for a powerful start to the day.

—*Annie Rundle, Muskego, WI*

Takes: 30 min. • **Makes:** 6 servings

- 1 pkg. (20 oz.) frozen sweet potato puffs
- 8 large eggs
- ⅓ cup 2% milk
- ¼ tsp. salt
- ⅛ tsp. pepper
- 1 cup cubed fully cooked ham
- 1 Tbsp. butter
  Shredded cheddar cheese and sliced green onions

1. Bake potato puffs according to package directions. In a large bowl, whisk eggs, milk, salt and pepper. Stir in ham.

2. In a large nonstick skillet, heat butter over medium heat. Add egg mixture; cook and stir until eggs are thickened and no liquid egg remains. Serve with potato puffs; sprinkle with cheese and green onions.

1 serving: 294 cal., 14g fat (4g sat. fat), 302mg chol., 752mg sod., 27g carb. (10g sugars, 2g fiber), 15g pro.

TEST KITCHEN TIP

You can also use frozen sweet potato hash browns in place of the puffs if you'd like.

SLOW-COOKER CHORIZO BREAKFAST CASSEROLE

My family asks for this slow-cooked casserole for breakfast and dinner. I serve it with white country gravy or mild salsa on the side—it's delightful either way.

—*Cindy Pruitt, Grove, OK*

Prep: 25 min. • **Cook:** 4 hours + standing
Makes: 8 servings

- 1 lb. fresh chorizo or bulk spicy pork sausage
- 1 medium onion, chopped
- 1 medium sweet red pepper, chopped
- 2 jalapeno peppers, seeded and chopped
- 1 pkg. (30 oz.) frozen shredded hash brown potatoes, thawed
- 1½ cups shredded Mexican cheese blend
- 12 large eggs
- 1 cup 2% milk
- ½ tsp. pepper
  Optional: chopped avocado, minced fresh cilantro and lime wedges

1. In a large skillet, cook chorizo, onion, red pepper and jalapenos over medium heat until cooked through and vegetables are tender, 7-8 minutes, breaking chorizo into crumbles; drain. Cool slightly.

2. In a greased 5-qt. slow cooker, layer a third of the potatoes, chorizo mixture and cheese. Repeat layers twice. In a large bowl, whisk the eggs, milk and pepper until blended; pour over top.

3. Cook, covered, on low 4-4½ hours or until the eggs are set and a thermometer reads 160°. Uncover and let stand for 10 minutes before serving. If desired, top servings with avocado, cilantro and lime wedges.

Note: Wear disposable gloves when cutting hot peppers; the oils can burn skin. Avoid touching your face.

1½ cups: 512 cal., 32g fat (12g sat. fat), 350mg chol., 964mg sod., 25g carb. (4g sugars, 2g fiber), 30g pro.

FRUITY WAFFLE PARFAITS

This recipe satisfied all of my cravings for breakfast when I was pregnant. I knew I was getting plenty of nutrition in each serving and it tasted wonderful.

—*Penelope Wyllie, San Francisco, CA*

Takes: 10 min. • **Makes:** 4 servings

- 4 frozen low-fat multigrain waffles
- ½ cup almond butter or creamy peanut butter
- 2 cups strawberry yogurt
- 2 large bananas, sliced
- 2 cups sliced fresh strawberries
  Toasted chopped almonds, optional
  Maple syrup, optional

1. Toast waffles according to the package directions. Spread each waffle with 2 Tbsp. almond butter. Cut waffles into bite-sized pieces.

2. Layer half of the yogurt, bananas, strawberries and waffle pieces into four parfait glasses. Repeat layers. If desired, top with toasted almonds and maple syrup. Serve immediately.

1 serving: 469 cal., 20g fat (4g sat. fat), 6mg chol., 337mg sod., 65g carb. (39g sugars, 8g fiber), 15g pro.

MINI SAUSAGE QUICHES

These bite-sized muffins are loaded with sausage and cheese. Their crescent roll bases make preparation a breeze. Serve the cuties at any brunch or potluck gathering.
—*Jan Mead, Milford, CT*

- -

Prep: 25 min. • **Bake:** 20 min.
Makes: 4 dozen

- ½ lb. bulk hot Italian sausage
- 2 Tbsp. dried minced onion
- 2 Tbsp. minced chives
- 1 tube (8 oz.) refrigerated crescent rolls
- 4 large eggs, lightly beaten
- 2 cups shredded Swiss cheese
- 1 cup 4% cottage cheese
- ⅓ cup grated Parmesan cheese
  Paprika

1. In a large skillet, brown sausage and onion over medium heat until meat is no longer pink, 4-5 minutes; drain. Stir in chives.

2. On a lightly floured surface, unroll crescent dough into one long rectangle; seal seams and perforations. Cut into 48 pieces. Press onto the bottom and up the sides of greased miniature muffin cups.

3. Fill each with about 2 tsp. of the sausage mixture. In a large bowl, combine the eggs and cheeses. Spoon 2 teaspoonfuls over sausage mixture. Sprinkle with paprika.

4. Bake at 375° until a knife inserted in the center comes out clean, 20-25 minutes. Cool for 5 minutes before removing from pans to wire racks. If desired, sprinkle with additional minced chives. Serve warm.

1 miniature muffin: 66 cal., 5g fat (2g sat. fat), 27mg chol., 116mg sod., 2g carb. (1g sugars, 0 fiber), 4g pro.

CAMPFIRE PANCAKES WITH PEANUT MAPLE SYRUP

My family loves eating s'mores around the campfire when we vacation at the lake. Campfire pancakes are my tribute to those happy times.

—*Cheryl Snavely, Hagerstown, MD*

Takes: 20 min.
Makes: 8 pancakes (¼ cup syrup)

- 1 pkg. (6½ oz.) chocolate chip muffin mix
- ⅔ cup 2% milk
- 1 large egg, lightly beaten
- ½ cup miniature marshmallows
- ¼ cup butterscotch chips
- ¼ cup maple syrup
- 1 Tbsp. chunky peanut butter

1. In a large bowl, combine muffin mix, milk and egg; stir just until moistened. Fold in the marshmallows and chips.

2. Lightly grease a griddle; heat over medium heat. Pour batter by ¼ cupfuls onto griddle. Cook until bubbles on top begin to pop and bottoms are golden brown. Turn; cook until second side is golden brown.

3. Meanwhile, microwave maple syrup and peanut butter in 10- to 20-second intervals until heated through. Serve with pancakes.

2 pancakes with 1 Tbsp. syrup mixture: 407 cal., 13g fat (7g sat. fat), 50mg chol., 386mg sod., 63g carb. (43g sugars, 2g fiber), 8g pro.

TEST KITCHEN TIP

For fast homemade freezer pancakes, prepare a batch and cool on a wire rack; freeze in a single layer on a baking sheet. When frozen, store in freezer containers. When ready to use, pop into the toaster or toaster oven to defrost and reheat.

BREAKFAST RELLENO

My family loves anything with southwestern flavor, so I turned classic chiles relleno into a hearty breakfast casserole. We became fans in an instant.

—*Joan Hallford, North Richland Hills, TX*

Prep: 10 min. • **Bake:** 35 min. + standing
Makes: 15 servings

- 1 pkg. (20 oz.) refrigerated shredded hash brown potatoes
- 1 can (27 to 28 oz.) whole green chilies
- 1 cup chunky salsa
- 1 lb. bulk pork sausage or fresh chorizo, cooked, drained and crumbled
- 2 cups shredded Mexican cheese blend
- 6 large eggs
- ½ cup 2% milk
- ¼ tsp. ground cumin
  Salt and pepper to taste
  Optional ingredients: warm flour tortillas (8 in.), sour cream and salsa

1. Preheat oven to 350°. In a greased 13x9-in. baking dish, layer half the potatoes; all the chilies, opened flat; all the salsa; half the sausage; and half the cheese. Cover with remaining potatoes, sausage and cheese.
2. Beat eggs and milk; add cumin, salt and pepper. Pour over potato mixture.
3. Bake, uncovered, until the eggs are set in center, 35-40 minutes. Let stand 15 minutes. If desired, serve with warm tortillas, sour cream and additional salsa.
1 piece: 210 cal., 13g fat (5g sat. fat), 105mg chol., 440mg sod., 11g carb. (3g sugars, 1g fiber), 10g pro.

BACON SWISS SQUARES

Not only does this savory breakfast-inspired pizza come together easily, but the irresistible combination of eggs, bacon and Swiss cheese keeps everyone asking for more.
—*Agarita Vaughan, Fairbury, IL*

Takes: 30 min. • **Makes:** 12 servings

- 2 **cups biscuit/baking mix**
- ½ **cup cold water**
- 8 **oz. sliced Swiss cheese**
- 1 **lb. sliced bacon, cooked and crumbled**
- 4 **large eggs, lightly beaten**
- ¼ **cup milk**
- ½ **tsp. onion powder**

1. In a large bowl, combine biscuit mix and water. Turn onto a floured surface; knead 10 times. Roll into a 14x10-in. rectangle.

2. Place on the bottom and ½ in. up sides of a greased 13x9-in. baking dish. Arrange cheese over dough. Sprinkle with bacon. In a large bowl, whisk the eggs, milk and onion powder; pour over bacon.

3. Bake at 425° until a knife inserted in the center comes out clean, 15-18 minutes. Cut into squares; serve immediately.

1 piece: 246 cal., 15g fat (6g sat. fat), 91mg chol., 470mg sod., 15g carb. (1g sugars, 1g fiber), 13g pro.

ROASTED VEGETABLE & GOAT CHEESE QUICHE

Roasting the veggies in this quiche intensifies their flavors. And the addition of fresh goat cheese lends a creamy tanginess.

—*Laura Davis, Chincoteague, VA*

Prep: 45 min. + chilling
Bake: 25 min. + standing
Makes: 6 servings

- 1   **sheet refrigerated pie crust**
- 1   **small eggplant, cut into 1-in. pieces**
- 1   **poblano pepper, cut into 1-in. pieces**
- 1   **medium tomato, cut into 1-in. pieces**
- 2   **garlic cloves, minced**
- 1   **Tbsp. olive oil**
- 2   **large eggs plus 2 large egg yolks**
- ¾   **cup half-and-half cream**
- 1   **tsp. kosher salt**
- ½   **tsp. pepper**
- 1   **log (4 oz.) fresh goat cheese, crumbled**

1. Unroll pie crust into an ungreased 9-in. tart pan. Do not prick crust with fork. Refrigerate 30 minutes. Preheat oven to 425°.

2. Line crust with a double thickness of foil. Fill with pie weights or dried beans. Bake on a lower oven rack until edges are golden brown, 10-12 minutes. Remove the foil and weights; bake until bottom is golden brown, 3-5 minutes longer. Cool on a wire rack.

3. In a large bowl, combine the eggplant, pepper, tomato and garlic. Add oil and toss to coat. Transfer to a greased 15x10x1-in. baking pan. Roast until tender, 15-20 minutes, stirring halfway.

4. Reduce oven setting to 375°. Spoon vegetables into crust. In a large bowl, whisk eggs, egg yolks, cream, salt and pepper until blended; pour over top. Sprinkle with cheese.

5. Bake on a lower oven rack on a baking sheet until a knife inserted in center comes out clean, about 25-30 minutes. Cover edges with foil to avoid overbrowning. Let stand for 10 minutes before cutting.

1 piece: 219 cal., 14g fat (7g sat. fat), 83mg chol., 471mg sod., 19g carb. (2g sugars, 0 fiber), 3g pro.

BLUEBERRY CRUNCH BREAKFAST BAKE

Fresh in-season blueberries make this a special breakfast, but frozen berries work just as well. My grandmother used to make this dish with strawberries, and I loved to eat it at her house.

—*Marsha Ketaner, Henderson, NV*

Prep: 15 min. • **Bake:** 30 min.
Makes: 12 servings

- 1   **loaf (16 oz.) day-old French bread, cut into 1-in. slices**
- 8   **large eggs**
- 1   **cup half-and-half cream**
- ½   **tsp. vanilla extract**
- 1   **cup old-fashioned oats**
- 1   **cup packed brown sugar**
- ¼   **cup all-purpose flour**
- ½   **cup cold butter**
- 2   **cups fresh or frozen blueberries**
- 1   **cup chopped walnuts**

1. Arrange half of the French bread slices in a greased 13x9-in. baking dish.

2. In a large bowl, whisk the eggs, cream and vanilla. Slowly pour half of the cream mixture over the bread. Top with the remaining bread and egg mixture. Let stand until the liquid is absorbed, about 5 minutes.

3. Meanwhile, in a small bowl, combine the oats, brown sugar and flour; cut in butter until crumbly. Sprinkle over top. Top with blueberries and walnuts.

4. Bake casserole, uncovered, at 375° until a knife inserted in the center comes out clean, 30-35 minutes. Let dish stand for 5 minutes before serving.

1 serving: 427 cal., 21g fat (8g sat. fat), 154mg chol., 351mg sod., 50g carb. (23g sugars, 3g fiber), 12g pro.

BERRY SMOOTHIE BOWL

We turned one of our favorite smoothies into a smoothie bowl and topped it with more fresh fruit and a few toasted almonds and coconut for a little crunch.
—Taste of Home *Test Kitchen*

- -

Takes: 5 min. • **Makes:** 2 servings

- 1   **cup fat-free milk**
- 1   **cup frozen unsweetened strawberries**
- ½   **cup frozen unsweetened raspberries**
- 3   **Tbsp. sugar**
- 1   **cup ice cubes**
      Optional: sliced fresh strawberries, fresh raspberries, chia seeds, fresh pumpkin seeds, unsweetened shredded coconut, sliced almonds

Place the milk, berries and sugar in a blender; cover and process until smooth. Add the ice cubes; cover and process until the mixture is smooth. Divide mixture between 2 serving bowls. If desired, add optional toppings.

1½ cups: 155 cal., 0 fat (0 sat. fat), 2mg chol., 54mg sod., 35g carb. (30g sugars, 2g fiber), 5g pro.

TEST KITCHEN TIP

To toast almonds or coconut, spread evenly in a 15x10x1-in. baking pan. Bake at 350° until lightly browned, 5-10 minutes, stirring occasionally. Or spread in a dry nonstick skillet and heat over low heat until lightly browned, stirring occasionally.

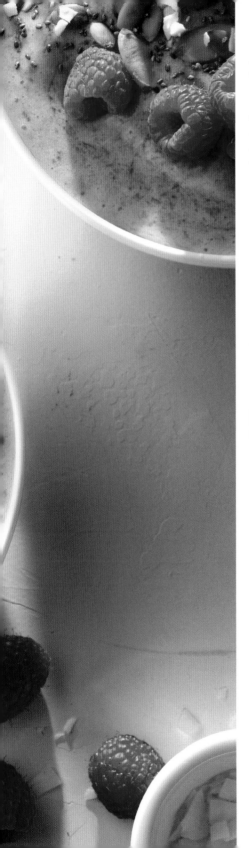

SAUSAGE & APPLE CORNBREAD BAKE

I make a cornbread-style bake with sausage, maple syrup and apples when we're craving a filling breakfast bake. It's sweet, savory and easy to make.
—*Stevie Wilson, Fremont, IA*

Prep: 15 min. + chilling
Bake: 30 min. + standing
Makes: 4 servings

- 1 lb. bulk pork sausage
- 4 medium tart apples, peeled and sliced (about 4 cups)
- 1 pkg. (8½ oz.) cornbread/muffin mix
- ⅓ cup 2% milk
- 1 large egg
   Maple syrup

1. Preheat oven to 400°. In a large skillet, cook sausage over medium heat until meat is no longer pink, 6-8 minutes, breaking into crumbles; drain. Transfer to a greased 8-in. square baking dish. Top with apples.
2. In a small bowl, combine muffin mix, milk and egg just until moistened. Pour over the apples. Bake, uncovered, until edges are golden brown and a toothpick inserted in center comes out clean, 30-40 minutes. Let stand 10 minutes before serving. Serve casserole with maple syrup.

1 serving: 618 cal., 34g fat (10g sat. fat), 111mg chol., 1209mg sod., 61g carb. (27g sugars, 6g fiber), 19g pro.

ROASTED TOMATO QUICHE

This cheesy quiche comes together quickly enough that I don't have to wake up extra early to get it on the table. That makes it a winner in my book!

—Elisabeth Larsen, Pleasant Grove, UT

- -

Prep: 45 min. • **Bake:** 40 min. + standing
Makes: 6 servings

- 1 **sheet refrigerated pie crust**
- 1 **cup grape tomatoes**
- 1 **Tbsp. olive oil**
- ⅛ **tsp. plus ½ tsp. salt, divided**
- ⅛ **tsp. plus ¼ tsp. pepper, divided**
- ½ **lb. bulk Italian sausage**
- 1 **small onion, chopped**
- 1 **pkg. (6 oz.) fresh baby spinach, chopped**
- 1 **cup shredded part-skim mozzarella cheese**
- 3 **large eggs**
- 1 **cup half-and-half cream**
- ½ **tsp. garlic powder**

1. Unroll crust into a 9-in. pie plate; flute edges. Line unpricked crust with a double thickness of heavy-duty foil. Fill with dried beans, uncooked rice or pie weights.

2. Bake at 450° for 8 minutes. Remove foil and weights; bake 5 minutes longer. Cool on a wire rack.

3. Place tomatoes in a 15x10x1-in. baking pan. Drizzle with oil; sprinkle with ⅛ tsp. each salt and pepper. Bake at 450° until skins blister, 8-10 minutes.

4. In a large skillet, cook sausage and onion over medium heat until sausage is no longer pink; drain. Remove sausage. In the same skillet, cook spinach until wilted, 4-5 minutes.

5. Combine sausage, tomatoes, spinach and cheese; transfer to crust. Whisk eggs, cream, garlic powder and remaining salt and pepper; pour over top.

6. Bake at 375° until a knife inserted in center comes out clean, about 40-45 minutes. Cover edges with foil during the last 15 minutes to prevent overbrowning if necessary. Let stand 10 minutes before serving.

Note: Let pie weights cool before storing. Beans and rice may be reused for pie weights, but not for cooking.

1 piece: 397 cal., 26g fat (11g sat. fat), 158mg chol., 725mg sod., 23g carb. (5g sugars, 1g fiber), 15g pro.

SLOW-COOKER SAUSAGE & WAFFLE BAKE

Here's an easy dish guaranteed to create excitement at breakfast. Nothing is missing from this sweet and savory combination. It's so wrong, it's right!
—*Courtney Lentz, Boston, MA*

- -

Prep: 20 min. • **Cook:** 5 hours + standing
Makes: 12 servings

- 2 **lbs. bulk spicy breakfast pork sausage**
- 1 **Tbsp. rubbed sage**
- ½ **tsp. fennel seed**
- 1 **pkg. (12.3 oz.) frozen waffles, cut into bite-sized pieces**
- 8 **large eggs**
- 1¼ **cups half-and-half cream**
- ¼ **cup maple syrup**
- ¼ **tsp. salt**
- ¼ **tsp. pepper**
- 2 **cups shredded cheddar cheese**
  Additional maple syrup

1. Fold two 18-in.-long pieces of foil into two 18x4-in. strips. Line the sides around the perimeter of a 5-qt. slow cooker with foil strips; spray with cooking spray.

2. In a large skillet, cook and crumble sausage over medium heat; drain. Add the sage and fennel seed.

3. Place waffles in slow cooker; top with sausage. In a bowl, mix eggs, cream, syrup and seasonings. Pour over the sausage and waffles. Top with cheese. Cook, covered, on low 5-6 hours or until set. Remove insert and let stand, uncovered, 15 minutes. Serve with additional maple syrup.

1 serving: 442 cal., 31g fat (12g sat. fat), 200mg chol., 878mg sod., 20g carb. (7g sugars, 1g fiber), 19g pro.

EGG-TOPPED WILTED SALAD

Tossed with a bright champagne vinegar dressing and topped with maple-chipotle bacon and sunny eggs, this is the ultimate brunch salad. But it's so delicious I'd gladly enjoy it any time of day!
—*Courtney Gaylord, Columbus, IN*

Prep: 20 min. • **Bake:** 25 min.
Makes: 4 servings

- 8 **bacon strips**
- 1 **tsp. packed brown sugar**
- ¼ **tsp. ground chipotle pepper**
- 1 **small red onion, halved and thinly sliced**
- 2 **Tbsp. champagne vinegar**
- 1 **tsp. sugar**
- ½ **tsp. pepper**
- 4 **large eggs**
- ¼ **tsp. salt**
- 8 **cups spring mix salad greens (about 5 oz.)**
- ½ **cup crumbled feta cheese**

1. Preheat oven to 350°. Place bacon on one half of a foil-lined 15x10x1-in. pan. Mix brown sugar and chipotle pepper; sprinkle evenly over bacon. Bake until bacon begins to shrink, about 10 minutes.

2. Using tongs, move bacon to other half of pan. Add onion to bacon drippings, stirring to coat. Return to oven; bake until bacon is crisp, about 15 minutes. Drain on paper towels, reserving 2 Tbsp. drippings.

3. In a small bowl, whisk together the vinegar, sugar, pepper and reserved bacon drippings. Coarsely chop bacon.

4. Place a large nonstick skillet coated with cooking spray over medium-high heat. Break eggs, one at a time, into skillet. Reduce heat to low; cook the eggs until desired doneness, turning after whites are set if desired. Sprinkle with salt.

5. Toss greens with dressing; divide among four dishes. Top with bacon, onion, cheese and eggs. Serve immediately.

1 serving: 279 cal., 20g fat (8g sat. fat), 216mg chol., 730mg sod., 10g carb. (3g sugars, 3g fiber), 17g pro.

BLUE CHEESE
POTATO CHIPS, PAGE 75

Party-Time Classics

Whether it's a holiday potluck, family reunion or casual get-together, these simply delightful snacks and drinks let the good times roll.

ASIAN PULLED PORK SANDWICHES

My pulled pork is a happy flavor mash-up of Vietnamese pho noodle soup and a banh mi sandwich. It's one seriously tasty slow-cooker dish.

—*Stacie Anderson, Virginia Beach, VA*

Prep: 15 min. • **Cook:** 7 hours
Makes: 18 servings

- ½ cup hoisin sauce
- ¼ cup seasoned rice vinegar
- ¼ cup reduced-sodium soy sauce
- ¼ cup honey
- 2 Tbsp. tomato paste
- 1 Tbsp. Worcestershire sauce
- 2 garlic cloves, minced
- 4 lbs. boneless pork shoulder roast
- 18 French dinner rolls (about 1¾ oz. each), split and warmed
  Optional toppings: shredded cabbage, julienned carrot, sliced jalapeno pepper, fresh cilantro or basil and Sriracha Asian hot chili sauce

1. In a small bowl, whisk the first seven ingredients until blended. Place roast in a 4- or 5-qt. slow cooker. Pour sauce mixture over top. Cook, covered, on low until pork is tender, 7-9 hours.

2. Remove roast; cool slightly. Skim fat from cooking juices. Coarsely shred pork with two forks. Return pork to slow cooker; heat through. Using tongs, serve pork on rolls, adding toppings as desired.

Freeze option: Freeze cooled meat mixture in freezer containers. To use, partially thaw in refrigerator overnight. Heat through in a saucepan, stirring occasionally; add a little broth if necessary. Serve as directed.

1 sandwich: 350 cal., 12g fat (4g sat. fat), 60mg chol., 703mg sod., 35g carb. (8g sugars, 1g fiber), 23g pro.

PINA COLADA FRUIT DIP

A taste of the tropics is always welcome and refreshing. This cool and creamy appetizer dip is also terrific to munch on after dinner.
—*Shelly Bevington, Hermiston, OR*

Takes: 15 min. • **Makes:** 2½ cups

- 1 pkg. (8 oz.) cream cheese, softened
- 1 jar (7 oz.) marshmallow creme
- 1 can (8 oz.) crushed pineapple, drained
- ½ cup sweetened shredded coconut
  Assorted fresh fruit or cubed pound cake

In a small bowl, beat cream cheese and marshmallow creme until fluffy. Fold in pineapple and coconut. Cover and chill until serving. Serve with fruit, pound cake or both.
¼ cup: 186 cal., 10g fat (6g sat. fat), 25mg chol., 96mg sod., 24g carb. (19g sugars, 0 fiber), 2g pro.

CHEESY BBQ BEEF DIP

Barbecued beef dip is a holiday staple in our house. My husband can't get enough!
—*Selena Swafford, Dalton, GA*

Takes: 30 min. • **Makes:** 8 servings

- 1 pkg. (8 oz.) cream cheese, softened
- 1 pkg. (15 oz.) refrigerated fully cooked barbecued shredded beef
- 1 cup shredded cheddar cheese
- ½ cup chopped red onion
- ¾ cup french-fried onions
  Optional toppings: chopped tomatoes, chopped red onion and minced fresh cilantro
  Tortilla chips

Preheat oven to 350°. Spread cream cheese on a greased 9-in. pie plate. Spread evenly with beef. Sprinkle with cheddar cheese and red onion. Bake until heated through, 15-20 minutes. Sprinkle with french-fried onions; bake 5 minutes. If desired, top with tomatoes, onion and cilantro. Serve with tortilla chips.
¼ cup: 279 cal., 19g fat (10g sat. fat), 57mg chol., 578mg sod., 16g carb. (10g sugars, 0 fiber), 12g pro.

BACON CHEESEBURGER BALLS

When I serve these, my husband and kids are often fooled into thinking we're having plain coated meatballs until they cut into the flavorful filling inside!

—*Cathy Lendvoy, Boharm, SK*

Prep: 25 min. • **Cook:** 10 min.
Makes: 3 dozen

- 1 large egg
- 1 envelope onion soup mix
- 1 lb. ground beef
- 2 Tbsp. all-purpose flour
- 2 Tbsp. 2% milk
- 1 cup shredded cheddar cheese
- 4 bacon strips, cooked and crumbled

COATING
- 2 large eggs
- 1 cup crushed Saltines (about 30 crackers)
- 5 Tbsp. canola oil

1. In a large bowl, combine egg and soup mix. Crumble beef over mixture and mix well. Divide into 36 portions; set aside. In another large bowl, combine the flour and milk until smooth. Add cheese and bacon; mix well.
2. Shape cheese mixture into 36 balls. Shape one beef portion around each cheese ball. In a shallow bowl, beat eggs for coating. Place cracker crumbs in another bowl. Dip the meatballs into eggs, then coat with crumbs.
3. Heat oil in a large cast-iron or other heavy skillet over medium heat. Cook meatballs until meat is no longer pink and coating is golden brown, 10-12 minutes.
3 balls: 222 cal., 16g fat (5g sat. fat), 90mg chol., 396mg sod., 7g carb. (1g sugars, 0 fiber), 13g pro.

HAM & CHEESE BISCUIT STACKS

These finger sandwiches are a pretty addition to any spread, yet filling enough to satisfy hearty appetites. I've served them at holidays, showers and tailgate parties.

—*Kelly Williams, Forked River, NJ*

Prep: 1 hour • **Bake:** 10 min. + cooling
Makes: 40 appetizers

- 4 tubes (6 oz. each) small refrigerated flaky biscuits (5 count each)
- ¼ cup stone-ground mustard

ASSEMBLY
- ½ cup butter, softened
- ¼ cup chopped green onions
- ½ cup stone-ground mustard
- ¼ cup mayonnaise
- ¼ cup honey
- 10 thick slices deli ham, quartered
- 10 slices Swiss cheese, quartered
- 2½ cups shredded romaine
- 20 pitted ripe olives, drained and patted dry
- 20 pimiento-stuffed olives, drained and patted dry
- 40 frilled toothpicks

1. Preheat oven to 400°. Cut biscuits in half to make half-circles; place 2 in. apart on ungreased baking sheets. Spread mustard over tops. Bake biscuits until golden brown, 8-10 minutes. Cool completely on wire racks.
2. Mix butter and green onions. In another bowl, mix mustard, mayonnaise and honey. Split each biscuit into two layers.
3. Spread biscuit bottoms with butter mixture; top with ham, cheese, romaine and biscuit tops. Spoon mustard mixture over tops. Thread one olive onto each toothpick; insert into stacks. Serve immediately.
1 appetizer: 121 cal., 7g fat (3g sat. fat), 16mg chol., 412mg sod., 11g carb. (2g sugars, 0 fiber), 4g pro.

ORANGE-GLAZED MEATBALLS

I love the sweet orange marmalade paired with the zip of a jalapeno in this sweet-and-sour glaze.

—*Bonnie Stallings, Martinsburg, WV*

Takes: 30 min. • **Makes:** 20 meatballs

1 **pkg. (22 oz.) frozen fully cooked angus beef meatballs**
1 **jar (12 oz.) orange marmalade**
¼ **cup orange juice**
3 **green onions, chopped, divided**
1 **jalapeno pepper, seeded and chopped**

1. Prepare the meatballs according to the package directions.
2. In a small saucepan, heat the orange marmalade, orange juice, half of the green onions and the jalapeno.
3. Place meatballs in a serving dish; pour glaze over the top and gently stir to coat. Garnish with remaining green onions.

1 meatball: 125 cal., 6g fat (3g sat. fat), 17mg chol., 208mg sod., 13g carb. (11g sugars, 1g fiber), 4g pro.

start WITH **FROZEN MEATBALLS**

CHERRY-ALMOND TEA MIX

Our family enjoys giving homemade gifts for Christmas, and hot beverage mixes are especially popular. This flavored tea is one of our favorites.
—*Andrea Horton, Kelso, WA*

Takes: 10 min.
Makes: 40 servings (2½ cups tea mix)

2¼ cups iced tea mix with lemon and sugar
2 envelopes (0.13 oz. each) unsweetened cherry Kool-Aid mix
2 tsp. almond extract
EACH SERVING
1 cup boiling or cold water

Place tea mix, Kool-Aid mix and extract in a food processor; pulse until blended. Store in an airtight container in a cool, dry place up to 6 months.

To prepare tea: Place 1 Tbsp. tea mix in a mug. Stir in 1 cup boiling or cold water until blended.

1 cup prepared tea: 41 cal., 0 fat (0 sat. fat), 0 chol., 1mg sod., 10g carb. (10g sugars, 0 fiber), 0 pro.

TEST KITCHEN TIP

Put leftover iced tea to good use by pouring it into an ice cube tray. The frozen tea cubes will keep the next day's drinks cool without diluting them.

BARBECUED MEATBALLS

Grape jelly and chili sauce are the secrets that make these meatballs so fantastic. If I'm serving them at a party, I make the meatballs and sauce in advance and reheat them right before guests arrive.
—*Irma Schnuelle, Manitowoc, WI*

Prep: 20 min. • **Cook:** 15 min.
Makes: about 3 dozen

½ cup dry bread crumbs
⅓ cup finely chopped onion
¼ cup whole milk
1 large egg, lightly beaten
1 Tbsp. minced fresh parsley
1 tsp. salt
1 tsp. Worcestershire sauce
½ tsp. pepper
1 lb. lean ground beef (90% lean)
¼ cup canola oil
1 bottle (12 oz.) chili sauce
1 jar (10 oz.) grape jelly

1. In a large bowl, combine the first eight ingredients. Crumble beef over mixture and mix well. Shape into 1-in. balls. In a large skillet, brown meatballs in oil on all sides.
2. Remove meatballs and drain. In the same skillet, combine chili sauce and jelly; cook and stir over medium heat until jelly has melted. Return meatballs to pan; heat through.

3 meatballs: 124 cal., 5g fat (1g sat. fat), 22mg chol., 394mg sod., 16g carb., trace fiber, 5g pro.

MARSHMALLOW FRUIT DIP

You can whip up this sweet and creamy dip in just 10 minutes. I like to serve it in a bowl surrounded by fresh-picked strawberries at spring brunches or luncheons.
—*Cindy Steffen, Cedarburg, WI*

Takes: 10 min. • **Makes:** 40 servings (5 cups)

- 1 pkg. (8 oz.) cream cheese, softened
- ¾ cup cherry yogurt
- 1 carton (8 oz.) frozen whipped topping, thawed
- 1 jar (7 oz.) marshmallow creme
  Assorted fresh fruit

In a large bowl, beat cream cheese and yogurt until blended. Fold in whipped topping and marshmallow creme. Serve with fruit.
2 Tbsp.: 56 cal., 3g fat (2g sat. fat), 7mg chol., 24mg sod., 6g carb. (5g sugars, 0 fiber), 1g pro.

BAKED ONION DIP

Some people like this cheesy dip so much that they can't tear themselves away from the appetizer table to eat their dinner.
—*Mona Zignego, Hartford, WI*

Prep: 5 min. • **Bake:** 40 min.
Makes: 16 servings (2 cups)

1 cup mayonnaise
1 cup chopped sweet onion
1 Tbsp. grated Parmesan cheese
¼ tsp. garlic salt
1 cup shredded Swiss cheese
   Minced fresh parsley, optional
   Assorted crackers

1. In a large bowl, combine mayonnaise, onion, Parmesan cheese and garlic salt; stir in Swiss cheese. Spoon into a 1-qt. baking dish.
2. Bake, uncovered, at 325° until golden brown, about 40 minutes. If desired, sprinkle with parsley. Serve with crackers.
2 Tbsp.: 131 cal., 13g fat (3g sat. fat), 11mg chol., 127mg sod., 1g carb. (1g sugars, 0 fiber), 2g pro.

---

5 INGREDIENTS

CHOCOLATE MOCHA DUSTED ALMONDS

I love to make recipes with nuts. These are chocolaty with a hint of coffee—elegant and addictive! I give them away as gifts; I've even made them for wedding favors.
—*Annette Scholz, Medaryville, IN*

Prep: 20 min. + chilling • **Makes:** 12 servings

1 cup dark chocolate chips
2 cups toasted whole almonds
¾ cup confectioners' sugar
3 Tbsp. baking cocoa
4½ tsp. instant coffee granules

1. Microwave the chocolate chips, covered, at 50% power, stirring once or twice, until melted, 3-4 minutes. Stir until smooth. Add almonds; mix until coated.
2. Meanwhile, combine the remaining ingredients. Transfer almonds to sugar mixture; toss to coat evenly. Spread over waxed paper-lined baking sheet.
3. Refrigerate until chocolate is set. Store in an airtight container in refrigerator.
About 3 Tbsp.: 270 cal., 19g fat (5g sat. fat), 0 chol., 12mg sod., 25g carb. (19g sugars, 4g fiber), 7g pro.

TEST KITCHEN TIP

Like spice? Add ½ teaspoon ground chipotle pepper or chili powder. Try this with any kind of nut. Just make sure you toast the nuts first to bring out all of their flavor.

CHRISTMAS PIZZA SQUARES

Looking to add a dash of Christmas color to your appetizer mix? Topped with roasted peppers, caramelized onions, beef and black olives, this popular pizza is as tasty as it is decorative on the table.
—*Margaret Pache, Mesa, AZ*

Prep: 45 min. • **Bake:** 20 min.
Makes: 15 servings

2 Tbsp. butter
1 tsp. canola oil
1 large onion, thinly sliced
1 lb. ground beef
½ tsp. salt
⅛ tsp. pepper
1 Tbsp. cornmeal
1 tube (13.8 oz.) refrigerated pizza crust
1½ cups shredded part-skim mozzarella cheese
1 jar (7 oz.) roasted red peppers, drained and sliced
1 medium tomato, seeded and diced
½ cup sliced ripe olives

1. In a nonstick skillet, heat butter and oil; add onion. Cook and stir over low heat until the onion is caramelized, 30-35 minutes. In another skillet, cook beef over medium heat until no longer pink; drain. Sprinkle with salt and pepper; set aside.
2. Sprinkle cornmeal into a greased 13x9-in. baking pan. Press the pizza dough into pan; prick dough with a fork. Bake at 400° for 10 minutes. Top with the beef, caramelized onion, cheese, red peppers, tomato and olives. Bake until the cheese is melted, 10-12 minutes longer. Cut into squares; serve warm.
1 square: 193 cal., 9g fat (4g sat. fat), 28mg chol., 371mg sod., 18g carb. (9g sugars, 1g fiber), 9g pro.

FAST FIX

CALZONE PINWHEELS

Not only do these pretty bites take advantage of convenient refrigerator crescent rolls, but they can be made ahead and popped in the oven right before company arrives. No one can eat just one, and people love the cheesy, fresh taste!

—*Lisa Smith, Bryan, OH*

Takes: 30 min. • **Makes:** 16 appetizers

- ½ cup shredded part-skim mozzarella cheese
- ½ cup part-skim ricotta cheese
- ½ cup diced pepperoni
- ¼ cup grated Parmesan cheese
- ¼ cup chopped fresh mushrooms
- ¼ cup finely chopped green pepper
- 2 Tbsp. finely chopped onion
- 1 tsp. Italian seasoning
- ¼ tsp. salt
- 1 pkg. (8 oz.) refrigerated crescent rolls
- 1 jar (14 oz.) pizza sauce, warmed

1. Preheat oven to 375°. In a small bowl, mix the first nine ingredients.
2. Unroll crescent dough and separate into four rectangles; press perforations to seal. Spread rectangles with cheese mixture to within ¼ in. of edges. Roll up jelly-roll style, starting with a short side; pinch seam to seal.
3. Using a serrated knife, cut each roll into four slices; place on a greased baking sheet, cut side down. Bake until golden brown, 12-15 minutes. Serve with pizza sauce.

1 appetizer: 118 cal., 7g fat (3g sat. fat), 11mg chol., 383mg sod., 8g carb. (3g sugars, 0 fiber), 4g pro.

DILLY CHEESE BALL

The whole family devours this herby cheese spread—even my son, the chef. Serve it with your favorite crackers.

—*Jane Vince, London, ON*

- -

Prep: 10 min. + chilling • **Makes:** 2½ cups

1	pkg. (8 oz.) cream cheese, softened
1	cup dill pickle relish, drained
¼	cup finely chopped onion
1½	cups shredded cheddar cheese
1	Tbsp. Worcestershire sauce
2	Tbsp. mayonnaise
2	Tbsp. minced fresh parsley
	Assorted crackers

Beat first six ingredients until smooth. Shape into a ball; wrap in plastic. Refrigerate several hours. Sprinkle with parsley; serve with assorted crackers.

2 Tbsp.: 100 cal., 8g fat (4g sat. fat), 22mg chol., 244mg sod., 5g carb. (1g sugars, 0 fiber), 3g pro.

5 INGREDIENTS | FAST FIX
SO-EASY SNACK MIX

I eat this tasty treat just as much as (if not more than) the kids! Have fun with it by adding other goodies into the mix, like nuts, cereal, pretzels and more.

—*Jeff King, Duluth, MN*

- -

Takes: 5 min. • **Makes:** 4 qt.

4	cups miniature cheddar cheese fish-shaped crackers
4	cups golden raisins
4	cups dried cherries
2	cups yogurt-covered raisins
2	cups miniature pretzels

Place all ingredients in a large bowl; toss to combine. Store in airtight containers.

½ cup: 195 cal., 3g fat (1g sat. fat), 1mg chol., 104mg sod., 42g carb. (29g sugars, 2g fiber), 2g pro.

BUFFALO MACARONI & CHEESE BITES

This pub-style appetizer turns comforting mac and cheese and Louisiana hot sauce into perfect munchies. Crispy and cheesy at the same time, these little bites are a wonderful meat-free option, too.
—*Ann Donnay, Milton, MA*

Prep: 45 min. + chilling • **Bake:** 15 min.
Makes: 2 dozen

- 1 pkg. (7¼ oz.) macaroni and cheese dinner mix
- 6 cups water
- 2 Tbsp. 2% milk
- 2 Tbsp. process cheese sauce
- 1 Tbsp. butter
- ¼ cup Louisiana-style hot sauce
- 1 cup all-purpose flour
- 1 large egg, beaten
- 1 can (6 oz.) French-fried onions, crushed
  Blue cheese salad dressing

1. Set cheese packet from dinner mix aside. In a large saucepan, bring water to a boil. Add the macaroni; cook until tender, 8-10 minutes. Drain. Stir in contents of the cheese packet, milk, cheese sauce and butter.

2. Press 2 tablespoonfuls into 24 greased miniature muffin cups. Cover and refrigerate for 3 hours or overnight.

3. Place the hot sauce, flour, egg and onions in separate shallow bowls. Remove macaroni bites from cups. Dip in the hot sauce and flour, then coat with egg and onions. Place 2 in. apart on a lightly greased baking sheet.

4. Bake bites at 400° until golden brown, 12-15 minutes. Serve with dressing.

1 appetizer: 104 cal., 5g fat (2g sat. fat), 11mg chol., 141mg sod., 13g carb. (1g sugars, 0 fiber), 2g pro.

start WITH
MAC & CHEESE DINNER MIX

FAST FIX

SWEET PEA PESTO CROSTINI

I made a healthier spin on my favorite celebrity chef's recipe by using hearty vegetable broth and less cheese. To top crostini, use less broth for a paste-like pesto. For use on pasta, add more broth for a sauce-like consistency.
—*Amber Massey, Argyle, TX*

Takes: 25 min. • **Makes:** 20 pieces

- 12 oz. fresh or frozen peas, thawed
- 4 garlic cloves, halved
- 1 tsp. rice vinegar
- ½ tsp. salt
- ⅛ tsp. lemon-pepper seasoning
- 3 Tbsp. olive oil
- ¼ cup shredded Parmesan cheese
- ⅓ cup vegetable broth
- 1 whole wheat French bread demi-baguette (about 6 oz. and 12 in. long)
- 2 cups cherry tomatoes (about 10 oz.), halved or quartered

1. Preheat broiler. Place peas, garlic, vinegar, salt and lemon pepper in a blender or food processor; pulse until well blended. Continue processing while gradually adding oil in a steady stream. Add cheese; pulse just until blended. Add broth; pulse until mixture reaches desired consistency.

2. Cut baguette into 20 slices, each ½ in. thick. Place on ungreased baking sheet. Broil 4-5 in. from heat until golden brown, 45-60 seconds per side. Remove to wire rack to cool.

3. To assemble crostini, spread each slice with about 1 Tbsp. pesto mixture; top with tomato pieces.

1 piece: 77 cal., 2g fat (0 sat. fat), 1mg chol., 190mg sod., 11g carb. (2g sugars, 1g fiber), 3g pro. **Diabetic exchanges:** ½ starch, ½ fat.

FAST FIX

MEXICAN DEVILED EGGS

My husband and I live on a beautiful lake and host lots of summer picnics and cookouts. I adapted this recipe to suit our tastes. Folks who are expecting the same old deviled eggs are surprised when they try this delightful, tangy variation.

—*Susan Klemm, Rhinelander, WI*

Takes: 15 min. • **Makes:** 8 servings

8	hard-boiled large eggs
½	cup shredded cheddar cheese
¼	cup mayonnaise
¼	cup salsa
2	Tbsp. sliced green onions
1	Tbsp. sour cream
	Salt to taste

1. Slice the eggs in half lengthwise; remove yolks and set whites aside. In a small bowl, mash yolks with cheese, mayonnaise, salsa, onions, sour cream and salt.
2. Stuff or pipe into egg whites. Serve immediately or chill until ready to serve.
2 stuffed egg halves: 159 cal., 13g fat (4g sat. fat), 223mg chol., 178mg sod., 1g carb. (1g sugars, 0 fiber), 8g pro.

5 INGREDIENTS | FAST FIX

CRANBERRY COCKTAIL

I adore the combination of flavors in this recipe. The secret is to thaw the lemonade so it's still slightly icy—this way the cocktail will be cool and refreshing. For a no-alcohol option, use peach juice and lemon-lime soda instead of schnapps and vodka.

—*Julie Danler, Bel Aire, KS*

Takes: 10 min. • **Makes:** 4 servings

	Ice cubes
4	oz. vodka
4	oz. peach schnapps liqueur
4	oz. thawed lemonade concentrate
4	oz. cranberry-raspberry juice
16	maraschino cherries

1. Fill shaker three-fourths full with ice cubes.
2. Add vodka, schnapps, lemonade concentrate and juice to shaker; cover and shake until condensation forms on outside of shaker, 10-15 seconds. Strain into four cocktail glasses. Place a skewer with four cherries in each glass.
1 serving: 226 cal., 0 fat (0 sat. fat), 0 chol., 4mg sod., 33g carb. (31g sugars, 0 fiber), 0 pro.

PIZZA ROLLS

This is my husband's homemade version of store-bought pizza rolls, and our family loves them. They take some time to make, but they are worth it—you get large batch to fill up the entire crew!
—*Julie Gaines, Normal, IL*

Prep: 50 min. • **Cook:** 5 min./batch
Makes: 32 rolls

- 4 **cups shredded pizza cheese blend or part-skim mozzarella cheese**
- 1 **lb. bulk Italian sausage, cooked and drained**
- 2 **pkg. (3 oz. each) sliced pepperoni, chopped**
- 1 **medium green pepper, finely chopped**
- 1 **medium sweet red pepper, finely chopped**
- 1 **medium onion, finely chopped**
- 2 **jars (14 oz. each) pizza sauce**
- 32 **egg roll wrappers**
   Oil for frying
   Additional pizza sauce for dipping, warmed, optional

1. In a large bowl, combine the cheese, sausage, pepperoni, peppers and onion. Stir in pizza sauce until combined. Place about ¼ cup filling in the center of each egg roll wrapper. Fold bottom corner over filling; fold sides toward center over filling. Moisten remaining corner with water and roll up tightly to seal.
2. In an electric skillet, heat 1 in. of oil to 375°. Fry pizza rolls until golden brown, 1-2 minutes on each side. Drain on paper towels. Serve with additional pizza sauce if desired.
1 roll: 297 cal., 19g fat (5g sat. fat), 28mg chol., 537mg sod., 22g carb. (2g sugars, 1g fiber), 9g pro.

ANTIPASTO BAKE

Stuffed with savory meats and cheeses, this hearty bake would satisfy an entire offensive line! It comes together quickly and bakes in under an hour, making it the perfect potluck bring-along. Introducing the all-star lineup in this ooey-gooey appetizer: salami, Swiss, pepperoni, Colby-Monterey Jack, prosciutto and provolone. A crisp topping finishes it off.
—*Brea Barclay, Green Bay, WI*

Prep: 20 min. • **Bake:** 45 min. + standing
Makes: 20 servings

- 2   tubes (8 oz. each) refrigerated crescent rolls
- ¼   lb. thinly sliced hard salami
- ¼   lb. thinly sliced Swiss cheese
- ¼   lb. thinly sliced pepperoni
- ¼   lb. thinly sliced Colby-Monterey Jack cheese
- ¼   lb. thinly sliced prosciutto
- ¼   lb. thinly sliced provolone cheese
- 2   large eggs
- ½   tsp. garlic powder
- ½   tsp. pepper
- 1   jar (12 oz.) roasted sweet red peppers, drained
- 1   large egg yolk, beaten

1. Preheat oven to 350°. Unroll one tube of crescent dough into one long rectangle; press perforations to seal. Press onto bottom and up sides of an ungreased 11x7-in. baking dish.
2. Layer meats and cheeses on dough in the order listed. Whisk eggs and seasonings until well blended; pour into dish. Top with roasted red peppers.
3. Unroll remaining tube of dough into a long rectangle; press perforations to seal. Place over filling; pinch seams tight. Brush with beaten egg yolk; cover with foil. Bake 30 minutes; remove foil. Bake until golden brown, 15-20 minutes. Let stand 20 minutes.
1 piece: 229 cal., 15g fat (7g sat. fat), 58mg chol., 662mg sod., 10g carb. (2g sugars, 0 fiber), 11g pro.

---

5 INGREDIENTS | FAST FIX
POLENTA PARMIGIANA

This warm Italian-flavored appetizer also makes a quick, filling lunch. I prefer this veggie version, but my kids like to add pepperoni or sausage to create mini pizzas.
—*Carolyn Kumpe, El Dorado, CA*

Takes: 30 min. • **Makes:** 16 appetizers

- 1   tube (1 lb.) polenta, cut into 16 slices
- ¼   cup olive oil
- 1   cup tomato basil pasta sauce, warmed
- ½   lb. fresh mozzarella cheese, cut into 16 slices
- ¼   cup grated Parmesan cheese
- ½   tsp. salt
- ⅛   tsp. pepper
      Fresh basil leaves, optional

1. Preheat oven to 425°. Place polenta in a greased 15x10x1-in. baking pan; brush with olive oil. Bake until edges are golden brown, 15-20 minutes.
2. Spoon pasta sauce over polenta slices. Top each with a mozzarella cheese slice; sprinkle with Parmesan cheese, salt and pepper. Bake until cheese is melted , 3-5 minutes longer. Garnish with basil if desired.
1 appetizer: 108 cal., 7g fat (3g sat. fat), 12mg chol., 273mg sod., 7g carb. (2g sugars, 1g fiber), 4g pro.

---

5 INGREDIENTS | FAST FIX | SHOWN ON PAGE 58
BLUE CHEESE POTATO CHIPS

Game day calls for something bold. I top potato chips with tomatoes, bacon and tangy blue cheese. I make two big pans, and they always disappear.
—*Bonnie Hawkins, Elkhorn, WI*

Takes: 15 min. • **Makes:** 10 servings

- 1   pkg. (8½ oz.) kettle-cooked potato chips
- 2   medium tomatoes, seeded and chopped
- 8   bacon strips, cooked and crumbled
- 6   green onions, chopped
- 1   cup crumbled blue cheese

1. Preheat broiler. In a 15x10x1-in. baking pan, arrange potato chips in an even layer. Top with remaining ingredients.
2. Broil 4-5 in. from heat until cheese begins to melt, 2-3 minutes. Serve immediately.
1 serving: 215 cal., 14g fat (5g sat. fat), 17mg chol., 359mg sod., 16g carb. (2g sugars, 1g fiber), 6g pro.

READER RAVE

"You gotta try this. It is so good and so different!"
—BONITO15, TASTEOFHOME.COM

DILLY VEGGIE PIZZA

This is one of my favorite ways to use up leftover chopped veggies. It's a cinch to prepare and you can change the mixture to match your kids' taste buds. Always popular at special events, it tastes just as good the next day.

—Heather Ahrens, Columbus, OH

Prep: 20 min. • **Bake:** 10 min. + cooling
Makes: 15 servings

- 1 tube (8 oz.) refrigerated crescent rolls
- 1½ cups vegetable dill dip
- 2 medium carrots, chopped
- 1 cup finely chopped fresh broccoli
- 1 cup chopped seeded tomatoes
- 4 green onions, sliced
- 1 can (2¼ oz.) sliced ripe olives, drained

1. Unroll the crescent dough into one long rectangle. Press dough onto the bottom of a greased 13x9-in. baking pan; seal seams. Bake at 375° until the crust is golden brown, 10-12 minutes. Cool crust completely on a wire rack.

2. Spread dip over crust; sprinkle with the carrots, broccoli, tomatoes, onions and olives. Cut into squares. Refrigerate leftovers.

1 piece: 225 cal., 20g fat (3g sat. fat), 12mg chol., 290mg sod., 11g carb. (3g sugars, 1g fiber), 2g pro.

ROASTED RED PEPPER TRIANGLES

For a sensational appetizer, sandwich this combo of full-flavored meats, cheeses and roasted red peppers between layers of flaky crescent dough. Have marinara sauce on hand for dipping.
—Amy Bell, Arlington, TN

Prep: 35 min. • **Bake:** 50 min.
Makes: 2 dozen

- 2 tubes (8 oz. each) refrigerated crescent rolls
- 1½ cups finely diced fully cooked ham
- 1 cup shredded Swiss cheese
- 1 pkg. (3 oz.) sliced pepperoni, chopped
- 8 slices provolone cheese
- 1 jar (12 oz.) roasted sweet red peppers, drained and cut into strips
- 4 large eggs
- ¼ cup grated Parmesan cheese
- 1 Tbsp. Italian salad dressing mix

1. Preheat oven to 350°. Unroll one tube of crescent dough into one long rectangle; press onto bottom and ¾ in. up sides of a greased 13x9-in. baking dish. Seal the seams and perforations. Top with half of the ham; layer with the Swiss cheese, pepperoni, provolone cheese and the remaining ham. Top with the red peppers.

2. In a small bowl, whisk eggs, Parmesan cheese and salad dressing mix; reserve ¼ cup. Pour remaining egg mixture over peppers.

3. On a lightly floured surface, roll out remaining crescent dough into a 13x9-in. rectangle; seal the seams and perforations. Place over filling; pinch edges to seal.

4. Bake, covered, for 30 minutes. Uncover; brush with reserved egg mixture. Bake until crust is golden brown, 20-25 minutes longer. Cool on a wire rack for 5 minutes. Cut into triangles. Serve warm.

1 piece: 165 cal., 10g fat (4g sat. fat), 50mg chol., 485mg sod., 8g carb. (2g sugars, 0 fiber), 8g pro.

SPINACH DIP IN A BREAD BOWL

I prepare this creamy spinach dip whenever I get together with friends. People can't believe how simple it is to make.
—Janelle Lee, Appleton, WI

Prep: 15 min. + chilling • **Makes:** 15 servings

- 2 cups sour cream
- 1 envelope (1 oz.) ranch salad dressing mix
- 1 pkg. (10 oz.) frozen chopped spinach, thawed and squeezed dry
- ¼ cup chopped onion
- ¾ tsp. dried basil
- ½ tsp. dried oregano
- 1 round loaf of bread (1 lb.) Raw vegetables

1. In a large bowl, combine the first six ingredients. Chill mixture for at least 1 hour. Cut a 1½-in. slice off the top of the loaf; set aside. Hollow out the bottom part, leaving a thick shell. Cut or tear the slice from the top of the loaf and the bread from inside into bite-sized pieces.
2. Fill the shell with dip; set on a large platter. Arrange the bread pieces and vegetables around it and serve immediately.
1 serving: 161 cal., 6g fat (4g sat. fat), 22mg chol., 571mg sod., 20g carb. (2g sugars, 1g fiber), 4g pro.

TEST KITCHEN TIP

When a recipe calls for frozen spinach, thawed and squeezed dry, use a salad spinner to easily get rid of the excess water.

FAST FIX
MEDITERRANEAN ARTICHOKE & RED PEPPER ROLL-UPS

I love these roll-ups because they're easy to make and tasty, too. They're delicious even without the sour cream dipping sauce.
—Donna Lindecamp, Morganton, NC

Takes: 30 min. • **Makes:** 2 dozen

- 1 can (14 oz.) water-packed artichoke hearts, rinsed, drained and finely chopped
- 4 oz. cream cheese, softened
- ⅓ cup grated Parmesan cheese
- ¼ cup crumbled feta cheese
- 2 green onions, thinly sliced
- 3 Tbsp. prepared pesto
- 8 flour tortillas (8 in.), warmed
- 1 jar (7½ oz.) roasted sweet red peppers, drained and cut into strips

SAUCE
- 1 cup sour cream
- 1 Tbsp. minced chives

1. In a small bowl, combine the artichokes, cream cheese, Parmesan cheese, feta cheese, green onions and pesto until blended. Spread ¼ cup mixture over each tortilla; top with red peppers and roll up tightly.
2. Place roll-ups 1 in. apart on a greased baking sheet. Bake at 350° until heated through, 12-15 minutes. Cut into thirds. Meanwhile, in a small bowl, combine sour cream and chives. Serve with rolls.
1 appetizer with 1 tsp. sauce: 112 cal., 6g fat (3g sat. fat), 14mg chol., 217mg sod., 11g carb. (1g sugars, 0 fiber), 4g pro.

REUBEN ROUNDS

Fans of the classic Reuben sandwich will go crazy for baked pastry spirals of corned beef, Swiss and sauerkraut. They're a breeze to make, and bottled Thousand Island dressing makes the perfect dipping sauce.

—*Cheryl Snavely, Hagerstown, MD*

Takes: 30 min. • **Makes:** 16 appetizers

- 1 **sheet frozen puff pastry, thawed**
- 6 **slices Swiss cheese**
- 5 **slices deli corned beef**
- ½ **cup sauerkraut, rinsed and well drained**
- 1 **tsp. caraway seeds**
- ¼ **cup Thousand Island salad dressing**

1. Preheat oven to 400°. Unfold puff pastry; layer with cheese, corned beef and sauerkraut to within ½-in. of edges. Roll up jelly-roll style. Trim ends and cut crosswise into 16 slices. Place on greased baking sheets, cut side down. Sprinkle with caraway seeds.
2. Bake until golden brown, 18-20 minutes. Serve with salad dressing.

1 appetizer: 114 cal., 7g fat (2g sat. fat), 8mg chol., 198mg sod., 10g carb. (1g sugars, 1g fiber), 3g pro.

start WITH FROZEN PUFF PASTRY

FESTIVE APPLE DIP

I came up with this layered peanut butter treat when my dad gave me a big bag of apples. The dip has been one of my favorites ever since. It's fantastic with apple slices, graham crackers, vanilla wafers, banana chunks or animal crackers.

—Theresa Tometich, Coralville, IA

Takes: 20 min. • **Makes:** 8 servings

1 pkg. (8 oz.) cream cheese, softened
½ cup creamy peanut butter
⅓ cup packed brown sugar
1 tsp. vanilla extract
½ cup miniature marshmallows
1 jar (11¾ oz.) hot fudge ice cream topping
2 Tbsp. chopped mixed nuts or peanuts
3 each medium red and green apples, cut into thin wedges
2 Tbsp. lemon juice

1. For dip, beat first four ingredients until smooth; stir in marshmallows. Spoon half of the mixture into a 3-cup bowl; top with half of the fudge topping. Repeat layers. Sprinkle with nuts.

2. To serve, toss apples with lemon juice. Serve with dip.

¼ cup dip with ¾ apple: 403 cal., 22g fat (9g sat. fat), 29mg chol., 218mg sod., 49g carb. (38g sugars, 3g fiber), 8g pro.

SLOW COOKER

HONEY BUFFALO MEATBALL SLIDERS

These little sliders deliver big Buffalo chicken flavor without the messiness of wings. The spicy-sweet meatballs are a hit at parties and potlucks and especially popular on game day.

—Julie Peterson, Crofton, MD

Prep: 10 min. • **Cook:** 2 hours
Makes: 6 servings

- ¼ cup packed brown sugar
- ¼ cup Louisiana-style hot sauce
- ¼ cup honey
- ¼ cup apricot preserves
- 2 Tbsp. cornstarch
- 2 Tbsp. reduced-sodium soy sauce
- 1 pkg. (24 oz.) frozen fully cooked Italian turkey meatballs, thawed
  Additional hot sauce, optional
  Bibb lettuce leaves
- 12 mini buns
  Crumbled blue cheese
  Ranch salad dressing, optional

1. In a 3- or 4-qt. slow cooker, mix first six ingredients until smooth. Stir in meatballs until coated. Cook, covered, on low until meatballs are heated through, 2-3 hours.
2. If desired, stir in additional hot sauce. Serve meatballs on lettuce-lined buns; top with cheese and, if desired, dressing.
2 sliders: 524 cal., 21g fat (6g sat. fat), 110mg chol., 1364mg sod., 61g carb. (29g sugars, 1g fiber), 28g pro.

BREADSTICK PIZZA

Make Monday fun-day with a hassle-free homemade pizza featuring refrigerated breadsticks as the crust. Feeding kids? Slice pieces into small strips and let them dip each strip into marinara sauce. They'll love it!
—*Mary Hankins, Kansas City, MO*

Prep: 25 min. • **Bake:** 20 min.
Makes: 12 servings

- 2   tubes (11 oz. each) refrigerated breadsticks
- ½   lb. sliced fresh mushrooms
- 2   medium green peppers, chopped
- 1   medium onion, chopped
- 1½ tsp. Italian seasoning, divided
- 4   tsp. olive oil, divided
- 1½ cups shredded cheddar cheese, divided
- 5   oz. Canadian bacon, chopped
- 1½ cups shredded part-skim mozzarella cheese
     Marinara sauce

1. Unroll refrigerated breadsticks into a greased 15x10x1-in. baking pan. Press onto bottom and up sides of pan; pinch seams to seal. Bake at 350° until set, 6-8 minutes.
2. Meanwhile, in a large skillet, saute the mushrooms, peppers, onion and 1 tsp. Italian seasoning in 2 tsp. oil until crisp-tender; drain.
3. Brush crust with remaining oil. Sprinkle with ¾ cup cheddar cheese; top with the vegetable mixture and Canadian bacon. Combine mozzarella cheese and remaining cheddar cheese; sprinkle over top. Sprinkle with remaining Italian seasoning.
4. Bake until cheese is melted and crust is golden brown, 20-25 minutes. Serve with marinara sauce.
Freeze option: Bake crust as directed, add toppings and cool. Securely wrap and freeze unbaked pizza. To use, unwrap pizza; bake as directed, increasing time as necessary.
1 piece: 267 cal., 11g fat (6g sat. fat), 27mg chol., 638mg sod., 29g carb. (5g sugars, 2g fiber), 13g pro.

BACON-ENCASED WATER CHESTNUTS

My husband and I do lots of entertaining, and we always start off each party with appetizers like these tempting hot bites.
—*Midge Scurlock, Creston, IA*

Prep: 10 min. • **Bake:** 50 min.
Makes: 32 appetizers

- 8   bacon strips
- 2   cans (8 oz. each) whole water chestnuts, drained
- ¾   cup ketchup
- 1   jar (2½ oz.) strained peach baby food
- ¼   cup sugar
     Dash salt

1. Cut bacon strips in half lengthwise and then in half widthwise. Wrap each bacon piece around a water chestnut; secure with a toothpick.
2. Place in an ungreased 13x9-in. baking dish. Bake, uncovered, at 350° for 25 minutes, turning once; drain if necessary.
3. In a small bowl, combine the remaining ingredients. Drizzle over water chestnuts. Bake until bacon is crisp, 25-35 minutes longer. Serve warm.
3 each: 155 cal., 11g fat (4g sat. fat), 12mg chol., 363mg sod., 14g carb. (8g sugars, 1g fiber), 2g pro.

LUSCIOUS LIME SLUSH

Guests go crazy for this sweet-tart refresher. If you prefer, swap in lemonade concentrate for the limeade.
—*Bonnie Jost, Manitowoc, WI*

Prep: 20 min. + freezing
Makes: 28 servings

- 9   cups water
- 4   individual green tea bags
- 2   cans (12 oz. each) frozen limeade concentrate, thawed
- 2   cups sugar
- 2   cups lemon rum or rum
- 7   cups lemon-lime soda, chilled

1. In a Dutch oven, bring water to a boil. Remove from the heat; add tea bags. Cover and steep for 3-5 minutes. Discard tea bags. Stir in limeade concentrate, sugar and rum.
2. Transfer to a 4-qt. freezer container; cool. Cover and freeze for 6 hours or overnight.
3. To use frozen limeade mixture: Combine the limeade mixture and soda in a 4-qt. pitcher. Or for one serving, combine ½ cup limeade mixture and ¼ cup soda in a glass. Serve immediately.
¾ cup: 177 cal., 0 fat (0 sat. fat), 0 chol., 7mg sod., 36g carb. (35g sugars, 0 fiber), 0 pro.

PRESSURE-COOKER BLACK BEAN CHICKEN NACHOS

Zeppelins, one of my favorite restaurants in Cedar Rapids, has the best chicken nachos. Their famous dish inspired me to create my own, but with the added convenience of using the pressure cooker. Fresh cilantro makes the dish pop with flavor.
—*Natalie Hess, Cedar Rapids, IA*

- -

Prep: 10 min. • **Cook:** 8 min. + releasing
Makes: 8 servings

- 1½ lbs. boneless skinless chicken breasts
- 2 jars (16 oz. each) black bean and corn salsa
- 1 medium green pepper, chopped
- 1 medium sweet red pepper, chopped
- 1 pkg. (12 oz.) tortilla chips
- 2 cups shredded Mexican cheese blend
  Optional ingredients: minced fresh cilantro, pickled jalapeno slices and sour cream

1. Place chicken, salsa and peppers in a 6-qt. electric pressure cooker. Lock lid; make sure vent is closed. Select manual setting; adjust pressure to high and set time for 8 minutes. When finished cooking, allow pressure to naturally release for 7 minutes and then quick-release any remaining pressure according to manufacturer's instructions.

2. Remove chicken; shred with two forks. Return to pressure cooker. Using a slotted spoon, serve chicken mixture over chips; sprinkle with cheese and, if desired, cilantro. Add toppings of choice.

1 serving: 280 cal., 11g fat (5g sat. fat), 72mg chol., 708mg sod., 20g carb. (5g sugars, 8g fiber), 27g pro.

5 INGREDIENTS

QUICK & EASY
BAKLAVA SQUARES

I love baklava but rarely indulged because it took so much time to make. Then a friend gave me this simple recipe. I've made these squares for family, friends and co-workers—they can't get enough. I'm always asked to bring them to special gatherings and parties, and I give them as gifts during the holidays.
—*Paula Marchesi, Lenhartsville, PA*

Prep: 20 min. • **Bake:** 30 min. + cooling
Makes: 2 dozen

- 1 lb. (4 cups) chopped walnuts
- 1½ tsp. ground cinnamon
- 1 pkg. (16 oz., 14x9-in. sheets) frozen phyllo dough, thawed
- 1 cup butter, melted
- 1 cup honey

1. Preheat oven to 350°. Coat a 13x9-in. baking dish with cooking spray. Combine walnuts and cinnamon.

2. Unroll the frozen phyllo dough. Layer two sheets of phyllo in prepared pan; brush with butter. Repeat with six more sheets of phyllo, brushing every other one with butter. (Keep remaining phyllo covered with a damp towel to prevent it from drying out.)

3. Sprinkle ½ cup nut mixture in pan; drizzle with 2 Tbsp. honey. Add two more phyllo sheets, brushing with butter; sprinkle another ½ cup nut mixture and 2 Tbsp. honey over phyllo. Repeat layers six times. Top with the remaining phyllo sheets, brushing every other one with butter. Using a sharp knife, score surface to make 24 squares. Bake until golden brown and crisp, 25-30 minutes. Cool on a wire rack 1 hour or before serving.

1 piece: 294 cal., 21g fat (6g sat. fat), 20mg chol., 145mg sod., 26g carb. (13g sugars, 2g fiber), 5g pro.

SHRIMP LOVER SQUARES

During the holiday season, my family enjoys having a variety of appetizers as a meal while playing a board game or watching a movie. These delicious shrimp squares are part of the buffet I prepare every year.

—Ardyce Piehl, Poynette, WI

Prep: 20 min. + chilling • **Makes:** 2 dozen

- 1 tube (8 oz.) refrigerated crescent rolls
- 1 pkg. (8 oz.) cream cheese, softened
- ¼ cup sour cream
- ½ tsp. dill weed
- ⅛ tsp. salt
- ½ cup seafood cocktail sauce
- 24 cooked medium shrimp, peeled and deveined
- ½ cup chopped green pepper
- ⅓ cup chopped onion
- 1 cup shredded Monterey Jack cheese

1. In a greased 13x9-in. baking dish, unroll crescent dough into one long rectangle; seal seams and perforations. Bake at 375° until golden brown, 10-12 minutes. Cool crust completely on a wire rack.

2. In a small bowl, beat the cream cheese, sour cream, dill and salt until smooth. Spread over the crust. Top with the seafood sauce, shrimp, green pepper, onion and cheese. Cover and refrigerate for 1 hour. Cut into 24 squares.

1 square: 109 cal., 7g fat (4g sat. fat), 32mg chol., 190mg sod., 5g carb. (2g sugars, 0 fiber), 5g pro.

FREEZE IT

COLLARD GREENS & PULLED PORK EGG ROLLS

It's fun to take remnants of ingredients from my pantry and create a brand-new meal. You can make wontons with this same filling for a bite-size snack.

—Melissa Pelkey Hass, Waleska, GA

Prep: 30 min. • **Bake:** 15 min.
Makes: 12 servings

- 1 lb. collard greens
- 1 cup refrigerated fully cooked barbecued shredded pork
- 1 pkg. (8 oz.) cream cheese, softened
- 1 small onion, finely chopped
- ¼ tsp. salt
- ⅛ tsp. pepper
- 1 pkg. (16 oz.) egg roll wrappers
- 2 Tbsp. butter, melted
  Thai sweet chili sauce

1. Trim collard greens, discarding thick ribs and stems. Coarsely chop leaves. In a large saucepan, bring ½ in. of water to a boil. Add greens; cook, covered, until they begin to wilt, 8-10 minutes. Drain, squeezing out as much water as possible.

2. Preheat oven to 425°. Combine greens, pork, cream cheese, onion and seasonings until well blended. With one corner of an egg roll wrapper facing you, place ¼ cup pork filling just below center of wrapper. (Cover remaining wrappers with a damp paper towel until ready to use.) Fold bottom corner over filling; moisten remaining wrapper edges with water. Fold side corners toward center over filling. Roll egg roll up tightly, pressing at tip to seal. Repeat until all filling is used.

3. Place egg rolls on a parchment-lined baking sheet; brush with melted butter. Bake until golden brown, 15-20 minutes. Serve with sweet chili sauce.

Freeze option: Cover and freeze unbaked egg rolls on waxed paper-lined baking sheets until firm. Transfer to freezer containers; return to freezer. To use, bake egg rolls as directed.

1 egg roll: 227 cal., 10g fat (5g sat. fat), 34mg chol., 472mg sod., 27g carb. (4g sugars, 2g fiber), 8g pro.

ARTICHOKE & SPINACH DIP PIZZA

When I have it in my pantry, I swap garlic oil for regular olive oil. It adds a little something extra without overpowering the toppings.
—*Shelly Bevington, Hermiston, OR*

Takes: 20 min. • **Makes:** 24 pieces

- 1 prebaked 12-in. pizza crust
- 1 Tbsp. olive oil
- 1 cup spinach dip
- 1 cup shredded part-skim mozzarella cheese
- 1 jar (7½ oz.) marinated quartered artichoke hearts, drained
- ½ cup oil-packed sun-dried tomatoes, patted dry and chopped
- ¼ cup chopped red onion

1. Preheat oven to 450°. Place crust on an ungreased pizza pan; brush with oil. Spread spinach dip over top. Sprinkle with cheese, artichokes, tomatoes and onion.

2. Bake until cheese is melted and edges are lightly browned, 8-10 minutes. Cut pizza into 24 pieces.

1 piece: 127 cal., 9g fat (2g sat. fat), 6mg chol., 213mg sod., 10g carb. (1g sugars, 0 fiber), 3g pro.

TEST KITCHEN TIP

If you don't have time to make a homemade pizza crust, you can use one of several convenience products. Thawed frozen bread dough, refrigerated pizza crust and shelf-stable pizza shells all make a suitable substitute.

start WITH
PREBAKED PIZZA CRUST

APPLE-GOUDA PIGS IN A BLANKET

Every year for New Year's I would make beef and cheddar pigs in a blanket. Now I use apple and Gouda for a new flavor combination.
—*Megan Weiss, Menomonie, WI*

Takes: 30 min. • **Makes:** 2 dozen

- 1 tube (8 oz.) refrigerated crescent rolls
- 1 small apple, peeled and cut into 24 thin slices
- 6 thin slices Gouda cheese, quartered
- 24 miniature smoked sausages
  Honey mustard salad dressing, optional

1. Preheat oven to 375°. Unroll the crescent dough and separate into eight triangles; cut each lengthwise into three thin triangles. On the wide end of each triangle, place one apple slice, one folded piece of cheese and one mini sausage; roll up tightly.

2. Place 1 in. apart on parchment-lined baking sheets, point side down. Bake until golden brown, 10-12 minutes. If desired, serve with honey mustard salad dressing.

1 appetizer: 82 cal., 6g fat (2g sat. fat), 11mg chol., 203mg sod., 5g carb. (1g sugars, 0 fiber), 3g pro.

STROMBOLI SANDWICH

I've made this sandwich many times for parties, and it gets terrific reviews. Add ingredients and spices to suit your tastes.
—*Leigh Lauer, Hummelstown, PA*

Prep: 20 min. + rising • **Bake:** 30 min.
Makes: 8-10 servings

- 2 loaves (1 lb. each) frozen bread dough, thawed
- ¼ lb. sliced ham
- ¼ lb. sliced pepperoni
- ¼ cup chopped onion
- ¼ cup chopped green pepper
- 1 jar (14 oz.) pizza sauce, divided
- ¼ lb. sliced mozzarella cheese
- ¼ lb. sliced bologna
- ¼ lb. sliced hard salami
- ¼ lb. slice Swiss cheese
- 1 tsp. dried basil
- 1 tsp. dried oregano
- ¼ tsp. garlic powder
- ¼ tsp. pepper
- 2 Tbsp. butter, melted

Let dough rise in a warm place until doubled. Punch down. Roll loaves together into one 15x12-in. rectangle. Layer ham and pepperoni on half of the dough (lengthwise). Sprinkle with onion and green pepper. Top with ¼ cup of pizza sauce. Layer mozzarella, bologna, salami and Swiss cheese over sauce. Sprinkle with basil, oregano, garlic powder and pepper. Spread another ¼ cup of pizza sauce on top. Fold plain half of dough over filling and seal edges well. Place on a greased 15x10x1-in. baking pan. Bake at 375° until golden brown, 30-35 minutes. Brush with melted butter. Heat the remaining pizza sauce and serve with sliced stromboli.

1 piece: 388 cal., 23g fat (10g sat. fat), 60mg chol., 1175mg sod., 28g carb. (5g sugars, 2g fiber), 19g pro.

---

5 INGREDIENTS | FREEZE IT

PROSCIUTTO PINWHEELS

These sensational appetizers look fancy but are easy to make. With just a few ingredients, they come together in a snap.
—*Kaitlyn Benito, Everett, WA*

Prep: 20 min. • **Bake:** 15 min.
Makes: 20 appetizers

- 1 sheet frozen puff pastry, thawed
- ¼ cup sweet hot mustard
- ¼ lb. sliced prosciutto or deli ham, chopped
- ½ cup shredded Parmesan cheese

1. Unfold puff pastry. Spread mustard over pastry to within ½ in. of edges. Sprinkle with prosciutto and cheese. Roll up one side to the middle of the dough; roll up the other side so the two rolls meet in the center. Using a serrated knife, cut into ½-in. slices.

2. Place on greased baking sheets. Bake at 400° until puffed and golden brown, 11-13 minutes. Serve warm.

Freeze option: Freeze cooled appetizers in freezer containers, separating layers with waxed paper. To use, reheat appetizers on a greased baking sheet in a preheated 400° oven until crisp and heated through.

1 appetizer: 86 cal., 5g fat (1g sat. fat), 6mg chol., 210mg sod., 8g carb. (0 sugars, 1g fiber), 3g pro.

CHICKEN PARMESAN SLIDER BAKE

Sliders are the perfect finger food for any get-together, and this flavorful chicken Parmesan version won't disappoint.
—*Nick Iverson, Denver, CO*

Prep: 20 min. • **Bake:** 25 min.
Makes: 1 dozen

- 24 oz. frozen breaded chicken tenders
- 1 pkg. (12 oz.) Hawaiian sweet rolls
- 1 pkg. (7½ oz.) sliced provolone and mozzarella cheese blend
- 1 jar (24 oz.) marinara sauce

TOPPING
- ½ cup butter, cubed
- 1 tsp. garlic powder
- 1 tsp. crushed red pepper flakes
- ¼ cup grated Parmesan cheese
- 2 Tbsp. minced fresh basil

1. Preheat oven to 375°. Prepare chicken tenders according to package directions. Meanwhile, without separating rolls, cut horizontally in half; arrange roll bottoms in a greased 13x9-in. baking dish. Spread half of cheese slices over roll bottoms. Bake until cheese is melted, 3-5 minutes.
2. Layer rolls with half of sauce, chicken tenders, remaining sauce and remaining cheese slices. Replace top halves of rolls.
3. For topping, microwave butter, garlic powder and red pepper flakes, covered, on high, stirring occasionally, until butter is melted. Pour over rolls; sprinkle with the cheese. Bake, uncovered, until golden brown and heated through, 20-25 minutes. Sprinkle with basil before serving.

1 slider: 402 cal., 23g fat (11g sat. fat), 62mg chol., 780mg sod., 34g carb. (10g sugars, 4g fiber), 17g pro.

9-LAYER GREEK DIP

Instead of the same ordinary taco or veggie dip at your next family event or potluck, try this light, cool and refreshing alternative.

—*Shawn Barto, Winter Garden, FL*

- -

Takes: 20 min. • **Makes:** 5 ½ cups

  1 **carton (10 oz.) hummus**
  1 **cup refrigerated tzatziki sauce**
  ½ **cup chopped green pepper**
  ½ **cup chopped sweet red pepper**
  ½ **cup chopped peeled cucumber**
  ½ **cup chopped water-packed artichoke hearts, drained**
  ½ **cup chopped pitted Greek olives, optional**
  ¼ **cup chopped pepperoncini**
  1 **cup crumbled feta cheese Baked pita chips**

In a 9-in. deep-dish pie plate, layer first six ingredients; top with olives, if desired, and pepperoncini. Sprinkle with feta cheese. Refrigerate until serving. Serve with baked pita chips.

¼ cup: 60 cal., 4g fat (1g sat. fat), 5mg chol., 210mg sod., 4g carb. (1g sugars, 1g fiber), 3g pro. **Diabetic exchanges:** ½ starch, ½ fat.

TEST KITCHEN TIP

For that fresh-from-the-kitchen taste, make your own tzatziki sauce to use in this dip. Combine ½ cup peeled, seeded and finely chopped cucumber with ½ cup plain Greek yogurt, 4 tsp. lemon juice, 1 Tbsp. chopped dill, 1 minced garlic clove, and salt and pepper to taste. Refrigerate until ready to use.

RAMEN SLIDERS

I grew up eating ramen and love it to this day. These sliders are a fun spin on my favorite type of noodle soup, which is topped with egg slices and kimchi.

—*Julie Teramoto, Los Angeles, CA*

- -

Prep: 40 min. • **Bake:** 20 min.
Bakes: 10 servings

- 1   pkg. (3 oz.) beef or pork ramen noodles
- 1   lb. ground beef
- 4   green onions, thinly sliced
- 2   hard-boiled large eggs, sliced
      Sriracha Asian hot chili sauce
      Kimchi, optional

1. Preheat oven to 350°. Grease 20 muffin cups. Cook noodles according to package directions, saving seasoning packet for meat mixture. Drain; divide the noodles among prepared muffin cups. Bake until crisp and light golden brown, 20-25 minutes. Remove from pans to wire racks to cool.

2. Meanwhile, combine the beef, green onions and reserved seasoning packet, mixing lightly but thoroughly. Shape into ten 2½-in.-round patties.

3. In a large nonstick skillet, cook burgers over medium heat until a thermometer reads 160°, 4-6 minutes on each side. Cut each egg into five slices. Serve the burgers on ramen buns with egg slices, chili sauce and, if desired, kimchi.

1 slider: 137 cal., 8g fat (3g sat. fat), 65mg chol., 185mg sod., 6g carb. (0 sugars, 0 fiber), 10g pro.

SALMON PARTY SPREAD

We're proud to serve our delicious Alaskan salmon to guests. Set out an assortment of crackers, and this slightly smoky spread will be gone in no time!
—*Kathy Crow, Cordova, AK*

Prep: 10 min. + chilling • **Makes:** 2 cups

- 1 pkg. (8 oz.) cream cheese, softened
- 1 can (7½ oz.) pink salmon, drained, flaked and cartilage removed
- 3 Tbsp. chopped fresh parsley
- 2 Tbsp. finely chopped green pepper
- 2 Tbsp. finely chopped sweet red pepper
- 2 tsp. lemon juice
- 1 tsp. prepared horseradish
- ½ tsp. liquid smoke, optional
  Finely chopped pecans or additional parsley
  Crackers

In a bowl, combine the first eight ingredients; stir until well blended. Cover mixture and chill 2-24 hours. Transfer to a serving bowl; if desired, sprinkle with pecans or parsley. Serve with crackers.

2 Tbsp.: 71 cal., 6g fat (3g sat. fat), 21mg chol., 115mg sod., 1g carb. (0 sugars, 0 fiber), 4g pro. (11g sugars, 1g fiber), 4g pro.

CREAMY CARAMEL DIP

Because I feed three hungry men (my husband, a member of the Royal Canadian Mounted Police, and our two boys), I love satisfying snacks that are easy to make. We all appreciate this cool, light fruit dip.
—Karen Laubman, Spruce Grove, AB

- -

Prep: 10 min. + chilling • **Makes:** 3½ cups

1	pkg. (8 oz.) cream cheese, softened
¾	cup packed brown sugar
1	cup sour cream
2	tsp. vanilla extract
2	tsp. lemon juice
1	cup cold milk
1	pkg. (3.4 oz.) instant vanilla pudding mix
	Assorted fresh fruit

1. In a bowl, beat cream cheese and brown sugar until smooth. Add the sour cream, vanilla, lemon juice, milk and pudding mix, beating well after each addition.
2. Cover and chill for at least 1 hour. Serve with assorted fresh fruit.
2 Tbsp.: 87 cal., 5g fat (3g sat. fat), 16mg chol., 83mg sod., 10g carb. (9g sugars, 0 fiber), 1g pro.

5 INGREDIENTS | FAST FIX
ASPARAGUS WITH HORSERADISH DIP

This is a terrific recipe for party season. Serve the asparagus on a decorative platter with lemon wedges on the side for a garnish. For a flavor variation, use chopped garlic in place of the horseradish.
—Lynn Caruso, Gilroy, CA

- -

Takes: 15 min. • **Makes:** 16 appetizers

32	fresh asparagus spears (about 2 lbs.), trimmed
1	cup reduced-fat mayonnaise
¼	cup grated Parmesan cheese
1	Tbsp. prepared horseradish
½	tsp. Worcestershire sauce

1. Place asparagus in a steamer basket; place in a large saucepan over 1 in. of water. Bring to a boil; cover and steam until crisp-tender, 2-4 minutes. Drain and immediately place in ice water. Drain and pat dry.
2. In a small bowl, combine the remaining ingredients. Serve with asparagus.
2 asparagus spears with 1 Tbsp. dip: 63 cal., 5g fat (1g sat. fat), 6mg chol., 146mg sod., 3g carb. (1g sugars, 0 fiber), 1g pro. **Diabetic exchanges:** 1 fat.

FAST FIX
CHEESY BEEF TACO DIP

Try this recipe for a warm, filling dip with a bit of a kick. It's a hit with my family, and party guests rave about it, too. Serve with crunchy tortilla chips so everyone can just dig in!
—Carol Smith, Sanford, NC

- -

Takes: 20 min. • **Makes:** 10 cups

2	lbs. ground beef
1	large onion, finely chopped
1	medium green pepper, finely chopped
1	lb. process cheese (Velveeta), cubed
1	lb. pepper jack cheese, cubed
1	jar (16 oz.) taco sauce
1	can (10 oz.) diced tomatoes and green chiles, drained
1	can (4 oz.) mushroom stems and pieces, drained and chopped
1	can (2¼ oz.) sliced ripe olives, drained
	Tortilla chips

In a large skillet, cook the beef, onion and green pepper over medium heat until meat is no longer pink; drain. Stir in the cheeses, taco sauce, tomatoes, mushrooms and olives. Cook and stir over low heat until cheese is melted. Serve warm with tortilla chips.
¼ cup: 127 cal., 9g fat (5g sat. fat), 30mg chol., 332mg sod., 3g carb. (2g sugars, 0 fiber), 9g pro.

FRIED CHICKEN & PULLED PORK CORNBREAD POPPERS

These fun little apps are an instant conversation starter wherever they're served. We love them on game day, but they'd be a hit at brunch, too.
—*Crystal Schlueter, Babbitt, MN*

- -

Takes: 25 min. • **Makes:** 2 dozen

- 2 oz. frozen popcorn chicken
- 1 pkg. (8½ oz.) cornbread/muffin mix
- 4 seeded jalapeno peppers or pickled jalapeno peppers, cut into 6 slices each
- ¼ cup refrigerated fully cooked barbecued pulled pork
- ½ cup maple syrup or honey
- 1 tsp. Sriracha Asian hot chili sauce, optional

1. Preheat oven to 400°. Bake popcorn chicken according to package directions. When cool enough to handle, cut chicken into 12 pieces.

2. Meanwhile, prepare cornbread mix according to package directions. Place a jalapeno slice in each of 24 foil-lined mini muffin cups. Fill each cup with 1 Tbsp. batter. Gently press a piece of popcorn chicken into the centers of half the cups. Spoon 1 tsp. pulled pork into the centers of remaining muffin cups.

3. Bake until muffins are golden brown, about 12 minutes. Serve poppers with maple syrup; if desired, whisk Sriracha sauce into syrup.

1 mini muffin: 74 cal., 2g fat (1g sat. fat), 10mg chol., 120mg sod., 13g carb. (7g sugars, 1g fiber), 2g pro.

SLOW COOKER

SLOW-COOKER SPINACH & ARTICHOKE DIP

It's easy to get my daughters to eat spinach and artichokes when this dip is on the table. We serve it with chips, toasted pita bread or fresh veggies.

—*Jennifer Stowell, Deep River, IA*

Prep: 10 min. • **Cook:** 2 hours
Makes: 8 cups

- 2 cans (14 oz. each) water-packed artichoke hearts, drained and chopped
- 2 pkg. (10 oz. each) frozen chopped spinach, thawed and squeezed dry
- 1 jar (15 oz.) Alfredo sauce
- 1 pkg. (8 oz.) cream cheese, cubed
- 2 cups shredded Italian cheese blend
- 1 cup shredded part-skim mozzarella cheese
- 1 cup shredded Parmesan cheese
- 1 cup 2% milk
- 2 garlic cloves, minced
  Assorted crackers and/or cucumber slices

In a greased 4-qt. slow cooker, combine the first nine ingredients. Cook, covered, on low until heated through, 2-3 hours. Serve with crackers and/or cucumber slices.

¼ cup: 105 cal., 7g fat (4g sat. fat), 21mg chol., 276mg sod., 5g carb. (1g sugars, 1g fiber), 6g pro.

READER RAVE

"I made this for a group of friends and they said it was the best artichoke dip they've ever had! And then they asked for the recipe. Delicious!"

—COUNTRY-GIRL99, TASTEOFHOME.COM

---

5 INGREDIENTS

TERIYAKI SALMON BUNDLES

If you're bored with the same old appetizers, give this flavorful one a try. You can arrange them on a platter or serve them on wooden skewers for easy dipping.

—*Diane Halferty, Corpus Christi, TX*

Prep: 30 min. • **Bake:** 20 min.
Makes: 32 appetizers (¾ cup sauce)

- 4 Tbsp. reduced-sodium teriyaki sauce, divided
- ½ tsp. grated lemon zest
- 2 Tbsp. lemon juice
- 1¼ lbs. salmon fillet, cut into 1-in. cubes
- 1 pkg. (17.3 oz.) frozen puff pastry, thawed
- ⅔ cup orange marmalade

1. Preheat oven to 400°. In a large bowl, whisk 2 Tbsp. teriyaki sauce, lemon zest and lemon juice. Add salmon; toss to coat. Marinate at room temperature 20 minutes.
2. Drain salmon, discarding marinade. Unfold puff pastry. Cut each sheet lengthwise into ½-in.-wide strips; cut crosswise in half. Overlap two strips of pastry, forming an "X." Place a salmon cube in the center. Wrap the pastry over salmon; pinch ends to seal. Place on a greased baking sheet, seam side down. Repeat. Bake bundles until golden brown, 18-20 minutes.
3. In a small bowl, mix orange marmalade and remaining teriyaki sauce. Serve sauce with salmon bundles.

1 appetizer with about 1 tsp. sauce: 120 cal., 6g fat (1g sat. fat), 9mg chol., 93mg sod., 13g carb. (4g sugars, 1g fiber), 4g pro.

HAM & CHEESE PUFFS

These marvelous little bites go over well with kids of all ages. The pop-in-your-mouth nibblers are perfect for a party, or to pair with soups and chili.
—*Marvin Buffington, Burlington, IA*

Takes: 30 min. • **Makes:** 2 dozen

- 1 pkg. (2½ oz.) thinly sliced deli ham, chopped
- 1 small onion, chopped
- ½ cup shredded Swiss cheese
- 1 large egg
- 1½ tsp. Dijon mustard
- ⅛ tsp. pepper
- 1 tube (8 oz.) refrigerated crescent rolls

1. Preheat oven to 375°. Combine the first six ingredients. Divide the crescent dough into 24 portions. Press into 24 greased mini muffin cups.

2. Spoon 1 Tbsp. ham mixture into each cup. Bake until golden brown, 13-15 minutes.

1 appetizer: 110 cal., 6g fat (2g sat. fat), 25mg chol., 263mg sod., 8g carb. (2g sugars, 0 fiber), 4g pro.

"These appetizers were the hit of the party! Easy to make and easy to warm up. My guests gobbled them up."
—PAGERD, TASTEOFHOME.COM

MINI MAC & CHEESE DOGS

We wanted to get creative with hot dogs, so we made a mac-and-cheesy one. Pile on the extra cheese, relish and even bacon.
—*Julie Peterson, Crofton, MD*

Prep: 25 min. + rising
Bake: 15 min. + cooling • **Makes:** 2 dozen

- 1 pkg. (16 oz.) frozen bread dough dinner rolls (12 count), thawed but still cold
- ½ cup panko (Japanese) bread crumbs
- 2 Tbsp. chopped onion
- 1 Tbsp. canola oil
- ¼ tsp. salt
- ⅛ tsp. pepper
- 12 bun-length beef hot dogs
- 1 pkg. (7¼ oz.) macaroni and cheese dinner mix

1. Let dough stand at room temperature until it's soft enough to shape, 15-20 minutes. Cut each dough roll in half; shape each half into a 3-in.-long mini hot dog bun. Place 2 in. apart on greased baking sheets.

2. Cover with greased plastic wrap; let rise in a warm place until almost doubled, about 45 minutes. Preheat oven to 350°.

3. Bake the mini buns until golden brown, 12-15 minutes. Remove from pans to wire racks to cool completely.

4. In a 15x10x1-in. baking pan, toss bread crumbs with onion, oil, salt and pepper. Bake at 350° until golden brown, stirring once, 5-7 minutes.

5. Cook hot dogs and macaroni and cheese according to package directions. To serve, cut hot dogs crosswise in half. Split buns; fill with hot dogs and macaroni and cheese. Sprinkle with toasted crumbs.

1 appetizer: 198 cal., 12g fat (5g sat. fat), 25mg chol., 446mg sod., 18g carb. (2g sugars, 1g fiber), 6g pro.

ANTIPASTO PLATTER

We entertain often, and antipasto is one of our favorite crowd-pleasers. Everyone loves having so many ingredients to nibble on. It's a satisfying change of pace from the usual chips and dip.

—*Teri Lindquist, Gurnee, IL*

Prep: 10 min. + chilling
Makes: 16 servings

- 1 jar (24 oz.) pepperoncini, drained
- 1 can (15 oz.) garbanzo beans or chickpeas, rinsed and drained
- 2 cups halved fresh mushrooms
- 2 cups halved cherry tomatoes
- ½ lb. provolone cheese, cubed
- 1 can (6 oz.) pitted ripe olives, drained
- 1 pkg. (3½ oz.) sliced pepperoni
- 1 bottle (8 oz.) Italian vinaigrette dressing
  Lettuce leaves

1. In a large bowl, combine pepperoncini, beans, mushrooms, tomatoes, cheese, olives and pepperoni. Pour vinaigrette over mixture; toss to coat.

2. Refrigerate mixture at least 30 minutes or overnight. Arrange on a lettuce-lined platter. Serve with toothpicks.

1 cup: 178 cal., 13g fat (4g sat. fat), 15mg chol., 852mg sod., 8g carb. (2g sugars, 2g fiber), 6g pro.

REUBEN WAFFLE POTATO APPETIZERS

I love Reubens, so I decided to turn the classic sandwich into a fun appetizer. Corned beef and sauerkraut atop waffle fries always gets people talking!

—*Gloria Bradley, Naperville, IL*

Prep: 30 min. • **Bake:** 10 min./batch
Makes: about 4 dozen

- 1 pkg. (22 oz.) frozen waffle-cut fries
- 4 oz. cream cheese, softened
- 2 cups shredded fontina cheese, divided
- ⅓ cup Thousand Island salad dressing
- 3 Tbsp. chopped sweet onion
- 1½ tsp. prepared horseradish
- 12 oz. sliced deli corned beef, coarsely chopped
- 1 cup sauerkraut, rinsed, well drained and chopped
- 2 Tbsp. minced fresh chives

1. Bake waffle fries according to package directions. Meanwhile, in a bowl, beat cream cheese, 1 cup fontina cheese, salad dressing, onion and horseradish until blended.

2. Remove fries from oven; reduce oven setting to 400°. Top each waffle fry with about ¼ oz. corned beef and 1 tsp. each cream cheese mixture, sauerkraut and remaining fontina cheese. Bake until cheese is melted, 8-10 minutes. Sprinkle with chives.

1 appetizer: 62 cal., 4g fat (2g sat. fat), 12mg chol., 168mg sod., 4g carb. (0 sugars, 0 fiber), 3g pro.

5 INGREDIENTS

ITALIAN MEATBALL BUNS

These soft little rolls come with a surprise inside—savory Italian meatballs. They're wonderful dipped in marinara sauce, making them fun for my grandkids and adults, too. I love how easy they are to put together.
—*Trina Linder-Mobley, Clover, SC*

Prep: 30 min. + rising • **Bake:** 15 min.
Makes: 2 dozen

- 12 frozen bread dough dinner rolls
- 1 pkg. (12 oz.) frozen fully cooked Italian meatballs, thawed
- 2 Tbsp. olive oil
- ¼ cup grated Parmesan cheese
- ¼ cup minced fresh basil
- 1½ cups marinara sauce, warmed

1. Let dough stand at room temperature until softened, 25-30 minutes.
2. Cut each roll in half. Wrap each portion around a meatball, enclosing the meatball completely; pinch dough firmly to seal. Place dough on greased baking sheets, seam side down. Cover with plastic wrap; let the dough rise in a warm place until almost doubled, 1½-2 hours.
3. Preheat oven to 350°. Bake buns until golden brown, 12-15 minutes. Brush tops with oil; sprinkle with cheese and basil. Serve with marinara sauce.
1 bun with 1 Tbsp. sauce: 112 cal., 5g fat (2g sat. fat), 8mg chol., 248mg sod., 12g carb. (2g

BUFFALO CHICKEN DEVILED EGGS

My daughter loves spicy Buffalo chicken and deviled eggs, so I combined the two. Make and chill a day ahead so the flavors mingle.
—*Robin Spires, Tampa, FL*

Prep: 25 min. + chilling • **Makes:** 2 dozen

- 12 hard-boiled large eggs
- ½ cup crumbled blue cheese, divided
- 2 celery ribs, finely chopped
- ½ cup mayonnaise
- ¼ cup finely chopped cooked chicken breast
- 3 Tbsp. minced fresh parsley
- 1 Tbsp. Buffalo wing sauce or 1 tsp. hot pepper sauce
- ⅛ tsp. pepper
  Additional Buffalo wing or hot pepper sauce, optional

1. Cut eggs lengthwise in half. Remove yolks, reserving whites. In a bowl, mash yolks and ¼ cup cheese. Stir in celery, mayonnaise, chicken, parsley, wing sauce and pepper.
2. Spoon filling into egg whites. Refrigerate, covered, at least 1 hour before serving. To serve, sprinkle tops with remaining cheese and, if desired, drizzle with additional Buffalo wing sauce.
1 stuffed egg half: 85 cal., 7g fat (2g sat. fat), 98mg chol., 111mg sod., 1g carb. (0 sugars, 0 fiber), 4g pro.

TAYLOR'S JALAPENO POPPERS

If you own a barbecue joint like I do, you may dream about barbecue in your sleep because you love it so much. Jalapeno poppers are another one of my favorite foods, and this recipe is a unique way to combine those two flavors. Try your own variation by stuffing the peppers with cooked chicken or beef.
—*Taylor Hicks, Las Vegas, NV*

Prep: 35 min. • **Cook:** 5 min./batch
Makes: 6 servings

- 6 large jalapeno peppers
  Oil for deep-fat frying
- 1 cup refrigerated fully cooked barbecued shredded pork (about 8 oz.)
- 1 cup shredded mild cheddar cheese
- ¼ cup barbecue sauce
- 1 cup all-purpose flour
- 1 cup cornstarch
- 3 tsp. salt
- 3 tsp. paprika
- 12 oz. beer
  White barbecue sauce, optional

1. Cut off stem end of each jalapeno. Using the tip of a small knife, remove the seeds and membrane. In a large saucepan, bring 8 cups water to a boil. Add the seeded jalapenos; cook, uncovered, just until crisp-tender, 2-3 minutes. Remove and immediately drop into ice water. Drain and pat completely dry.
2. In an electric skillet or deep fryer, heat oil to 375°. In a small bowl, mix pork, cheese and barbecue sauce; spoon into jalapenos. In another bowl, whisk flour, cornstarch, salt and paprika; stir in beer just until moistened.
3. Using tongs, dip stuffed jalapenos into batter; fry in batches until golden brown, 3-4 minutes. Drain on paper towels. If desired, serve with white barbecue sauce.
1 appetizer: 209 cal., 8g fat (4g sat. fat), 30mg chol., 870mg sod., 23g carb. (8g sugars, 1g fiber), 10g pro.

FAST FIX | FREEZE IT
MINI GRILLED CHEESE

If you're looking for a great make-ahead snack, try these mini sammies. They're nice to have in the freezer to pull out for a quick lunch with soup or a salad. My family loves to nibble on them anytime.
—*Anita Curtis, Camarillo, CA*

Takes: 30 min. • **Makes:** 8 dozen

- 1 cup butter, softened
- 2 jars (5 oz. each) sharp American cheese spread, softened
- 1 large egg
- 1 can (4 oz.) chopped green chiles, drained
- ¼ cup salsa
- 2 cups shredded cheddar cheese
- 2 loaves (1½ lbs. each) thinly sliced sandwich bread, crusts removed

1. Preheat oven to 350°. Cream butter, cheese spread and egg until smooth. Stir in chiles, salsa and cheddar cheese. Spread about 1 Tbsp. cheese mixture on each slice of one loaf of bread.
2. Top with remaining bread; spread with more cheese mixture. Cut each sandwich into four triangles; place on a greased baking sheet lined with parchment. Bake until cheese is melted, 10 to 15 minutes.
Freeze option: To freeze, place in a single layer on a baking sheet. Freeze 1 hour. Transfer to an airtight container in the freezer. To bake frozen, preheat oven to 350°. Place on a greased baking sheet lined with parchment. Bake until grilled cheese sandwiches are bubbly and browned, 15-20 minutes.
2 triangles: 102 cal., 7g fat (4g sat. fat), 22mg chol., 213mg sod., 8g carb. (1g sugars, 0 fiber), 3g pro.

EASY IRISH CREAM

Stir up this fast and easy recipe for a fall or winter gathering. There's plenty of coffee flavor in every cozy cup.
—*Anna Hansen, Park City, UT*

Takes: 15 min. • **Makes:** 5 cups

- 2 **cups half-and-half cream**
- 1 **can (13.4 oz.) dulce de leche or sweetened condensed milk**
- 1¼ **cups Irish whiskey**
- ¼ **cup chocolate syrup**
- 2 **Tbsp. instant coffee granules**
- 2 **tsp. vanilla extract**
  Hot brewed coffee or ice cubes

Pulse first six ingredients in a blender until smooth. Stir 1-2 Tbsp. into a mug of hot coffee. Or if you prefer an iced drink, pour 1-2 Tbsp. Irish cream and about 8 oz. cold coffee over ice.

½ cup: 415 cal., 21g fat (13g sat. fat), 79mg chol., 116mg sod., 35g carb. (34g sugars, 0 fiber), 4g pro.

WARM BROCCOLI CHEESE DIP

When my family gathers for a party, this flavorful, creamy dip is always on the menu. We all love the zip from the jalapeno pepper and the crunch of the broccoli.

—Barbara Maiol, Conyers, GA

Prep: 15 min. • **Cook:** 2½ hours
Makes: 5½ cups

2   jars (8 oz. each) process cheese sauce
1   can (10¾ oz.) condensed cream of chicken soup, undiluted
3   cups frozen chopped broccoli, thawed and drained
½   lb. fresh mushrooms, chopped
2   Tbsp. chopped seeded jalapeno pepper
    Assorted fresh vegetables

In a 1½-qt. slow cooker, combine the cheese sauce and soup. Cover and cook on low for 30 minutes or until cheese is melted, stirring occasionally. Stir in the broccoli, mushrooms and jalapeno. Cover and cook on low until vegetables are tender, 2-3 hours. Serve with assorted fresh vegetables.

¼ cup: 47 cal., 3g fat (2g sat. fat), 7mg chol., 277mg sod., 3g carb. (1g sugars, 1g fiber), 2g pro.

Note: Wear disposable gloves when cutting hot peppers; the oils can burn skin. Avoid touching your face.

MEXICAN FONDUE

This irresistible fondue has become such a favorite with family and friends, I make it for all kinds of occasions throughout the year. It's fun to serve with fondue forks, but regular skewers work, too.

—*Nella Parker, Hersey, MI*

Prep: 15 min. • **Cook:** 1½ hours
Makes: 4½ cups

- 1 can (14¾ oz.) cream-style corn
- 1 can (14½ oz.) diced tomatoes, drained
- 3 Tbsp. chopped green chiles
- 1 tsp. chili powder
- 1 pkg. (16 oz.) process cheese (Velveeta), cubed
  French bread cubes

1. In a small bowl, combine the corn, tomatoes, green chiles and chili powder. Stir in cheese. Pour mixture into a 1½-qt. slow cooker coated with cooking spray.
2. Cover and cook on high until cheese is melted, 1½ hours, stirring every 30 minutes. Serve warm with bread cubes.

¼ cup: 105 cal., 6g fat (4g sat. fat), 20mg chol., 421mg sod., 7g carb. (3g sugars, 1g fiber), 5g pro.

LOADED PULLED PORK CUPS

Potato nests are simple to make and surprisingly handy for pulled pork, cheese, sour cream and other toppings. Make, bake and collect the compliments.
—*Melissa Sperka, Greensboro, NC*

- -

Prep: 40 min. • **Bake:** 25 min.
Makes: 1½ dozen

 1 pkg. (20 oz.) refrigerated shredded hash brown potatoes
 ¾ cup shredded Parmesan cheese
 2 large egg whites, beaten
 1 tsp. garlic salt
 ½ tsp. onion powder
 ¼ tsp. pepper
 1 carton (16 oz.) refrigerated fully cooked barbecued shredded pork
 1 cup shredded Colby-Monterey Jack cheese
 ½ cup sour cream
 5 bacon strips, cooked and crumbled
   Minced chives

1. Preheat oven to 450°. In a large bowl, mix hash browns, Parmesan cheese, egg whites and seasonings until blended. Divide potatoes among 18 well-greased muffin cups; press onto bottoms and up sides to form cups.

2. Bake until edges are dark golden brown, 22-25 minutes. Carefully run a knife around sides of each cup. Cool for 5 minutes before removing from the pans to a serving platter. Meanwhile, heat the pulled pork according to package directions.

3. Sprinkle cheese into cups. Top with pork, sour cream and bacon; sprinkle with chives. Serve warm.

1 pulled pork cup: 129 cal., 6g fat (3g sat. fat), 19mg chol., 439mg sod., 11g carb. (4g sugars, 0 fiber), 8g pro.

CHICKEN & BROCCOLI RABE
SOUP WITH
TORTELLINI, PAGE 128

CHAPTER 3

Shortcut Soups & Breads

Nothing beats the old-fashioned goodness of aromatic, fresh-baked bread and a steaming bowl of nourishing soup. These come together quickly with heartwarming rewards.

MUSHROOM CHEESE BREAD

My savory grilled bread is a nice complement to a hot bowl of soup or chili. For a fun flavor twist, we sometimes use half cheddar cheese and half mozzarella.

—*Dolly McDonald, Edmonton, AB*

- -

Takes: 15 min. • **Makes:** 12 servings

- 1 cup shredded part-skim mozzarella cheese
- 1 can (4 oz.) mushroom stems and pieces, drained
- ⅓ cup mayonnaise
- 2 Tbsp. shredded Parmesan cheese
- 2 Tbsp. chopped green onion
- 1 loaf (1 lb.) unsliced French bread

1. In a small bowl, combine the mozzarella cheese, mushrooms, mayonnaise, Parmesan cheese and onion. Cut loaf of French bread in half lengthwise; spread cheese mixture over cut sides.

2. Grill, covered, over indirect heat or broil 4 in. from the heat until lightly browned, 5-10 minutes. Slice and serve warm.

1 serving: 180 cal., 8g fat (2g sat. fat), 10mg chol., 347mg sod., 20g carb. (1g sugars, 1g fiber), 6g pro.

READER RAVE

"This is an amazing recipe. Very tasty and quick to make. We serve it often, either as an appetizer or beside a soup for supper. I usually do about 1½ times the cheese mixture as we like a lot of the gooey, bubbly warm topping."

— DABAKER55126, TASTEOFHOME.COM

5 INGREDIENTS | SLOW COOKER

SLOW-COOKED BEEF VEGETABLE SOUP

Convenient frozen veggies and hash browns make this meaty soup a snap to mix up. Simply brown the ground beef, then stir everything together to simmer all day. It's wonderful served with bread and a salad.

—*Carol Calhoun, Sioux Falls, SD*

- -

Prep: 10 min. • **Cook:** 8 hours
Makes: 10 servings (2½ qt.)

1. lb. ground beef
1. can (46 oz.) tomato juice
1. pkg. (16 oz.) frozen mixed vegetables, thawed
2. cups frozen cubed hash brown potatoes, thawed
1. envelope onion soup mix

1. In a large skillet, cook beef over medium heat until no longer pink; drain. Transfer to a 5-qt. slow cooker. Stir in the tomato juice, mixed vegetables, potatoes and soup mix.
2. Cover and cook on low for 8-10 hours.
1 cup: 139 cal., 4g fat (2g sat. fat), 22mg chol., 766mg sod., 16g carb. (6g sugars, 3g fiber), 11g pro.

GREEN ONION ROLLS

Better double the batch—these savory, elegant rolls will disappear fast.
—*Jane Kroeger, Key Largo, FL*

Prep: 30 min. + rising • **Bake:** 20 min.
Makes: 1 dozen

- 1 Tbsp. butter
- 1½ cups chopped green onions
- ½ tsp. pepper
- ¾ tsp. garlic salt, optional
- 1 loaf (1 lb.) frozen bread dough, thawed
- ½ cup shredded part-skim mozzarella cheese
- ⅓ cup grated Parmesan cheese

1. Preheat oven to 375°. In a large skillet, heat butter over medium-high heat; saute green onions until tender. Stir in pepper and, if desired, garlic salt. Remove from heat.
2. On a lightly floured surface, roll dough into a 12x8-in. rectangle. Spread with onion mixture. Sprinkle with cheeses.
3. Roll up jelly-roll style, starting with a long side; pinch seam to seal. Cut into 12 slices; place in greased muffin cups. Cover with greased plastic wrap; let rise in a warm place until doubled, about 30 minutes. Preheat oven to 375°.
4. Bake until golden brown, 18-20 minutes. Remove from pan to a wire rack. Serve warm.
1 roll: 142 cal., 4g fat (1g sat. fat), 7mg chol., 415mg sod., 20g carb. (2g sugars, 2g fiber), 6g pro.

READER RAVE

"Prepared as directed, except used garlic powder as that is what I had on hand. All gobbled up in minutes. A keeper recipe!"
—NAOMIE, TASTEOFHOME.COM

SLOW COOKER
TURKEY CHILI

I've taken my mother's milder recipe for chili and made it thicker and more robust. It's a favorite, especially in fall and winter.
—*Celesta Zanger, Bloomfield Hills, MI*

Prep: 20 min. • **Cook:** 6½ hours
Makes: 12 servings (3 qt.)

- 1 lb. lean ground turkey
- ¾ cup chopped celery
- ¾ cup chopped onion
- ¾ cup chopped green pepper
- 2 Tbsp. chili powder
- 1 tsp. ground cumin
- ¼ tsp. pepper
- ⅛ to ¼ tsp. cayenne pepper
- 2 cans (14½ oz. each) no-salt-added diced tomatoes, undrained
- 1 jar (24 oz.) meatless pasta sauce
- 1 can (16 oz.) hot chili beans, undrained
- 1½ cups water
- ½ cup frozen corn
- 1 can (16 oz.) kidney beans, rinsed and drained
- 1 can (15 oz.) pinto beans, rinsed and drained
  Sour cream, cubed avocado, diced jalapeno peppers, optional

1. In a large skillet, cook and crumble turkey with celery, onion and pepper over medium-high heat until no longer pink, 6-8 minutes. Transfer to a 5-qt. slow cooker. Stir in the seasonings, tomatoes, pasta sauce, chili beans, water and corn.
2. Cook, covered, on high 1 hour. Reduce setting to low; cook, covered, until flavors are blended, 5-6 hours.
3. Stir in kidney and pinto beans; cook, covered, on low 30 minutes longer. If desired, serve with sour cream, avocado and jalapeno.
1 cup: 200 cal., 4g fat (1g sat. fat), 26mg chol., 535mg sod., 29g carb. (8g sugars, 8g fiber), 15g pro.

5 INGREDIENTS
HERBED PARMESAN BREAD

I've been making my Parmesan bread for so many years, I can no longer recall where I got the recipe! Thanks to a convenient baking mix, a freshly made loaf gets in the oven fast.

—*Lesley Archer, Chapala, Mexico*

Prep: 10 min. • **Bake:** 35 min. + cooling
Makes: 1 loaf (12 slices)

- 3¾ cups biscuit/baking mix
- 1 cup plus 2 Tbsp. grated Parmesan cheese, divided
- 1 tsp. Italian seasoning
- ½ tsp. salt
- 1 large egg, room temperature
- 1 can (5 oz.) evaporated milk
- ¾ cup water

1. Preheat oven to 350°. In a large bowl, combine the biscuit mix, 1 cup cheese, Italian seasoning and salt. In a small bowl, whisk egg, milk and water. Stir into dry ingredients just until moistened. Transfer to a greased 8x4-in. loaf pan. Sprinkle with remaining cheese.
2. Bake until a toothpick inserted in the center comes out clean, 35-40 minutes. Cool 10 minutes before removing from pan to a wire rack.

1 slice: 207 cal., 9g fat (4g sat. fat), 28mg chol., 702mg sod., 25g carb. (2g sugars, 1g fiber), 7g pro.

FAST FIX
WEEKNIGHT TURKEY TORTILLA SOUP

This is now my family's most requested soup—so much so that they will make sure I have leftover turkey. You can spice up this soup and make it more filling by adding smoked sausage or andouille and some Cajun seasoning to taste.

—*Gail Lucas, Olive Branch, MS*

Takes: 30 min. • **Makes:** 8 servings (3 qt.)

- 1 Tbsp. olive oil
- 1 large onion, chopped
- 1 garlic clove, minced
- 6 cups reduced-sodium chicken broth
- 1 can (15 oz.) diced tomatoes, undrained
- 1 can (4 oz.) chopped green chiles
- 1 envelope reduced-sodium taco seasoning
- 2 cups cubed cooked turkey
- 2 cups frozen corn (about 10 oz.), thawed
- ⅓ cup minced fresh cilantro
  Optional toppings: tortilla strips, shredded Monterey Jack cheese, sliced avocado and lime wedges

In a Dutch oven, heat oil over medium-high heat. Add onion; cook and stir until tender, 1-2 minutes. Add garlic; cook 1 minute longer. Add the broth, tomatoes, chiles and taco seasoning; bring to a boil. Reduce the heat; simmer 5 minutes. Add turkey and corn; heat through. Stir in cilantro before serving. Serve with toppings of your choice.

1½ cups: 144 cal., 3g fat (1g sat. fat), 35mg chol., 846mg sod., 16g carb. (6g sugars, 2g fiber), 14g pro.

TEST KITCHEN TIP

If you want to add even more spice to this tortilla soup, use a can of diced jalapeno peppers instead of chopped green chiles. For extra heartiness, stir in a can of black beans or pinto beans.

CHICKEN, ASPARAGUS & CORN CHOWDER

Chicken, asparagus and corn combine for a light, comforting soup that's easy to whip up with common ingredients. If I have rotisserie chicken on hand, I toss that in.

—*Jennifer Vo, Irvine, CA*

- -

Takes: 30 min. • **Makes:** 4 servings

2	Tbsp. olive oil
¾	cup cut fresh asparagus (1-in. pieces)
1	small onion, finely chopped
2	Tbsp. all-purpose flour
½	tsp. salt
¼	tsp. garlic powder
⅛	to ¼ tsp. pepper
1	can (14½ oz.) chicken broth
½	cup fat-free half-and-half
1½	cups cubed cooked chicken breast
¾	cup frozen corn

1. In a large saucepan, heat oil over medium heat. Add asparagus and onion; cook and stir until tender, 3-4 minutes.

2. Stir in flour, salt, garlic powder and pepper until blended; gradually stir in the chicken broth and half-and-half. Bring mixture to a boil, stirring constantly; cook and stir until slightly thickened, 3-5 minutes. Add chicken and corn; heat through.

1 cup: 215 cal., 9g fat (1g sat. fat), 43mg chol., 800mg sod., 15g carb. (4g sugars, 1g fiber), 19g pro.

FARMHOUSE HAM CHOWDER

Leftover ham and veggies add body to this nourishing chowder, but ranch dressing is the secret ingredient that gives it zest. A little smoked Gouda adds a nice touch.
—Lisa Renshaw, Kansas City, MO

- -

Prep: 10 min. • **Cook:** 30 min.
Makes: 8 servings (2 qt.)

½ cup finely chopped onion
½ cup finely chopped celery
½ cup chopped sweet red pepper
2 Tbsp. butter
¼ cup all-purpose flour
1 envelope ranch salad dressing mix
4¼ cups whole milk
2 cups frozen cubed hash
   brown potatoes, thawed
2 cups frozen corn, thawed
2 cups cubed fully cooked ham
1 tsp. minced fresh thyme
   or ¼ tsp. dried thyme
½ cup shredded smoked Gouda cheese

1. In a large saucepan, saute the onion, celery and red pepper in butter until crisp-tender. Stir in flour and dressing mix until blended; gradually stir in milk. Bring to a boil; cook and stir until thickened, about 2 minutes.
2. Add the potatoes, corn, ham and thyme. Bring to a boil. Reduce the heat; simmer, uncovered, for 8-10 minutes to allow flavors to blend. Stir in cheese until blended.
1 cup: 267 cal., 11g fat (6g sat. fat), 48mg chol., 1288mg sod., 29g carb. (8g sugars, 2g fiber), 14g pro.

DID YOU KNOW?

Chowder is a chunky, thick, rich soup frequently made with seafood or vegetables (such as corn), but it can be made with other meat such as ham or poultry. Chowders have a milk or cream base and may be thickened with flour.

FAST FIX
QUICK CHICKEN & WILD RICE SOUP

My mother-in-law raves about the chicken and rice soup I serve at our house. I tweaked the recipe several times to get it just right.
—Teresa Jacobson, St. Johns, FL

- -

Takes: 30 min. • **Makes:** 4 servings (2 qt.)

1 pkg. (6.2 oz.) fast-cooking
   long grain and wild rice mix
2 Tbsp. butter
1 small onion, finely chopped
1 celery rib, finely chopped
1 medium carrot, finely chopped
1 garlic clove, minced
2 Tbsp. all-purpose flour
3 cups 2% milk
1½ cups chicken broth
2 cups cubed cooked chicken

1. Cook the rice mix according to the package directions.
2. Meanwhile, in a large saucepan, heat butter over medium-high heat. Add onion, celery and carrot; cook and stir until tender, 6-8 minutes. Add the garlic; cook 1 minute longer. Stir in flour until blended; gradually whisk in the milk and broth. Bring to a boil, stirring constantly; cook and stir until slightly thickened, 1-2 minutes.
3. Stir in the chicken and the rice mixture; heat through.
2 cups: 465 cal., 15g fat (7g sat. fat), 94mg chol., 1095mg sod., 50g carb. (12g sugars, 2g fiber), 32g pro.

S'MORES MONKEY BREAD MUFFINS

When it comes to mini versions of anything, I'm sold. These muffins are ooey-gooey individual-sized monkey breads made with frozen dinner rolls. They couldn't be easier to make, and kids love them.
—Tina Butler, Royse City, TX

- -

Prep: 35 min. • **Bake:** 15 min.
Makes: 1 dozen

15 frozen bread dough dinner
    rolls, thawed but still cold
1⅓ cups graham cracker crumbs
½ cup sugar
6 Tbsp. butter, cubed
1 cup miniature semisweet
   chocolate chips, divided
¾ cup miniature marshmallows
ICING
1 cup confectioners' sugar
½ tsp. butter, softened
1 to 2 Tbsp. 2% milk

1. Preheat oven to 375°. Line 12 muffin cups with foil liners.
2. Using a sharp knife, cut each dinner roll into four pieces. In a shallow bowl, mix the graham cracker crumbs and sugar. In a large microwave-safe bowl, microwave butter until melted. Dip three pieces of dough in butter, then roll in crumb mixture to coat; place in a prepared muffin cup. Repeat until all muffin cups are filled. Sprinkle the tops with ¾ cup chocolate chips and marshmallows.
3. Toss the remaining dough pieces with remaining butter, rewarming the butter if necessary. Place two additional dough pieces into each muffin cup; sprinkle with remaining chocolate chips.
4. Bake until golden brown, 15-20 minutes. Cool 5 minutes before removing from pan to a wire rack. Mix icing ingredients; spoon over tops. Serve warm.
1 muffin: 351 cal., 13g fat (6g sat. fat), 16mg chol., 337mg sod., 57g carb. (29g sugars, 3g fiber), 6g pro.

FAST FIX

GARLIC KNOTS

Here's a handy bread that can be made in no time flat. Refrigerated biscuits make preparation simple. The classic Italian flavors complement a variety of meals.
—*Jane Paschke, University Park, FL*

- -

Takes: 30 min. • **Makes:** 2½ dozen

1	tube (12 oz.) refrigerated buttermilk biscuits
¼	cup canola oil
3	Tbsp. grated Parmesan cheese
1	tsp. garlic powder
1	tsp. dried oregano
1	tsp. dried parsley flakes

1. Preheat oven to 400°. Cut each biscuit into thirds. Roll each piece into a 3-in. rope and tie into a knot; tuck ends under. Place 2 in. apart on a greased baking sheet. Bake until golden brown, 8-10 minutes.

2. In a large bowl, combine the remaining ingredients; add the warm knots and gently toss to coat.

1 roll: 46 cal., 2g fat (0 sat. fat), 0 chol., 105mg sod., 6g carb. (0 sugars, 0 fiber), 1g pro.
Diabetic exchanges: ½ starch, ½ fat.

ARBORIO RICE & WHITE BEAN SOUP

Soup is the ultimate comfort food. This one is satisfying, low in fat and comes together in less than 30 minutes.
—*Deanna McDonald, Muskegon, MI*

Takes: 30 min. • **Makes:** 4 servings (1¾ qt.)

- 1 Tbsp. olive oil
- 3 garlic cloves, minced
- ¾ cup uncooked arborio rice
- 1 carton (32 oz.) vegetable broth
- ¾ tsp. dried basil
- ½ tsp. dried thyme
- ¼ tsp. dried oregano
- 1 pkg. (16 oz.) frozen broccoli-cauliflower blend
- 1 can (15 oz.) cannellini beans, rinsed and drained
- 2 cups fresh baby spinach
  Lemon wedges, optional

1. In a large saucepan, heat oil over medium heat; saute garlic 1 minute. Add rice; cook and stir 2 minutes. Stir in broth and herbs; bring to a boil. Reduce heat; simmer, covered, until rice is al dente, about 10 minutes.

2. Stir in frozen vegetables and beans; cook, covered, over medium heat until heated through and rice is tender, 8-10 minutes, stirring occasionally. Stir in spinach until wilted. If desired, serve with lemon wedges.

1¾ cups: 303 cal., 4g fat (1g sat. fat), 0 chol., 861mg sod., 52g carb. (2g sugars, 6g fiber), 9g pro.

HEALTH TIP

Neutral flavor and tender skin make white beans a versatile addition to any soup or stew. They add almost 4 grams of fiber per serving in this recipe. If you want to cut some of the sodium, use reduced-sodium broth.

GUMBO IN A JIFFY

Here's a yummy dish that's a cinch to make. My husband loves the kick that Italian sausage gives this quick gumbo.
—*Amy Flack, Homer City, PA*

Takes: 20 min. • **Makes:** 6 servings (1½ qt.)

- 1 pkg. (12 oz.) smoked sausage
- 1 can (14½ oz.) diced tomatoes with green peppers and onions, undrained
- 1 can (14½ oz.) chicken broth
- ½ cup water
- 1 cup uncooked instant rice
- 1 can (7 oz.) whole kernel corn, drained
  Sliced green onions, optional

In a large saucepan, cook sliced sausage until browned on both sides. Stir in the tomatoes, broth and water; bring to a boil. Stir in rice and corn; cover and remove from the heat. Let stand for 5 minutes. If desired, top with sliced green onions.

1 cup: 204 cal., 6g fat (2g sat. fat), 30mg chol., 884mg sod., 23g carb. (6g sugars, 2g fiber), 13g pro. **Diabetic exchanges:** 1½ lean meat, 1½ vegetable, 1 starch.

HERBED BREAD TWISTS

A blend of herbs and a sprinkling of sesame seeds dress up frozen bread dough. The twists look fancy but they're easy to make.
—*Deb Stapert, Comstock Park, MI*

Prep: 30 min. + rising • **Bake:** 10 min.
Makes: 2 dozen

- ¼ cup butter, softened
- ¼ tsp. garlic powder
- ¼ tsp. each dried basil, marjoram and oregano
- 1 loaf (1 lb.) frozen bread dough, thawed
- ¾ cup shredded part-skim mozzarella cheese
- 1 large egg
- 1 Tbsp. water
- 4 tsp. sesame seeds

1. In a small bowl, combine the butter and seasonings. On a lightly floured surface, roll dough into a 12-in. square. Spread with butter mixture to within ½ in. of edges; sprinkle with mozzarella cheese.

2. Fold dough into thirds. Cut widthwise into 24 strips. Twist each strip twice; pinch ends to seal. Place twists 2 in. apart on greased baking sheets. Cover and let rise in a warm place until doubled, about 40 minutes.

3. Beat the egg and water; brush over dough. Sprinkle with sesame seeds. Bake at 375° until light golden brown, 10-12 minutes. Remove from pans to wire racks.

1 twist: 84 cal., 4g fat (2g sat. fat), 17mg chol., 140mg sod., 10g carb. (1g sugars, 1g fiber), 3g pro.

ABC SOUP

Instead of opening a can of alphabet soup, why not make some from scratch? Kids of all ages love this traditional soup with a tomato base, ground beef and letter-shaped pasta.
—*Sharon Brockman, Appleton, WI*

Takes: 30 min.
Makes: 11 servings (2¾ qt.)

- 1 lb. ground beef
- 1 medium onion, chopped
- 2 qt. tomato juice
- 1 can (15 oz.) mixed vegetables, undrained
- 1 cup water
- 2 beef bouillon cubes
- 1 cup uncooked alphabet pasta
   Salt and pepper to taste

In a large saucepan, cook beef and onion over medium heat until the meat is no longer pink; drain. Add tomato juice, vegetables, water and bouillon; bring to a boil. Add pasta. Cook, uncovered, until pasta is tender, 6-8 minutes, stirring frequently. Add the salt and pepper.

1 cup: 148 cal., 4g fat (2g sat. fat), 19mg chol., 858mg sod., 19g carb. (7g sugars, 2g fiber), 10g pro.

NAVY BEAN VEGETABLE SOUP

My family likes bean soup, so I came up with this enticing version. The leftovers—if there are any—are even better the next day!
—*Eleanor Mielke, Mitchell, SD*

Prep: 15 min. • **Cook:** 9 hours
Makes: 12 servings (3 qt.)

- 4 medium carrots, thinly sliced
- 2 celery ribs, chopped
- 1 medium onion, chopped
- 2 cups cubed fully cooked ham
- 1½ cups dried navy beans
- 1 envelope vegetable recipe mix (Knorr)
- 1 envelope onion soup mix
- 1 bay leaf
- ½ tsp. pepper
- 8 cups water

In a 5-qt. slow cooker, combine the first nine ingredients. Stir in water. Cover and cook on low until the beans are tender, 9-10 hours. Discard bay leaf.

1 cup: 157 cal., 2g fat (1g sat. fat), 12mg chol., 763mg sod., 24g carb. (4g sugars, 8g fiber), 11g pro.

MUSHROOM TORTELLINI SOUP

This nutritious veggie soup eats like a meal thanks to cheese tortellini. It's a real comfort on a cold or rainy day.
—*Jen Lucas, Baldwinville, MA*

- -

Takes: 25 min. • **Makes:** 6 servings (2 qt.)

- 2 Tbsp. olive oil
- ½ lb. sliced fresh mushrooms
- 2 garlic cloves, minced
- 4 cups vegetable broth
- 1 can (14½ oz.) diced tomatoes with basil, oregano and garlic, undrained
- 1 pkg. (19 oz.) frozen cheese tortellini
- 2 cups fresh baby spinach, coarsely chopped
- ⅛ tsp. pepper
  Shredded Parmesan cheese, optional

1. In a Dutch oven, heat oil over medium-high heat. Add the mushrooms; cook and stir until tender, 6-8 minutes. Add the garlic; cook 1 minute longer.

2. Add broth and tomatoes; bring to a boil. Add tortellini; cook, uncovered, just until tortellini float (do not boil), 3-4 minutes. Stir in spinach and pepper; cook just until spinach is wilted. If desired, serve with cheese.

1⅓ cups: 261 cal., 10g fat (3g sat. fat), 14mg chol., 1084mg sod., 32g carb. (5g sugars, 3g fiber), 10g pro.

SLOW COOKER

SLOW-COOKER SPICY PORK CHILI

Tender pork adds extra heartiness to this flavorful slow-cooked chili. Feel free to use boneless pork roast, pork tenderloin or boneless pork chops.

—Taste of Home *Test Kitchen*

Prep: 10 min. • **Cook:** 6 hours
Makes: 6 servings (2 ½ qt.)

- 2 lbs. boneless pork, cut into ½-in. cubes
- 1 Tbsp. canola oil
- 1 can (28 oz.) crushed tomatoes
- 2 cups frozen corn
- 1 can (15 oz.) black beans, rinsed and drained
- 1 cup chopped onion
- 2 cups beef broth
- 1 can (4 oz.) chopped green chiles
- 1 Tbsp. chili powder
- 1 tsp. minced garlic
- ½ tsp. salt
- ½ tsp. cayenne pepper
- ½ tsp. pepper
- ¼ cup minced fresh cilantro
  Shredded cheddar cheese, optional

1. In a large skillet, cook the pork in oil over medium-high heat until pork is browned, 5-6 minutes. Transfer pork and drippings to a 5-qt. slow cooker. Stir in the tomatoes, corn, beans, onion, broth, chiles, chili powder, garlic, salt, cayenne and pepper.
2. Cover and cook on low until pork is tender, 6-7 hours Stir in cilantro. Serve with cheese if desired.

1¾ cups: 395 cal., 12g fat (4g sat. fat), 89mg chol., 1055mg sod., 34g carb. (9g sugars, 8g fiber), 39g pro.

5 INGREDIENTS | FAST FIX
MONKEY BREAD BISCUITS

Classic monkey bread is a sweetly spiced breakfast treat. I came up with an easy dinner version featuring garlic and Italian seasoning the crowd will love.
—*Dana Johnson, Scottsdale, AZ*

Takes: 20 min. • **Makes:** 1 dozen

- 1   tube (16.3 oz.) large refrigerated flaky biscuits
- 3   Tbsp. butter, melted
- 1   garlic clove, minced
- ½   tsp. Italian seasoning
- ¼   cup grated Parmesan cheese
     Additional Italian seasoning

1. Preheat oven to 425°. Separate biscuits; cut each biscuit into six pieces. In a large bowl, combine butter, garlic and Italian seasoning; add biscuit pieces and toss to coat.

2. Place four pieces in each of 12 greased muffin cups. Sprinkle with the cheese and additional Italian seasoning. Bake until golden brown, 8-10 minutes. Serve warm.

1 biscuit: 159 cal., 9g fat (3g sat. fat), 9mg chol., 418mg sod., 16g carb. (3g sugars, 1g fiber), 3g pro.

SLOW COOKER
SLOW-COOKED MEXICAN BEEF SOUP

My family loves this Mexican take on beef stew, and I'm happy to make it since it's so simple. Serve with cornbread instead of corn chips to make it an even more filling meal.
—*Angela Lively, Conroe, TX*

Prep: 15 min. • **Cook:** 6 hours
Makes: 6 servings (2 qt.)

- 1   lb. beef stew meat (1¼-in. pieces)
- ¾   lb. potatoes (about 2 medium), cut into ¾-in. cubes
- 2   cups frozen corn (about 10 oz.), thawed
- 2   medium carrots, cut into ½-in. slices
- 1   medium onion, chopped
- 2   garlic cloves, minced
- 1½ tsp. dried oregano
- 1   tsp. ground cumin
- ½   tsp. salt
- ¼   tsp. crushed red pepper flakes
- 2   cups beef stock
- 1   can (10 oz.) diced tomatoes and green chiles, undrained
       Sour cream and tortilla chips, optional

In a 5- or 6-qt. slow cooker, combine first 12 ingredients. Cook, covered, on low until meat is tender, 6-8 hours. If desired, serve with sour cream and chips.

1⅓ cups: 218 cal., 6g fat (2g sat. fat), 47mg chol., 602mg sod., 24g carb. (5g sugars, 3g fiber), 19g pro. **Diabetic exchanges:** 2 lean meat, 1½ starch.

ITALIAN CHICKEN MEATBALL & BEAN SOUP

In North Dakota, it's pretty common for winter temperatures to fall below zero. Satisfying soups like this are a must.
—*Noelle Myers, Grand Forks, ND*

Prep: 35 min. • **Cook:** 15 min.
Makes: 8 servings (3 qt.)

- 1   large egg, lightly beaten
- ½   cup savory herb or chicken stuffing mix, crushed
- ¼   tsp. salt
- 1   lb. ground chicken
SOUP
- 1   Tbsp. olive oil
- 3   celery ribs, chopped
- 2   medium carrots, chopped
- 1   small onion, chopped
- 2   tsp. Italian seasoning
- 2   garlic cloves, minced
- 3   cans (15 oz. each) cannellini beans, rinsed and drained
- 6   cups reduced-sodium chicken broth
- 1½ tsp. grated lemon zest
- 5   oz. fresh baby spinach (about 6 cups)
- 2   Tbsp. lemon juice

1. Preheat oven to 400°. In a large bowl, combine egg, stuffing mix and salt. Add the chicken; mix lightly but thoroughly. Shape into 1¼-in. balls. Place meatballs in a greased 15x10x1-in. baking pan. Bake until cooked through, 14-17 minutes.

2. Meanwhile, in a 6-qt. stockpot, heat oil over medium heat. Add celery, carrots and onion; cook and stir until the carrots are softened, 5-7 minutes. Stir in Italian seasoning and garlic; cook 1 minute longer.

3. Add beans, broth and lemon zest; bring to a boil. Reduce heat to low. Stir in spinach and meatballs; cook just until spinach is wilted. Stir in lemon juice.

1½ cups: 265 cal., 8g fat (2g sat. fat), 61mg chol., 828mg sod., 30g carb. (2g sugars, 8g fiber), 20g pro.

CHICKEN & BROCCOLI RABE SOUP WITH TORTELLINI

With chicken, pasta and a bold tomato broth, this hearty and inviting soup is comfort food at its best. Extra protein from the tortellini makes this a meal on its own.
—*Cyndy Gerken, Naples, FL*

- -

Prep: 15 min. • **Cook:** 45 min.
Makes: 10 servings (3¼ qt.)

- 1 lb. broccoli rabe
- ½ tsp. ground nutmeg
- ¼ tsp. pepper, divided
- 2 Tbsp. olive oil
- ¼ lb. diced pancetta or 4 bacon strips, chopped
- 1 large onion, chopped
- 4 garlic cloves, minced
- 2 cartons (32 oz. each) chicken stock
- 1 can (15 oz.) tomato sauce
- 3 fresh thyme sprigs
- 3 Tbsp. minced fresh parsley
- 1 bay leaf
- ¼ cup grated Parmesan cheese
- 1 rotisserie chicken, skin removed, shredded
- 1 pkg. (19 oz.) frozen cheese tortellini
  Additional grated Parmesan cheese

1. Fill a Dutch oven two-thirds full with water; bring to a boil. Cut ½ in. off ends of broccoli rabe; trim woody stems. Coarsely chop the stems and leaves; add to the boiling water. Cook, uncovered, just until crisp-tender, 1-2 minutes. Drain and remove from pan; sprinkle with the nutmeg and ⅛ tsp. pepper.

2. In same Dutch oven, heat olive oil over medium heat. Add the pancetta; cook until brown and crisp, 4-5 minutes. Add onion and the remaining pepper; cook until tender, 3-4 minutes. Stir in garlic; cook 1 minute longer. Add the next six ingredients and broccoli rabe; bring to a boil. Reduce heat; simmer, covered, 30 minutes. Meanwhile, cook the tortellini according to package directions; drain.

3. Discard bay leaf and thyme sprigs from soup. Add chicken to soup; heat through. To serve, spoon tortellini into individual bowls; pour soup into bowls. Sprinkle with additional Parmesan cheese.

1⅓ cups: 328 cal., 13g fat (4g sat. fat), 72mg chol., 1058mg sod., 24g carb. (3g sugars, 3g fiber), 28g pro.

TEST KITCHEN TIP

To mix it up, try Thai-flavored chicken broth in place of some or all of the chicken stock.

SAVORY BISCUIT-BREADSTICKS

I love to experiment in the kitchen and find creative ways to dress up simple ingredients, like refrigerated biscuits. The results usually are a big hit, like these superfast breadsticks.
—*Billy Hensley, Mount Carmel, TN*

Takes: 20 min. • **Makes:** 10 breadsticks

- ½ cup grated Parmesan cheese
- 2 tsp. dried minced garlic
- ¼ tsp. crushed red pepper flakes
- 1 tube (12 oz.) refrigerated buttermilk biscuits
- 2 Tbsp. olive oil

Preheat the oven to 400°. In a shallow bowl, mix the cheese, garlic and pepper flakes. Roll each biscuit into a 6-in. rope. Brush lightly with oil; roll in the cheese mixture. Place on a greased baking sheet. Bake until golden brown, 8-10 minutes.

1 breadstick: 142 cal., 8g fat (2g sat. fat), 3mg chol., 353mg sod., 16g carb. (2g sugars, 0 fiber), 3g pro.

ITALIAN HERB & CHEESE BREADSTICKS

Thanks to the convenience of frozen bread dough, these delectable breadsticks take just minutes to make. Dip the cheesy bites into warm marinara sauce.

—*Rebekah Beyer, Sabetha, KS*

- -

Prep: 20 min. • **Bake:** 20 min.
Makes: 2 dozen

- 1 loaf (1 lb.) frozen bread dough, thawed
- ⅓ cup butter, softened
- 1 Tbsp. Italian seasoning
- 1 garlic clove, minced
- ¾ cup shredded part-skim mozzarella cheese
- ½ cup grated Parmesan cheese, divided Marinara sauce, warmed, optional

1. On a lightly floured surface, roll dough into a 12-in. square. In a small bowl, mix butter, Italian seasoning and garlic; spread over dough. Sprinkle the mozzarella cheese and ¼ cup Parmesan cheese over butter mixture. Fold dough in thirds over filling; pinch seams to seal.
2. Cut crosswise into twenty-four ½-in.-wide strips. Twist each strip 2-3 times. Place 2 in. apart on greased baking sheets. Cover and let rise until almost doubled, about 30 minutes.
3. Preheat oven to 375°. Sprinkle with remaining Parmesan cheese. Bake until golden brown, 20-22 minutes. If desired, serve with marinara sauce.

1 breadstick: 93 cal., 4g fat (2g sat. fat), 10mg chol., 180mg sod., 10g carb. (1g sugars, 1g fiber), 3g pro.

VEGGIE CHEESE SOUP

My niece makes this in a slow cooker by putting in all the ingredients except the cheese. When the veggies are tender, she adds the cubed cheese and 5 minutes later, a tasty and nutritious meal is served.

—*Jean Hall, Rapid City, SD*

- -

Prep: 15 min. • **Cook:** 25 min.
Makes: 9 servings (1½ qt.)

- 1 medium onion, chopped
- 1 celery rib, chopped
- 2 small red potatoes, cut into ½-in. cubes
- 2¾ cups water
- 2 tsp. reduced-sodium chicken bouillon granules
- 1 Tbsp. cornstarch
- ¼ cup cold water
- 1 can (10¾ oz.) reduced-fat reduced-sodium condensed cream of chicken soup, undiluted
- 3 cups frozen California-blend vegetables, thawed
- ½ cup chopped fully cooked lean ham
- 8 oz. reduced-fat process cheese (Velveeta), cubed

1. In a large saucepan coated with a cooking spray, cook onion and celery over medium heat until onion is tender. Stir in the potatoes, water and bouillon. Bring to a boil. Reduce heat; cover and simmer for 10 minutes.
2. Combine the cornstarch and cold water until smooth; gradually stir into soup. Return to a boil; cook and stir until mixture is slightly thickened, 1-2 minutes. Stir in condensed soup until blended.
3. Reduce heat; add vegetables and ham. Cook and stir until vegetables are tender. Stir in cheese until melted.

¾ cup: 115 cal., 4g fat (2g sat. fat), 15mg chol., 682mg sod., 13g carb. (4g sugars, 1g fiber), 8g pro.

TURKEY SAUSAGE, BUTTERNUT SQUASH & KALE SOUP

Kale and butternut squash are two of my favorite fall veggies. This recipe combines them into a warm and comforting soup. If you love sweet potatoes, use those in place of the butternut squash.

—*Laura Koch, Lincoln, NE*

- -

Prep: 20 min. • **Cook:** 30 min.
Makes: 10 servings (2½ qt.)

- 1 pkg. (19½ oz.) Italian turkey sausage links, casings removed
- 1 medium butternut squash (about 3 lbs.), peeled and cubed
- 2 cartons (32 oz. each) reduced-sodium chicken broth
- 1 bunch kale, trimmed and coarsely chopped (about 16 cups)
- ½ cup shaved Parmesan cheese

1. In a stockpot, cook sausage over medium heat until no longer pink, 8-10 minutes, breaking into crumbles.
2. Add squash and broth; bring to a boil. Gradually stir in kale, allowing it to wilt slightly between additions. Return to a boil. Reduce heat; simmer, uncovered, until vegetables are tender, 15-20 minutes. Top servings with shaved Parmesan cheese.

1 cup: 163 cal., 5g fat (2g sat. fat), 23mg chol., 838mg sod., 20g carb. (5g sugars, 5g fiber), 13g pro.

CHEESE-FILLED GARLIC ROLLS

To change up plain old dinner rolls, I added mozzarella cheese. Now my family wants them at every gathering. I don't mind, even in a time crunch.

—Rosalie Fittery, Philadelphia, PA

Prep: 20 min. + rising • **Bake:** 15 min.
Makes: 2 dozen

- 1 loaf (1 lb.) frozen bread dough, thawed
- 24 cubes part-skim mozzarella cheese (¾ in. each, about 10 oz.)
- 3 Tbsp. butter, melted
- 2 tsp. minced fresh parsley
- 1 garlic clove, minced
- ½ tsp. Italian seasoning
- ½ tsp. crushed red pepper flakes
- 2 Tbsp. grated Parmigiano-Reggiano cheese

1. Divide the dough into 24 portions. Shape each portion around a cheese cube to cover completely; pinch to seal. Place each roll in a greased muffin cup, seam side down. Cover with kitchen towels; let rise in a warm place until doubled, about 30 minutes. Preheat oven to 350°.
2. In a small bowl, mix butter, parsley, garlic, Italian seasoning and pepper flakes. Brush over rolls; sprinkle with cheese. Bake until golden brown, 15-18 minutes.
3. Cool 5 minutes before removing from pans. Serve warm.
1 roll: 103 cal., 5g fat (2g sat. fat), 12mg chol., 205mg sod., 10g carb. (1g sugars, 1g fiber), 5g pro.

5 INGREDIENTS | FAST FIX
EASY PARMESAN BISCUITS

This recipe is simple but so good. Children love to dip the biscuits in butter and coat them with the cheese.

—Linda Becker, Olympia, WA

Takes: 15 min. • **Makes:** 5 biscuits

- 1 tube (6 oz.) refrigerated buttermilk biscuits, separated into 5 biscuits
- 3 Tbsp. butter, melted
- ½ cup grated Parmesan cheese

Preheat oven to 400°. Dip both sides of the biscuits into melted butter, then into cheese. Place 1 in. apart in a well-greased 9-in. round pan. Bake until golden brown, 8-11 minutes. Serve warm.
1 biscuit: 177 cal., 10g fat (6g sat. fat), 25mg chol., 462mg sod., 16g carb. (0 sugars, 0 fiber), 6g pro.

FAST FIX
BROCCOLI-CHICKEN RICE SOUP

I transformed leftover cooked chicken and rice into this tasty soup. It even passed the company test so I knew it was a keeper.

—Karen Reed, Middletown, OH

Takes: 30 min. • **Makes:** 6 servings (2½ qt.)

- 4 cups whole milk
- 2 cans (14½ oz. each) chicken broth
- 1 envelope ranch salad dressing mix
- 2 cups fresh broccoli florets
- ½ lb. process cheese (Velveeta), cubed
- 3 cups cooked rice
- 2 cups cubed cooked chicken

In a Dutch oven, combine milk, broth and dressing mix; bring to a boil. Add broccoli; cook, uncovered, until tender, 3-5 minutes. Stir in process cheese until melted. Add the rice and chicken; heat soup through, stirring occasionally.
1⅔ cups: 442 cal., 19g fat (10g sat. fat), 98mg chol., 1571mg sod., 38g carb. (11g sugars, 1g fiber), 28g pro.

SALMON SWEET POTATO SOUP

I created this recipe as a healthier alternative to whitefish chowder, which is a favorite in the area where I grew up. Salmon and sweet potatoes boost the nutrition, and the slow cooker makes this soup convenient.

—*Matthew Hass, Ellison Bay, WI*

Prep: 20 min. • **Cook:** 5½ hours
Makes: 8 servings (3 qt.)

- 1 Tbsp. olive oil
- 1 medium onion, chopped
- 1 medium carrot, chopped
- 1 celery rib, chopped
- 3 garlic cloves, minced
- 2 medium sweet potatoes, peeled and cut into ½-in. cubes
- 1½ cups frozen corn, thawed
- 6 cups reduced-sodium chicken broth
- 1 tsp. celery salt
- 1 tsp. dill weed
- ½ tsp. salt
- ¾ tsp. pepper
- 1½ lbs. salmon fillets, skin removed and cut into ¾-in. pieces
- 1 can (12 oz.) fat-free evaporated milk
- 2 Tbsp. minced fresh parsley

1. In a large skillet, heat oil over medium heat. Add onion, carrot and celery; cook and stir until tender, 4-5 minutes. Add garlic; cook 1 minute longer. Transfer to a 5-qt. slow cooker. Add the next seven ingredients. Cook, covered, on low until sweet potatoes are tender, 5-6 hours.

2. Stir in salmon, milk and parsley. Cook, covered, until fish just begins to flake easily with a fork, 30-40 minutes longer.

1½ cups: 279 cal., 10g fat (2g sat. fat), 45mg chol., 834mg sod., 26g carb. (13g sugars, 3g fiber), 22g pro. **Diabetic exchanges:** 3 lean meat, 1½ starch, ½ fat.

MOM'S CHOCOLATE BREAD

My mom made this divine chocolaty bread for holidays or by special request, but it makes any old morning even better. I always think of our family when I smell it baking.
—*Rachel Rhodes, Hartsville, SC*

Prep: 10 min. • **Bake:** 30 min. + cooling
Makes: 1 loaf (12 slices)

- 4 **Tbsp. sugar, divided**
- 3 **Tbsp. all-purpose flour**
- 1 **Tbsp. cold butter**
- 1 **to 3 Tbsp. ground cinnamon**
- 1 **tube (8 oz.) refrigerated crescent rolls**
- ⅔ **cup semisweet chocolate chips**
- 1 **Tbsp. butter, melted**

1. Preheat oven to 375°. For streusel, in a small bowl, mix 3 Tbsp. sugar and flour; cut in butter until crumbly. Reserve half of the streusel for topping. Stir cinnamon and remaining sugar into remaining streusel.
2. Unroll crescent dough into one long rectangle; press perforations to seal. Sprinkle with chocolate chips and cinnamon mixture. Roll up jelly-roll style, starting with a long side; pinch seam to seal. Fold roll in half lengthwise; transfer to a greased 8x4-in. loaf pan. Brush with butter; sprinkle with reserved streusel.
3. Bake until golden brown, 30-35 minutes. Cool in pan 10 minutes before removing to a wire rack to cool completely.
1 slice: 164 cal., 9g fat (4g sat. fat), 5mg chol., 165mg sod., 21g carb. (11g sugars, 2g fiber), 2g pro.

CHICKEN GNOCCHI PESTO SOUP

After tasting a similar soup at a restaurant, I created this quick and tasty version.
—*Deanna Smith, Des Moines, IA*

- -

Takes: 25 min. • **Makes:** 4 servings (1½ qt.)

- 1 jar (15 oz.) roasted garlic Alfredo sauce
- 2 cups water
- 2 cups rotisserie chicken, roughly chopped
- 1 tsp. Italian seasoning
- ¼ tsp. salt
- ¼ tsp. pepper
- 1 pkg. (16 oz.) potato gnocchi
- 3 cups coarsley chopped fresh spinach
- 4 tsp. prepared pesto

In a large saucepan, combine the first six ingredients; bring to a gentle boil, stirring occasionally. Stir in gnocchi and spinach; cook until gnocchi float, 3-8 minutes. Top each serving with pesto.

Note: Look for potato gnocchi in the pasta or frozen foods section.

1½ cups: 586 cal., 26g fat (11g sat. fat), 158mg chol., 1650mg sod., 56g carb. (3g sugars, 4g fiber), 31g pro.

READER RAVE

"I am so thrilled with this recipe. It became my favorite winter soup. I have made it with broccoli, and mushrooms and less spinach; no chicken or with bacon. It is very quick, and can be changed easily with what you have on hand. Yummy!"
—HOOVER1030, TASTEOFHOME.COM

DILL CHICKEN SOUP

I could eat soup for every meal, all year long. I particularly like dill and spinach—they add a brightness to this light and healthy soup.
—*Robin Haas, Jamaica Plain, MA*

- -

Takes: 30 min. • **Makes:** 6 servings (2 qt.)

- 1 Tbsp. canola oil
- 2 medium carrots, chopped
- 1 small onion, coarsely chopped
- 2 garlic cloves, minced
- ½ cup uncooked whole wheat orzo pasta
- 1½ cups coarsely shredded rotisserie chicken
- 6 cups reduced-sodium chicken broth
- 1½ cups frozen peas (about 6 oz.)
- 8 oz. fresh baby spinach (about 10 cups)
- 2 Tbsp. chopped fresh dill or 1 Tbsp. dill weed
- 2 Tbsp. lemon juice
  Coarsely ground pepper, optional

1. In a 6-qt. stockpot, heat oil over medium heat. Add carrots, onion and garlic; saute until carrots are tender, 4-5 minutes.

2. Stir in orzo, chicken and broth; bring to a boil. Reduce the heat; simmer, uncovered, 5 minutes. Stir in peas, spinach and dill; return to a boil. Reduce heat; simmer, uncovered, until orzo is tender, 3-4 minutes. Stir in lemon juice. If desired, top each serving with coarsely ground pepper.

1⅓ cups: 198 cal., 6g fat (1g sat. fat), 31mg chol., 681mg sod., 20g carb. (4g sugars, 5g fiber), 18g pro. **Diabetic exchanges:** 2 lean meat, 1 starch, 1 vegetable, ½ fat.

MUFFIN-TIN TAMALE CAKES

We needed snack inspiration beyond peanut butter and jelly. These muffin tamales have all of the flavor without the fuss. Pair with skewered fruit.
—*Suzanne Clark, Phoenix, AZ*

Prep: 25 min. • **Bake:** 20 min.
Makes: 2 dozen

- 2 pkg. (8½ oz. each) cornbread/muffin mix
- 1 can (14¾ oz.) cream-style corn
- 2 large eggs, room temperature, lightly beaten
- 1½ cups shredded reduced-fat Mexican cheese blend, divided
- 1½ cups chopped cooked chicken breast
- ¾ cup red enchilada sauce

1. Preheat oven to 400°. In a large bowl, combine muffin mix, corn and eggs; stir just until moistened. Stir in 1 cup cheese. In another bowl, toss chicken breast with enchilada sauce.

2. Fill each of 24 foil-lined or greased muffin cups with 2 Tbsp. batter. Place 1 Tbsp. chicken mixture into center of each; cover with about 1 Tbsp. batter.

3. Bake until golden brown, 13-15 minutes. Sprinkle tops with remaining cheese. Bake until cheese is melted, 3-5 minutes longer. Cool 5 minutes before removing from pan to wire racks. Serve warm. Refrigerate leftovers.

1 muffin: 137 cal., 5g fat (2g sat. fat), 28mg chol., 313mg sod., 18g carb. (5g sugars, 2g fiber), 7g pro. **Diabetic exchanges:** 1 starch, 1 lean meat.

start WITH
CORNBREAD/ MUFFIN MIX

KIDS' FAVORITE CHILI

This sweet and easy chili is sure to warm up the whole family on chilly nights. The recipe has been in my family for three generations.
—*Terri Keeney, Greeley, CO*

Takes: 25 min. • **Makes:** 4 servings (1½ qt.)

- 1 lb. ground turkey
- ½ cup chopped onion
- 1 can (15¾ oz.) pork and beans
- 1 can (14½ oz.) diced tomatoes, undrained
- 1 can (10¾ oz.) condensed tomato soup, undiluted
- 1 Tbsp. brown sugar
- 1 Tbsp. chili powder

In a large saucepan, cook turkey and onion over medium heat until meat is no longer pink; drain. Stir in the remaining ingredients. Bring to a boil. Reduce heat; cover and simmer until heated through, 15-20 minutes.

1½ cups: 359 cal., 10g fat (2g sat. fat), 75mg chol., 908mg sod., 43g carb. (20g sugars, 9g fiber), 30g pro.

READER RAVE

"This is my new go-to chili recipe! The ultimate comfort food and a perfect dinner for the winter months."
—GINA KAPFHAMER, TASTEOFHOME.COM

CHEESY PIZZA ROLLS

The cast-iron skillet browns these delicious rolls to perfection. My family can't get enough. Use whatever pizza toppings your family likes best.
—*Dorothy Smith, El Dorado, AR*

Prep: 15 min. • **Bake:** 25 min.
Makes: 8 appetizers

- 1 loaf (1 lb.) frozen pizza dough, thawed
- ½ cup pasta sauce
- 1 cup shredded part-skim mozzarella cheese, divided
- 1 cup coarsely chopped pepperoni (about 64 slices)
- ½ lb. bulk Italian sausage, cooked and crumbled
- ¼ cup grated Parmesan cheese
  Minced fresh basil, optional
  Crushed red pepper flakes, optional

1. Preheat oven to 400°. On a lightly floured surface, roll dough into a 16x10-in. rectangle. Brush with the pasta sauce to within ½ in. of the edges.

2. Sprinkle with ½ cup mozzarella cheese, pepperoni, sausage and Parmesan. Roll up jelly-roll style, starting with a long side; pinch seam to seal. Cut into eight slices. Place in a greased 9-in. cast-iron skillet or greased 9-in. round baking pan, cut side down.

3. Bake 20 minutes; sprinkle with remaining mozzarella cheese. Bake until golden brown, 5-10 minutes more. If desired, serve rolls with minced fresh basil and crushed red pepper flakes.

1 appetizer: 355 cal., 19g fat (7g sat. fat), 42mg chol., 978mg sod., 29g carb. (3g sugars, 0 fiber), 14g pro.

SHRIMP EGG DROP SOUP

Who knew that egg drop soup could be so easy? It's just three simple steps to this better-than-restaurant-quality soup with just the right blend of veggies and shrimp.
—Taste of Home *Test Kitchen*

Takes: 30 min. • **Makes:** 4 servings (1¼ qt.)

- 4 tsp. cornstarch
- ½ tsp. soy sauce
- ⅛ tsp. ground ginger
- 1½ cups cold water, divided
- 2 cans (14½ oz. each) chicken broth
- 1½ cups frozen home-style egg noodles
- 1 cup frozen broccoli florets, thawed and coarsely chopped
- ½ cup julienned carrot
- 1 large egg, lightly beaten
- ½ lb. cooked medium shrimp, peeled and deveined

1. In a small bowl, combine the cornstarch, soy sauce, ground ginger and ½ cup cold water; set aside.
2. In a large saucepan, combine broth and remaining water. Bring to a simmer; add noodles. Cook, uncovered, for 15 minutes. Add the broccoli and carrot; simmer until noodles are tender, 3-4 minutes longer.
3. Drizzle beaten egg into hot soup, stirring constantly. Stir cornstarch mixture and add to the pan. Bring to a boil; cook and stir until slightly thickened, about 2 minutes. Add the shrimp; heat through.
1¼ cups: 241 cal., 4g fat (1g sat. fat), 196mg chol., 1050mg sod., 30g carb. (3g sugars, 2g fiber), 18g pro.

WEEKNIGHT TACO SOUP

This soup turned out delicious on the first try, when I was working without a recipe. You could also add cooked ground beef or cubed stew meat dredged in seasoned flour and browned for a heartier meal.
—Amanda Swartz, Goderich, ON

Takes: 30 min. • **Makes:** 6 servings (2½ qt.)

- 1 Tbsp. canola oil
- 1 large onion, chopped
- 1 medium sweet red pepper, chopped
- 1 medium green pepper, chopped
- 1 can (28 oz.) diced tomatoes, undrained
- 3 cups vegetable broth
- 1 can (15 oz.) pinto beans, rinsed and drained
- 1½ cups frozen corn
- 1 envelope taco seasoning
- ¼ tsp. salt
- ¼ tsp. pepper
- 1 pkg. (8.8 oz.) ready-to-serve long grain rice
- 1 cup sour cream
  Optional toppings: shredded cheddar cheese, crushed tortilla chips and additional sour cream

1. In a Dutch oven, heat oil over medium heat. Add onion and peppers; cook and stir until crisp-tender, 3-5 minutes.
2. Add tomatoes, broth, beans, corn, taco seasoning, salt and pepper; bring to a boil. Reduce the heat; simmer, uncovered, until the vegetables are tender, 10-15 minutes. Reduce heat. Stir in rice and sour cream; heat through. Serve with toppings as desired.
Freeze option: Freeze cooled soup in freezer containers. To use, partially thaw in refrigerator overnight. Heat through in a saucepan, stirring occasionally; add a little broth if necessary.
1¾ cups: 333 cal., 12g fat (5g sat. fat), 9mg chol., 1288mg sod., 49g carb. (10g sugars, 7g fiber), 9g pro.

HAM & BROCCOLI CORNBREAD

Leftovers haunt me. Often nobody wants to eat them, and I hate to see food go to waste. A cornbread casserole is an excellent way to leverage many combinations of leftover meat and veggies into new exciting meals that everyone will love.

—*Fay Moreland, Wichita Falls, TX*

Prep: 15 min. • **Bake:** 35 min. + cooling
Makes: 12 servings

- 5 Tbsp. butter, divided
- 2 large eggs, room temperature
- 1 cup 2% milk
- ½ cup sour cream
  Pinch cayenne pepper
- 2 pkg. (8½ oz. each) cornbread/muffin mix
- 2 cups chopped fresh broccoli
- 1½ cups shredded sharp cheddar cheese
- 1½ cups cubed fully cooked ham
- 3 green onions, thinly sliced

1. Preheat oven to 375°. Place 3 Tbsp. butter in a 12-in. cast-iron skillet; place pan in oven until butter is melted, 3-5 minutes. Carefully tilt pan to coat bottom and sides with butter.

2. Melt remaining butter. In a large bowl, whisk together eggs, milk, sour cream, cayenne pepper and melted butter until blended. Add muffin mixes; stir just until moistened. Fold in remaining ingredients. Pour into hot pan.

3. Bake until cornbread is golden brown and a toothpick inserted in center comes out clean, 35-40 minutes. Let stand 15 minutes before serving.

1 piece: 338 cal., 18g fat (9g sat. fat), 73mg chol., 700mg sod., 31g carb. (10g sugars, 3g fiber), 12g pro.

SPICY PEANUT CHICKEN CHILI

After spending time in the Southwest, I discovered Mexican peanut chicken and thought it would be fun to make it into a chili. Chipotle peppers give it a nice spice that's extra warming on a cold day.
—*Crystal Schlueter, Babbitt, MN*

Takes: 30 min. • **Makes:** 6 servings (2 qt.)

- 1 can (15 oz.) pinto beans, rinsed and drained
- 1 can (14½ oz.) Mexican diced tomatoes, undrained
- 1 can (14½ oz.) no-salt-added diced tomatoes, undrained
- 1 can (14½ oz.) reduced-sodium chicken broth
- 1 pkg. (12 oz.) frozen southwestern corn
- 3 Tbsp. creamy peanut butter
- 1 to 2 Tbsp. minced chipotle peppers in adobo sauce
- 2 tsp. chili powder
- ½ tsp. ground cinnamon
- 3 cups coarsely shredded rotisserie chicken
- 6 Tbsp. reduced-fat sour cream
  Minced fresh cilantro, optional

1. Place the first nine ingredients in a 6-qt. stockpot; bring to a boil. Reduce the heat; simmer, covered, until flavors are blended, about 15 minutes.

2. Stir in chicken; heat through. Serve with sour cream and, if desired, cilantro.

Freeze option: Freeze cooled chili in freezer containers. To use, partially thaw in refrigerator overnight. Heat through in a saucepan, stirring occasionally; add a little broth if necessary.

1⅓ cups chili with 1 Tbsp. sour cream: 368 cal., 13g fat (3g sat. fat), 67mg chol., 797mg sod., 33g carb. (11g sugars, 6g fiber), 30g pro.

CORN CHOWDER WITH POTATOES

I developed this soup out of two other recipes to create my own low-calorie favorite. It turned out so well that I entered it in my county fair and won a blue ribbon.
—*Alyce Wyman, Pembina, ND*

Prep: 15 min. • **Cook:** 30 min.
Makes: 6 servings (1½ qt.)

- 1 small onion, chopped
- 1 garlic clove, minced
- 1½ cups cubed peeled potatoes
- ¼ cup shredded carrot
- 2 cups water
- 2 tsp. dried parsley flakes
- 2 tsp. reduced-sodium chicken bouillon granules
- ¼ tsp. salt
- ⅛ tsp. pepper
- 1 can (14¾ oz.) cream-style corn
- 1½ cups fat-free milk, divided
- 3 bacon strips, cooked and crumbled
- 3 Tbsp. all-purpose flour
- ½ cup cubed reduced-fat process cheese (Velveeta)
- ½ cup beer or nonalcoholic beer
- ½ tsp. liquid smoke, optional

1. Place a large saucepan coated with cooking spray over medium heat. Add the onion and garlic; cook and stir until tender. Add the potatoes, carrot, water, parsley flakes and seasonings. Bring to a boil. Reduce the heat; cook, covered, until the potatoes are tender, 15-20 minutes.
2. Stir in corn, 1¼ cups milk and bacon. In a small bowl, mix flour and remaining milk until smooth; stir into soup. Bring to a boil; cook and stir until thickened, about 2 minutes. Add cheese; stir until melted. Stir in beer and, if desired, liquid smoke; heat through.

1 cup: 179 cal., 3g fat (1g sat. fat), 9mg chol., 681mg sod., 31g carb. (8g sugars, 2g fiber), 8g pro.

READER RAVE

"We loved this! My husband and I both thought the liquid smoke was what made it. Without it, it might have been bland. Just don't use too much."
—JHEVNER, TASTEOFHOME.COM

SLOW COOKER

HEARTY HOMEMADE CHICKEN NOODLE SOUP

This satisfying homemade soup with a hint of cayenne is brimming with vegetables, chicken and noodles. The recipe came from my father-in-law, but I made some adjustments to give it my own spin.
—*Norma Reynolds, Overland Park, KS*

Prep: 20 min. • **Cook:** 5½ hours
Makes: 12 servings (3 qt.)

- 12 fresh baby carrots, cut into ½-in. pieces
- 4 celery ribs, cut into ½-in. pieces
- ¾ cup finely chopped onion
- 1 Tbsp. minced fresh parsley
- ½ tsp. pepper
- ¼ tsp. cayenne pepper
- 1½ tsp. mustard seed
- 2 garlic cloves, peeled and halved
- 1¼ lbs. boneless skinless chicken breast halves
- 1¼ lbs. boneless skinless chicken thighs
- 4 cans (14½ oz. each) chicken broth
- 1 pkg. (9 oz.) refrigerated linguine
  Coarsely ground pepper and additional minced fresh parsley, optional

1. In a 5-qt. slow cooker, combine the first six ingredients. Place mustard seed and garlic on a double thickness of cheesecloth; bring up corners of cloth and tie with kitchen string to form a bag. Place in slow cooker. Add chicken and broth. Cover and cook on low until meat is tender, 5-6 hours.
2. Discard spice bag. Remove chicken; cool slightly. Stir linguine into soup; cover and cook on high until tender, about 30 minutes. Cut chicken into pieces and return to soup; heat through. Sprinkle with coarsely ground pepper and additional parsley if desired.

1 cup: 199 cal., 6g fat (2g sat. fat), 73mg chol., 663mg sod., 14g carb. (2g sugars, 1g fiber), 22g pro. **Diabetic exchanges:** 3 lean meat, 1 starch.

SWISS & CARAWAY FLATBREADS

My mom came across this rustic-looking flatbread recipe many years ago and always made it on Christmas Eve. Now I make it for my own family throughout the year. It's easy to double or cut in half depending on how many you're serving.
—*Diane Berger, Sequim, WA*

- -

Prep: 20 min. + rising • **Bake:** 10 min.
Makes: 2 loaves (16 pieces each)

- 2   **loaves (1 lb. each) frozen bread dough, thawed**
- ¼   **cup butter, melted**
- ¼   **cup canola oil**
- 1   **Tbsp. dried minced onion**
- 1   **Tbsp. Dijon mustard**
- 2   **tsp. caraway seeds**
- 1   **tsp. Worcestershire sauce**
- 1   **Tbsp. dry sherry, optional**
- 2   **cups shredded Swiss cheese**

1. On a lightly floured surface, roll each portion of dough into a 15x10-in. rectangle. Transfer to two greased 15x10x1-in. baking pans. Cover with kitchen towels; let rise in a warm place until doubled, about 45 minutes.
2. Preheat oven to 425°. Using fingertips, press several dimples into dough. In a small bowl, whisk the melted butter, oil, onion, mustard, caraway seeds, Worcestershire sauce and, if desired, sherry until blended; brush over the dough. Sprinkle with cheese. Bake until golden brown, 10-15 minutes. Serve warm.

Freeze option: Cut cooled flatbreads into pieces. Freeze in freezer containers. To use, reheat flatbreads on an ungreased baking sheet in a preheated 425° oven until heated through.
1 piece: 134 cal., 6g fat (2g sat. fat), 10mg chol., 199mg sod., 14g carb. (1g sugars, 1g fiber), 5g pro.

start WITH
FROZEN BREAD DOUGH

PORK EDAMAME SOUP

My husband grew up in a traditional Asian household, and he gives this soup high marks for authentic taste. I think the Asian hot chili sauce is what makes the dish, but any type of hot sauce would give it a delicious kick!

—*Kari Sue, Bend, OR*

- -

Prep: 25 min. • **Cook:** 4 hours 10 min.
Makes: 6 servings (2¼ qt.)

- 4 tsp. canola oil
- 2 lbs. boneless country-style pork ribs, trimmed, cut into 1-in. cubes
- 2 medium carrots, cut into 1-in. pieces
- 1 medium sweet red pepper, cut into 1-in. pieces
- 1 can (8 oz.) sliced water chestnuts, drained
- 6 garlic cloves, minced
- 2 Tbsp. soy sauce
- 1 Tbsp. hoisin sauce
- 1 Tbsp. minced fresh gingerroot
- 2 tsp. Sriracha Asian hot chili sauce
- 2 cans (14½ oz. each) chicken broth
- 1 pkg. (10 oz.) frozen shelled edamame, thawed
- 1 pkg. (3 oz.) ramen noodles
  Thinly sliced green onions, optional

1. In a large skillet, heat oil over medium-high heat. Brown pork in batches. Remove to a 5-qt. slow cooker. Stir in all the remaining ingredients except edamame, noodles and green onions.

2. Cook, covered, on low until the meat and vegetables are tender, 4-5 hours. Stir in the edamame. Break up noodles slightly; stir into soup, discarding or saving seasoning packet for another use. Cook, covered, on low until noodles are al dente, 10-15 minutes.

3. Serve immediately. If desired, top with green onions.

1½ cups: 455 cal., 23g fat (7g sat. fat), 90mg chol., 1134mg sod., 25g carb. (6g sugars, 4g fiber), 36g pro.

CHUNKY CREAMY CHICKEN SOUP

I am a stay-at-home mom who relies on my slow cooker for fast, nutritious meals with minimal prep time and cleanup. I knew this recipe was a winner when I didn't have any leftovers and my husband asked me to make it again.

—Nancy Clow, Mallorytown, ON

Prep: 15 min. • **Cook:** 4½ hours
Makes: 7 servings (1¾ qt.)

- 1½ lbs. boneless skinless chicken breasts, cut into 2-in. strips
- 2 tsp. canola oil
- ⅔ cup finely chopped onion
- 2 medium carrots, chopped
- 2 celery ribs, chopped
- 1 cup frozen corn
- 2 cans (10¾ oz. each) condensed cream of potato soup, undiluted
- 1½ cups chicken broth
- 1 tsp. dill weed
- 1 cup frozen peas
- ½ cup half-and-half cream

1. In a large skillet over medium-high heat, brown the chicken in oil. Transfer to a 5-qt. slow cooker; add the onion, carrots, celery and corn.

2. In a large bowl, whisk the soup, broth and dill until blended; stir into slow cooker. Cover and cook on low until chicken and vegetables are tender, about 4 hours.

3. Stir in the peas and cream. Cover and cook the soup until heated through, about 30 minutes longer.

1 cup: 229 cal., 7g fat (3g sat. fat), 66mg chol., 629mg sod., 17g carb. (5g sugars, 3g fiber), 24g pro.

FAST FIX
EASY TORTELLINI SPINACH SOUP

This is the easiest soup you will ever make—take it from me! I always keep the ingredients on hand so if I'm feeling under the weather or just plain busy, I can throw together this delicious soup in a flash.

—Angela Lively, Conroe, TX

Takes: 20 min. • **Makes:** 8 servings (3 qt.)

- 16 frozen fully cooked Italian meatballs (about 1 lb.)
- 1 can (14½ oz.) fire-roasted diced tomatoes, undrained
- ¼ tsp. Italian seasoning
- ¼ tsp. pepper
- 2 cartons (32 oz. each) chicken stock
- 2 cups frozen cheese tortellini (about 8 oz.)
- 3 oz. fresh baby spinach (about 4 cups)
  Shredded Parmesan cheese, optional

1. Place the first five ingredients in a 6-qt. stockpot; bring to a boil. Reduce the heat; simmer, covered, 10 minutes.

2. Return to a boil. Add the tortellini; cook, uncovered, until the meatballs are heated through and tortellini are tender, 3-5 minutes, stirring occasionally. Stir in the spinach until wilted. Serve immediately. If desired, top with Parmesan cheese.

1½ cups: 177 cal., 8g fat (4g sat. fat), 18mg chol., 949mg sod., 14g carb. (3g sugars, 1g fiber), 12g pro.

PESTO PULL-APART BREAD

I combined some of my favorite flavors in an easy bread to complement our Italian meals. I make the pesto, oven-dried tomatoes and roasted red peppers, but store-bought versions will work just as well.
—*Sue Gronholz, Beaver Dam, WI*

Prep: 10 min. • **Bake:** 30 min.
Makes: 16 servings

- 1 tube (16.3 oz.) large refrigerated buttermilk biscuits
- ¼ cup olive oil
- 2 Tbsp. prepared pesto
- ¼ cup sun-dried tomatoes (not packed in oil)
- ¼ cup roasted sweet red peppers, drained and diced
- ¼ cup sliced ripe olives
- 1 cup shredded mozzarella and provolone cheese blend
  Additional prepared pesto, optional

1. Preheat oven to 350°. Cut each biscuit into 4 pieces. Combine the olive oil and pesto. Dip biscuit pieces into pesto mixture until coated; place in an 8-in. round baking pan. Top with sun-dried tomatoes, roasted red peppers and ripe olives.

2. Bake until bread is golden brown, about 25 minutes. Sprinkle with cheese; return to oven, and bake until melted, 5 minutes longer. Cut into wedges or pull apart; serve warm with additional pesto if desired.

1 serving: 152 cal., 9g fat (3g sat. fat), 5mg chol., 410mg sod., 13g carb. (2g sugars, 1g fiber), 3g pro.

FRENCH LENTIL & CARROT SOUP

It's amazing how just a few key ingredients can make such a difference in the outcome of a dish. This soup boasts a blend of fragrant herbs that gives it its signature flavor. Using finely chopped rotisserie chicken makes this recipe perfect for a busy weeknight meal, but you can leave the chicken out altogether if you prefer.
—*Colleen Delawder, Herndon, VA*

Prep: 15 min. • **Cook:** 6¼ hours
Makes: 6 servings (2¼ qt.)

- 5 large carrots, peeled and sliced
- 1½ cups dried green lentils, rinsed
- 1 shallot, finely chopped
- 2 tsp. herbes de Provence
- ½ tsp. pepper
- ¼ tsp. kosher salt
- 6 cups reduced-sodium chicken broth
- 2 cups cubed rotisserie chicken
- ¼ cup heavy whipping cream

1. Combine the first seven ingredients in a 5- or 6-qt. slow cooker; cover. Cook, on low until lentils are tender, 6-8 hours.
2. Stir in the chicken and cream. Cover and continue cooking until heated through, about 15 minutes.

1½ cups: 338 cal., 8g fat (3g sat. fat), 53mg chol., 738mg sod., 39g carb. (5g sugars, 7g fiber), 29g pro. **Diabetic exchanges:** 3 lean meat, 2 starch, 1 vegetable.

TEST KITCHEN TIP

Herbes de Provence is a blend of fragrant dry herbs reminiscent of the Provence region in the south of France. Typical blends include rosemary, thyme, savory, oregano, marjoram and other herbs. Some varieties contain lavender. Look for herbes de Provence in the spice aisle.

HONEY-SQUASH DINNER ROLLS

Dinner rolls take on a rich autumnal color when you add squash to the dough. Feel free to use any variety of frozen winter squash. If you prefer fresh, mashed butternut or acorn work well. I've even use cooked carrots with good results. Bake these in a cast-iron skillet for a beautiful, rustic presentation.
—*Marcia Whitney, Gainesville, FL*

Prep: 40 min. + rising • Bake: 20 min.
Makes: 2 dozen

- 2 pkg. (¼ oz. each) active dry yeast
- 2 tsp. salt
- ¼ tsp. ground nutmeg
- 6 to 6½ cups all-purpose flour
- 1¼ cups 2% milk
- ½ cup butter, cubed
- ½ cup honey
- 1 pkg. (12 oz.) frozen mashed winter squash, thawed (about 1⅓ cups)
- 1 large egg, lightly beaten
   Poppy seeds, salted pumpkin seeds or pepitas, or sesame seeds

1. In a large bowl, mix yeast, salt, nutmeg and 3 cups flour. In a small saucepan, heat milk, butter and honey to 120°-130°. Add to the dry ingredients; beat on medium speed for 2 minutes. Add squash; beat on high for 2 minutes. Stir in enough remaining flour to form a soft dough (dough will be sticky).
2. Turn dough onto a floured surface; knead until smooth and elastic, 6-8 minutes. Place in a greased bowl, turning once to grease the top. Cover with plastic wrap and let rise in a warm place until doubled, about 1 hour.
3. Punch down the dough. Turn onto a lightly floured surface; divide and shape into 24 balls. Divide between two greased 9-in. cast-iron skillets or round baking pans. Cover with kitchen towels; let rise in a warm place until doubled, about 45 minutes.
4. Preheat oven to 375°. Brush tops with beaten egg; sprinkle with seeds. Bake until dark golden brown, 20-25 minutes. Cover loosely with foil during the last 5-7 minutes if needed to prevent overbrowning. Remove from pans to wire racks; serve warm.

1 roll: 186 cal., 5g fat (3g sat. fat), 19mg chol., 238mg sod., 32g carb. (6g sugars, 1g fiber), 4g pro. **Diabetic exchanges:** 2 starch, 1 fat.

FAST FIX
CHEESY CREAM OF ASPARAGUS SOUP

Kids may not want to try a vegetable soup, but once they spoon up a mouthful of this cheesy variety, the flavor will keep them coming back for more.
—*Muriel Lerdal, Humboldt, IA*

Takes: 25 min. • Makes: 6 servings (1 qt.)

- 2 pkg. (12 oz. each) frozen cut asparagus
- ¼ cup butter
- 2 Tbsp. all-purpose flour
- 4 cups whole milk
- 1 cup shredded Monterey Jack cheese
- 4 to 5 drops hot pepper sauce
- 1½ tsp. salt
- ¾ to 1 tsp. pepper
   Roasted asparagus tips, optional

1. Prepare the asparagus according to the package directions; drain and set aside. In a large saucepan, melt butter. Stir in the flour until smooth; gradually add milk. Bring to a boil; cook and stir until thickened, about 2 minutes. Cool slightly.
2. Pour half of the thickened milk mixture into a blender; add half of the asparagus. Cover and process until very smooth; return soup to the saucepan. Repeat with the remaining milk mixture and asparagus. Stir in the cheese, hot pepper sauce, salt and pepper; heat through (do not boil). If desired, top with roasted asparagus tips.
¾ cup: 261 cal., 19g fat (12g sat. fat), 59mg chol., 852mg sod., 12g carb. (9g sugars, 1g fiber), 12g pro.

SPINACH & TORTELLINI SOUP

My tomato-flavored broth is the perfect base for cheese tortellini and fresh spinach. Add extra garlic and Italian seasoning to suit your family's tastes.
—*Debbie Wilson, Burlington, NC*

- -

Takes: 20 min. • **Makes:** 6 servings (2 qt.)

- 1 tsp. olive oil
- 2 garlic cloves, minced
- 1 can (14½ oz.) no-salt-added diced tomatoes, undrained
- 3 cans (14½ oz. each) vegetable broth
- 2 tsp. Italian seasoning
- 1 pkg. (9 oz.) refrigerated cheese tortellini
- 4 cups fresh baby spinach
   Shredded Parmesan cheese and freshly ground pepper

1. In a large saucepan, heat oil over medium heat. Add garlic; cook and stir 1 minute. Stir in tomatoes, broth and Italian seasoning; bring to a boil. Add tortellini; bring to a gentle boil. Cook, uncovered, just until the tortellini are tender, 7-9 minutes.

2. Stir in spinach. Sprinkle servings with cheese and pepper.

1⅓ cups: 164 cal., 5g fat (2g sat. fat), 18mg chol., 799mg sod., 25g carb. (4g sugars, 2g fiber), 7g pro.

CONFETTI CORNBREAD

My grandmother Virginia always served Southwest cornbread with meals. To honor her, I created a recipe that cuts down on prep but doesn't skimp on flavor.
—*Angie Price, Bradford, TN*

Prep: 20 min. • **Bake:** 50 min.
Makes: 12 servings

2 pkg. (8½ oz. each) cornbread/muffin mix
¼ tsp. cayenne pepper
2 large eggs, room temperature
1 can (14¾ oz.) cream-style corn
½ cup buttermilk
¼ cup plus 1½ tsp. canola oil, divided
1 cup shredded cheddar cheese
1 small onion, chopped
1 can (4 oz.) chopped green chiles
1 jar (2 oz.) pimiento strips, drained
1 jalapeno pepper, seeded and chopped

1. Preheat oven to 350°. In large bowl, combine muffin mixes and cayenne pepper. In another bowl, mix eggs, corn, buttermilk and ¼ cup oil until blended. Add to the dry ingredients; stir just until moistened. Fold in the cheese, onion, chiles, pimiento strips and jalapeno.

2. Brush the remaining oil onto bottom of a 13x9-in. baking pan; place in oven until hot, 4-5 minutes. Pour batter into hot pan. Bake until the edges are golden brown and a toothpick inserted in center comes out clean, 50-60 minutes. Cool in pan on a wire rack. Serve warm.

1 piece: 299 cal., 14g fat (4g sat. fat), 42mg chol., 547mg sod., 36g carb. (10g sugars, 3g fiber), 7g pro.

ROSEMARY CHEDDAR MUFFINS

My stepmother gave me this recipe nearly 30 years ago. We have enjoyed these luscious biscuitlike muffins ever since. You might not even need butter!
—*Bonnie Stallings, Martinsburg, WV*

Takes: 25 min. • **Makes:** 1 dozen

- 2 **cups self-rising flour**
- ½ **cup shredded sharp cheddar cheese**
- 1 **Tbsp. minced fresh rosemary or 1 tsp. dried rosemary, crushed**
- 1¼ **cups 2% milk**
- 3 **Tbsp. mayonnaise**

1. Preheat oven to 400°. In a large bowl, combine the flour, cheese and rosemary. In another bowl, combine milk and mayonnaise; stir into dry ingredients just until moistened. Spoon into 12 greased muffin cups.

2. Bake 8-10 minutes or until lightly browned and toothpick inserted in muffin comes out clean. Cool 5 minutes before removing from pan to a wire rack. Serve warm.

Note: As a substitute for each cup of self-rising flour, place 1½ tsp. baking powder and ½ tsp. salt in a measuring cup. Add all-purpose flour to measure 1 cup.

1 muffin: 121 cal., 5g fat (2g sat. fat), 8mg chol., 300mg sod., 16g carb. (1g sugars, 0 fiber), 4g pro.

"My family enjoyed these and asked me to make them again. I used fresh rosemary from my garden and finely shredded cheddar cheese."
—WJAMANDA, TASTEOFHOME.COM

ZESTY GARBANZO SAUSAGE SOUP

Even the busiest home cooks will have time to whip up this Cajun-inspired soup. If your family prefers spicier flavors, use medium salsa instead of mild.
—*Priscilla Doyle, Lutz, FL*

Prep: 20 min. • **Cook:** 6½ hours
Makes: 7 servings (2½ qt.)

- 2 **cans (15 oz. each) garbanzo beans or chickpeas, rinsed and drained**
- 3 **cups water**
- 1 **jar (16 oz.) mild salsa**
- 1 **can (14½ oz.) diced tomatoes, undrained**
- 2 **celery ribs, chopped**
- 1 **cup sliced fresh or frozen okra**
- 1 **medium onion, chopped**
- 2 **tsp. Cajun seasoning**
- 1 **lb. smoked kielbasa or Polish sausage, cut into 1-in. pieces**

In a 5-qt. slow cooker, combine the first eight ingredients. Cover and cook on low until vegetables are tender, 6-8 hours. Stir in the kielbasa. Cover and cook soup until heated through, about 30 minutes longer.

1½ cups: 370 cal., 20g fat (6g sat. fat), 43mg chol., 1514mg sod., 32g carb. (9g sugars, 6g fiber), 14g pro.

CHEESE & GARLIC BISCUITS

My biscuits won the Best Quick Bread division at my county fair. One of the judges liked it so much, she asked for the recipe! These buttery, savory biscuits go with just about anything.

—*Gloria Jarrett, Loveland, OH*

- -

Takes: 20 min. • **Makes:** 2½ dozen.

2½ cups biscuit/baking mix
¾ cup shredded sharp cheddar cheese
1 teaspoon garlic powder
1 teaspoon ranch salad dressing mix
1 cup buttermilk

TOPPING:
½ cup butter, melted
1 tablespoon minced chives
½ teaspoon garlic powder
½ teaspoon ranch salad dressing mix
¼ teaspoon pepper

1. In a large bowl, combine the baking mix, cheese, garlic powder and salad dressing mix. Stir in buttermilk just until moistened. Drop the batter by tablespoonfuls onto greased baking sheets.

2. Bake at 450° for 6-8 minutes or until golden brown. Meanwhile, combine topping ingredients. Brush over biscuits. Serve warm.

1 biscuit: 81 cal., 5g fat (3g sat. fat), 11mg chol., 176mg sod., 7g carb. (1g sugar, 0 fiber), 2g pro.

WHITE BEAN & CHICKEN ENCHILADA SOUP

My daughter loves foods with a creamy texture, my husband has a penchant for spice and I have a fondness for white beans. This soup pleases us all! I garnish it with jalapenos, sour cream and green onions.
—*Darcy Gonzalez, Palmdale, CA*

Prep: 15 min. • **Cook:** 20 min.
Makes: 8 servings (3 qt.)

- 4 cans (15½ oz. each) great northern beans, rinsed and drained
- 3 boneless skinless chicken breasts (6 oz. each), cubed
- ½ medium onion, chopped
- 1 garlic clove, minced
- 2 cups frozen corn, thawed
- 1 can (10¾ oz.) condensed cream of chicken soup, undiluted
- 1 carton (32 oz.) reduced-sodium chicken broth
- 1 Tbsp. ground cumin
- 2 seeded and chopped jalapeno peppers, divided
- 1 tsp. pepper
- 2 green onions, chopped
  Sour cream, shredded cheddar cheese and tortilla chips
  Fresh cilantro leaves, optional

1. In a large stockpot, combine first eight ingredients. Add 1 chopped jalapeno and the ground pepper. Bring to a boil. Reduce heat; simmer, covered, until the chicken is no longer pink and soup is heated through, 15-20 minutes.
2. Serve with remaining chopped jalapeno; top with the green onions, sour cream, cheese and tortilla chips. If desired, add fresh cilantro leaves.
1½ cups: 301 cal., 5g fat (1g sat. fat), 41mg chol., 1121mg sod., 37g carb. (1g sugars, 12g fiber), 25g pro.

SLOW-COOKED MEATBALL SOUP

I try to sneak as many vegetables into my daughter's diet as I can. This savory soup with meatballs and pasta does the trick. Best of all, the whole family loves it.
—*Kymm Wills, Phoenix, AZ*

Prep: 15 min. • **Cook:** 5¼ hours
Makes: 10 servings (3½ qt.)

- 3 medium carrots, sliced
- 2 celery ribs, sliced
- 1 small onion, chopped
- 1 bay leaf
- 1 tsp. Italian seasoning
- ¼ tsp. pepper
- 1 pkg. (24 oz.) frozen fully cooked Italian meatballs, thawed
- 1 carton (32 oz.) beef broth
- 2 cans (14½ oz. each) Italian diced tomatoes, undrained
- 2 cups water
- ¾ cup dry red wine or additional water
- ¾ cup ditalini or other small pasta
- 4 cups fresh baby spinach (about 5 oz.)
  Grated Parmesan cheese

1. Place the first 11 ingredients in a 6-qt. slow cooker. Cook, covered, on low until the vegetables are tender and the flavors are blended, 5-6 hours.
2. Stir in pasta; cook, covered, on high until pasta is tender, 15-20 minutes. Discard the bay leaf; stir in spinach until wilted. Serve with cheese.
Note: This recipe was tested with Johnsonville Classic Italian Style Meatballs.
1⅓ cups: 288 cal., 16g fat (7g sat. fat), 33mg chol., 1173mg sod., 23g carb. (7g sugars, 3g fiber), 15g pro.

CHEESE BROCCOLI SOUP

Basic ingredients have never tasted or looked so good. The green broccoli florets and the brilliant orange carrots make my rich soup a colorful addition to any table.
—*Evelyn Massner, Oakville, IA*

Prep: 5 min. • **Cook:** 30 min.
Makes: 8 servings (2 qt.)

- 2 cups sliced fresh carrots
- 2 cups broccoli florets
- 1 cup sliced celery
- 1½ cups chopped onion
- ½ cup butter
- ¾ cup all-purpose flour
- 1 can (10½ oz.) condensed chicken broth, undiluted
- 4 cups whole milk
- ½ lb. process cheese (Velveeta), cubed

1. In a large saucepan, bring 2 qt. water to a boil. Add carrots, broccoli and celery; cover and boil for 5 minutes. Drain and set aside.
2. In the same saucepan, saute onion in butter. Add flour and stir to make smooth paste. Gradually add chicken broth and milk. Cook until mixture thickens, 8-10 minutes. Add vegetables; heat until tender. Add cheese; heat until cheese is melted.
1 cup: 472 cal., 31g fat (19g sat. fat), 88mg chol., 1033mg sod., 32g carb. (17g sugars, 3g fiber), 18g pro.

READER RAVE

"I made soup this for a group of friends and they all raved about it, saying it was some of the best they've ever had. I did make a few changes: I added minced garlic to the sauteed onions and substituted some dry white wine for some of the chicken broth."
—AMY THE MIDWIFE, TASTEOFHOME.COM

HEARTY VEGETABLE SOUP

A friend gave me the idea to use V8 juice in soup because it provides more robust flavor. This recipe calls for lots of frozen veggies, making it both easy and healthy.
—*Janice Steinmetz, Somers, CT*

Prep: 25 min. • **Cook:** 1 hour 20 min.
Makes: 16 servings (4 qt.)

- 1 Tbsp. olive oil
- 8 medium carrots, sliced
- 2 large onions, chopped
- 4 celery ribs, chopped
- 1 large green pepper, seeded and chopped
- 1 garlic clove, minced
- 2 cups chopped cabbage
- 2 cups frozen cut green beans (about 8 oz.)
- 2 cups frozen peas (about 8 oz.)
- 1 cup frozen corn (about 5 oz.)
- 1 can (15 oz.) garbanzo beans or chickpeas, rinsed and drained
- 1 bay leaf
- 2 tsp. chicken bouillon granules
- 1½ tsp. dried parsley flakes
- 1 tsp. salt
- 1 tsp. dried marjoram
- 1 tsp. dried thyme
- ½ tsp. dried basil
- ¼ tsp. pepper
- 4 cups water
- 1 can (28 oz.) diced tomatoes, undrained
- 2 cups V8 juice

1. In a stockpot, heat oil over medium-high heat; saute carrots, onions, celery and green pepper until crisp-tender. Add garlic; cook and stir for 1 minute. Stir in the remaining ingredients; bring to a boil.
2. Reduce the heat; simmer, covered, until the vegetables are tender, 1 to 1½ hours. Remove bay leaf.
1 cup: 105 cal., 2g fat (0 sat. fat), 0 chol., 488mg sod., 20g carb. (9g sugars, 5g fiber), 4g pro. **Diabetic exchanges:** 1 starch.

5 INGREDIENTS | FAST FIX | FREEZE IT

CHEDDAR CORN DOG MUFFINS

I wanted a change from ordinary hot dogs in a bun, so I made corn dog muffins. I added jalapenos to this kid-friendly recipe and that won my husband over, too.
—*Becky Tarala, Palm Coast, FL*

Takes: 25 min. • **Makes:** 9 muffins

- 1 pkg. (8½ oz.) cornbread/muffin mix
- ⅔ cup 2% milk
- 1 large egg, room temperature, lightly beaten
- 5 turkey hot dogs, sliced
- ½ cup shredded sharp cheddar cheese
- 2 Tbsp. finely chopped pickled jalapeno, optional

1. Preheat oven to 400°. Line nine muffin cups with foil liners.

2. In a small bowl, combine the muffin mix, milk and egg; stir in the hot dogs, cheese and, if desired, jalapeno. Fill prepared muffin cups three-fourths full.

3. Bake until a toothpick inserted in center comes out clean, 14-18 minutes. Cool for 5 minutes before removing from pan to a wire rack. Serve warm. Refrigerate leftovers.

Freeze option: Freeze cooled muffins in freezer containers. To use, microwave each muffin on high for 30-60 seconds or until heated through.

1 muffin: 216 cal., 10g fat (4g sat. fat), 46mg chol., 619mg sod., 23g carb. (7g sugars, 2g fiber), 8g pro.

FAST FIX

TURKEY & DUMPLING SOUP

To show some love at a family gathering, I fill a large stockpot with this rich and comforting turkey soup brimming with veggies, potatoes and dumplings.
—*Lea Lidel, Leander, TX*

Takes: 30 min. • **Makes:** 8 servings (3½ qt.)

- 1 Tbsp. olive oil
- 2 celery ribs, chopped
- ½ cup chopped onion
- 1½ lbs. red potatoes (about 5 medium), cut into ½-in. cubes
- 3½ cups frozen mixed vegetables (about 16 oz.)
- ½ tsp. pepper
- ½ tsp. dried thyme
- 2 cartons (32 oz. each) reduced-sodium chicken broth
- 2½ cups coarsely shredded cooked turkey or chicken
- 2 cups biscuit/baking mix
- ⅔ cup 2% milk

1. In a 6-qt. stockpot, heat oil over medium heat; saute celery and onion until tender, 3-4 minutes. Stir in the potatoes, mixed vegetables, seasonings and broth; bring to a boil. Reduce the heat; cook, covered, until the potatoes are almost tender, 8-10 minutes. Add turkey; bring mixture to a simmer.
2. Meanwhile, stir baking mix and milk until a soft dough forms; drop by tablespoonfuls on top of simmering soup. Cook, covered, on low heat until a toothpick inserted in the dumplings comes out clean, 8-10 minutes.
1¾ cups: 350 cal., 8g fat (2g sat. fat), 46mg chol., 1036mg sod., 47g carb. (7g sugars, 6g fiber), 23g pro.

5 INGREDIENTS | FAST FIX

QUICK FOCACCIA BREAD

Green olives complement my speedy version of the beloved Italian bread. Try the focaccia with minestrone or Italian wedding soup, or serve it with an antipasto tray for a satisfying appetizer everyone will love.
—*Ivy Laffoon, Ceres, CA*

Takes: 30 min. • **Makes:** 8 servings

- 1 loaf (1 lb.) frozen bread dough, thawed
- ½ cup sliced pimiento-stuffed olives
- ½ cup shredded Colby-Monterey Jack cheese
- ½ cup shredded Parmesan cheese
- 1 tsp. Italian seasoning
- 2 Tbsp. olive oil

1. On an ungreased baking sheet, pat dough into a 12x6-in. rectangle. Build up edges slightly. Top with olives, cheeses and Italian seasoning; press gently into dough. Drizzle with oil.
2. Bake at 350° until the cheese is melted and golden brown, 15-20 minutes. Let stand for 5 minutes before slicing.
1 slice: 249 cal., 11g fat (3g sat. fat), 10mg chol., 623mg sod., 31g carb. (2g sugars, 2g fiber), 9g pro.

**FAVORITE CHEESY POTATOES,
PAGE 210**

CHAPTER 4

Scrumptious Salads & Sides

Here you'll find easy-prep salads and side dishes for all occasions—everything from traditional holiday casseroles to fruity, fanciful picnic salads.

COLORFUL SPIRAL PASTA SALAD

Make this bright salad your next make-and-take dish. This tricolor toss-up with broccoli, tomatoes, olives and a convenient bottled dressing is the easiest one you could take.

—*Amanda Cable, Boxford, MA*

- -

Takes: 20 min.
Makes: 14 servings

1	pkg. (12 oz.) tricolor spiral pasta
4	cups fresh broccoli florets
1	pint grape tomatoes
1	can (6 oz.) pitted ripe olives, drained
⅛	tsp. salt
⅛	tsp. pepper
1½	cups Italian salad dressing with roasted red pepper and Parmesan

1. In a Dutch oven, cook pasta according to the package directions, adding the broccoli during the last 2 minutes of cooking. Drain and rinse in cold water.

2. Transfer to a large bowl. Add tomatoes, olives, salt and pepper. Drizzle with salad dressing; toss to coat. Chill until serving.

¾ cup: 149 cal., 4g fat (0 sat. fat), 0 chol., 513mg sod., 24g carb. (4g sugars, 2g fiber), 4g pro.

READER RAVE

"This is the best salad for home or to take anywhere. You can add any vegetables you like—fresh sweet peppers, onion, mushrooms, asparagus and chopped carrots—and the bowl always ends up cleaned of the last bit. If you keep it a day or so, the flavors are even better. I especially like feta cheese or Parmesan cheese."

—6COWS RUNNING, TASTEOFHOME.COM

SCALLOPED POTATOES & HAM

I adapted an oven recipe to cook in the slow cooker while I'm away. It's ready to eat when I get home, making it a winner in my book!
—*Joni Hilton, Rocklin, CA*

Prep: 25 min. • **Cook:** 8 hours
Makes: 16 servings

- 1 can (10¾ oz.) condensed cheddar cheese soup, undiluted
- 1 can (10¾ oz.) condensed cream of mushroom soup, undiluted
- 1 cup 2% milk
- 10 medium potatoes, peeled and thinly sliced
- 3 cups cubed fully cooked ham
- 2 medium onions, chopped
- 1 tsp. paprika
- 1 tsp. pepper

1. In a small bowl, combine the soups and milk. In a greased 5-qt. slow cooker, layer half of the potatoes, ham, onions and soup mixture. Repeat layers. Sprinkle with paprika and pepper.

2. Cover and cook on low until potatoes are tender, 8-10 hours.

¾ cup: 167 cal., 4g fat (1g sat. fat), 17mg chol., 630mg sod., 25g carb. (4g sugars, 2g fiber), 8g pro.

TANGY BACON GREEN BEANS

My grandma's Pennsylvania Dutch-style recipe turns plain old green beans into a tangy cross between three-bean and German potato salad.
—*Sharon Tipton, Casselberry, FL*

- -

Takes: 30 min. • **Makes:** 12 servings

- 2 lbs. frozen whole green beans
- 12 bacon strips, chopped
- 2 medium onions, halved and sliced
- 2 Tbsp. cornstarch
- 1¼ cups water
- ¼ cup packed brown sugar
- ¼ cup cider vinegar
- 1½ tsp. salt
- 1 tsp. ground mustard

1. Cook beans according to the package directions. Meanwhile, in a 6-qt. stockpot, cook bacon over medium heat until crisp, stirring occasionally. With a slotted spoon, remove bacon to paper towels; reserve the drippings.

2. In same pan, saute the onions in bacon drippings over medium heat until tender and lightly browned, 7-9 minutes. In a bowl, whisk remaining ingredients until smooth; add to the pan. Bring to a boil; cook and stir until thickened, 1-2 minutes.

3. Drain beans and add to warm dressing; toss and heat through. Top with bacon.

1 serving: 173 cal., 11g fat (4g sat. fat), 18mg chol., 483mg sod., 13g carb. (7g sugars, 2g fiber), 5g pro.

HEALTH TIP

Not only can using frozen veggies save prep time, they're just as healthy as fresh—sometimes they're even more nutritious— because they're picked at the peak of ripeness.

CRUNCHY RAMEN SALAD

This salad is a knockout for potlucks and picnics. I tote the veggies in a bowl, dressing in a jar and noodles in a bag. Then toss them up together just before it's time to eat.
—*LJ Porter, Bauxite, AR*

- -

Takes: 25 min.
Makes: 16 servings

- 1 Tbsp. plus ½ cup olive oil, divided
- ½ cup slivered almonds
- ½ cup sunflower kernels
- 2 pkg. (14 oz. each) coleslaw mix
- 12 green onions, chopped (about 1½ cups)
- 1 medium sweet red pepper, chopped
- ⅓ cup cider vinegar
- ¼ cup sugar
- ⅛ tsp. pepper
- 2 pkg. (3 oz. each) chicken ramen noodles

1. In a large skillet, heat 1 Tbsp. oil over medium heat. Add slivered almonds and sunflower kernels; cook until toasted, about 4 minutes. Cool.

2. In a large bowl, combine the coleslaw mix, onions and red pepper. In a small bowl, whisk the vinegar, sugar, pepper, contents of ramen seasoning packets and remaining oil. Pour over the salad; toss to coat. Refrigerate until serving. Break noodles into small pieces. Just before serving, stir in noodles, almonds and sunflower kernels.

¾ cup: 189 cal., 13g fat (2g sat. fat), 0 chol., 250mg sod., 16g carb. (6g sugars, 3g fiber), 4g pro.

5 INGREDIENTS | FAST FIX

SALSA RICE

You can adjust the heat level in this popular rice dish by selecting a salsa—mild, medium or hot—that suits your tastes. It's a quick and delicious way to round out burritos or tacos.
—*Molly Ingle, Canton, NC*

- -

Takes: 15 min. • **Makes:** 5 servings

1½ cups water
1½ cups chunky salsa
2   cups uncooked instant rice
1   to 1½ cups shredded Colby-
     Monterey Jack cheese

In a saucepan, bring water and salsa to a boil. Stir in rice. Remove from the heat; cover and let stand for 5 minutes. Stir in cheese; cover and let stand for 30 seconds or until cheese is melted.

1 serving: 232 cal., 4g fat (3g sat. fat), 12mg chol., 506mg sod., 35g carb. (3g sugars, 3g fiber), 9g pro. **Diabetic exchanges:** 2 starch, 1 lean meat.

READER RAVE

"We loved this rice! Made it for Taco Tuesday and it was a hit."
—CHICKLUVS2COOK, TASTEOFHOME.COM

5 INGREDIENTS | FAST FIX

NECTARINE & BEET SALAD

Beets and nectarines sprinkled with feta cheese make a scrumptious new blend for a mixed green salad. The combination of ingredients may seem an unusual, but I guarantee it will become a new favorite.
—*Nicole Werner, Ann Arbor, MI*

- -

Takes: 10 min. • **Makes:** 8 servings

2　pkg. (5 oz. each) spring
　　mix salad greens
2　medium nectarines, sliced
½　cup balsamic vinaigrette
1　can (14½ oz.) sliced beets, drained
½　cup crumbled feta cheese

On a serving dish, toss greens and nectarines with vinaigrette. Top with beets and cheese; serve immediately.
1 cup: 84 cal., 4g fat (1g sat. fat), 4mg chol., 371mg sod., 10g carb. (6g sugars, 3g fiber), 3g pro. **Diabetic exchanges:** 2 vegetable, ½ fat.

READER RAVE

"I definitely liked this. A nice, different salad. I added an extra nectarine and used a 4-ounce container of feta and some salt. Super easy and makes quite a bit since it uses two bags of salad. I'll make it again."
—LAURA70, TASTEOFHOME.COM

5 INGREDIENTS

GREEN PEA CASSEROLE

This has been my family's favorite vegetable casserole for over 20 years now. The kids request it again and again for holiday dinners.
—*Barbara Preneta, Unionville, CT*

Prep: 15 min. • **Bake:** 20 min.
Makes: 8 servings

- 5 cups frozen peas (about 20 oz.), thawed
- 1 celery rib, chopped
- ½ cup mayonnaise
- ⅓ cup chopped onion
- ¼ tsp. salt
- ¼ tsp. pepper
- 1 pkg. (6 oz.) stuffing mix

Preheat oven to 350°. Mix first six ingredients; transfer to a greased 11x7-in baking dish. Prepare stuffing mix according to package directions. Spread over pea mixture. Bake casserole, uncovered, until lightly browned, 20-25 minutes.

⅔ cup: 293 cal., 17g fat (5g sat. fat), 16mg chol., 581mg sod., 29g carb. (6g sugars, 5g fiber), 7g pro.

AUNT MARION'S FRUIT SALAD DESSERT

My Aunt Marion, my namesake, is like a grandma to me. She gave me the recipe for this luscious fruit salad, which goes to all our family reunions, snowmobile club picnics and hunt club suppers...and I always go home with an empty bowl!
—*Marion LaTourette, Honesdale, PA*

Prep: 20 min. + chilling
Makes: 10 servings (2½ qt.)

- 1 can (20 oz.) pineapple chunks, drained
- 1 can (15¼ oz.) sliced peaches, drained and cut into bite-size pieces
- 1 can (11 oz.) mandarin oranges, drained
- 3 bananas, sliced
- 2 unpeeled red apples, cut into bite-sized pieces

FRUIT SAUCE

- 1 cup cold whole milk
- ¾ cup sour cream
- ⅓ cup thawed orange juice concentrate
- 1 pkg. (3.4 oz.) instant vanilla pudding mix

In a large bowl, combine the fruits; set aside. Whisk sauce ingredients until smooth. Gently fold into fruits. Cover and chill for 3-4 hours before serving.

1 cup: 218 cal., 5g fat (3g sat. fat), 7mg chol., 86mg sod., 44g carb. (37g sugars, 3g fiber), 2g pro.

READER RAVE

"Delicious! I've been making this since I saw it in Taste of Home magazine 15 or 20 years ago. It is by far my most requested dish for family gatherings and potlucks."
—JENNY, TASTEOFHOME.COM

start WITH
FROZEN PEAS

CREAMY CARROT CASSEROLE

My mom and I developed this recipe to see if there was a carrot dish that people who don't care for carrots would enjoy. So far, I haven't met anyone who doesn't like this casserole.
—*Laurie Heward, Fillmore, UT*

- -

Prep: 15 min. • **Bake:** 30 min.
Makes: 8 servings

1½ **lbs. carrots, sliced or 1 pkg. (20 oz.) frozen sliced carrots, thawed**
1 **cup mayonnaise**
1 **Tbsp. grated onion**
1 **Tbsp. prepared horseradish**
¼ **cup shredded cheddar cheese**
2 **Tbsp. crushed Ritz crackers**

1. Preheat oven to 350°. Place 1 in. of water in a large saucepan; add carrots. Bring to a boil. Reduce heat; cover and simmer until crisp-tender, 7-9 minutes. Drain, reserving ¼ cup cooking liquid. Transfer carrots to a 1½-qt. baking dish.
2. In a small bowl, combine the mayonnaise, onion, horseradish and reserved cooking liquid; spread evenly over carrots. Sprinkle with cheese; top with cracker crumbs. Bake, uncovered, for 30 minutes.
¾ cup: 238 cal., 22g fat (4g sat. fat), 6mg chol., 241mg sod., 10g carb. (4g sugars, 2g fiber), 2g pro.

SLOW-COOKED WILD RICE

This recipe is a family heirloom—so much so that I asked permission from Mom before passing it along. It has traveled to weddings, baptisms, birthdays and anniversaries, and it always makes people smile.

—*Janet Mahowald, Rice Lake, WI*

- -

Prep: 15 min. • **Cook:** 4 hours • **Makes:** 8 cups

- 1 **lb. bulk pork sausage**
- 4 **celery ribs, chopped**
- 1 **small onion, chopped**
- 1 **can (10¾ oz.) condensed cream of mushroom soup, undiluted**
- 1 **can (10¾ oz.) condensed cream of chicken soup, undiluted**
- 1 **cup uncooked wild rice**
- 1 **can (4 oz.) mushroom stems and pieces, drained**
- 3 **cups chicken broth**

1. In a large skillet, cook and crumble sausage with celery and onion over medium heat until sausage is no longer pink and vegetables are tender, 6-8 minutes; drain. Transfer to a 3-qt. slow cooker. Add soups, rice and mushrooms. Stir in broth.

2. Cook, covered, on low until rice is tender, 4-5 hours.

¾ cup: 236 cal., 14g fat (4g sat. fat), 30mg chol., 1059mg sod., 19g carb. (2g sugars, 2g fiber), 9g pro.

DID YOU KNOW?

Wild rice is a dark-hulled, aquatic grass native to North America. It has a chewy texture and nutty flavor. Grains expand three to four times their original size and some of the kernels may pop, allowing you to see the white insides. Wild rice should be rinsed before cooking.

CASHEW-CHICKEN ROTINI SALAD

I've tried many chicken salad recipes over the years, but this is my favorite. It's fruity and refreshing, and the cashews add a wonderful crunch. Every time I bring it to a potluck or picnic, I get rave reviews.
—*Kara Cook, Elk Ridge, UT*

Prep: 30 min. + chilling • **Makes:** 12 servings

- 1 pkg. (16 oz.) spiral or rotini pasta
- 4 cups cubed cooked chicken
- 1 can (20 oz.) pineapple tidbits, drained
- 1½ cups sliced celery
- ¾ cup thinly sliced green onions
- 1 cup seedless red grapes
- 1 cup seedless green grapes
- 1 pkg. (5 oz.) dried cranberries
- 1 cup ranch salad dressing
- ¾ cup mayonnaise
- 2 cups salted cashews

1. Cook pasta according to the package directions. Meanwhile, in a large bowl, combine the chicken, pineapple, celery, onions, grapes and cranberries. Drain the pasta and rinse in cold water; stir into the chicken mixture.

2. In a small bowl, whisk the ranch dressing and mayonnaise. Pour over salad and toss to coat. Cover and refrigerate for at least 1 hour. Just before serving, stir in cashews.

1⅓ cups: 661 cal., 37g fat (6g sat. fat), 44mg chol., 451mg sod., 59g carb. (24g sugars, 4g fiber), 23g pro.

CHILLED FRUIT CUPS

These cute cups are easy to assemble ahead of time to serve a crowd as part of brunch or any time of day. They're a convenient and colorful addition to the spread.
—*Andrea Hawthorne, Bozeman, MT*

Prep: 10 min. + freezing • **Makes:** 18 servings

- 1 can (12 oz.) frozen pineapple juice concentrate, thawed
- 1 can (6 oz.) frozen orange juice concentrate, thawed
- 1 cup water
- 1 cup sugar
- 2 Tbsp. lemon juice
- 3 medium firm bananas, sliced
- 1 pkg. (16 oz.) frozen unsweetened strawberries
- 1 can (15 oz.) mandarin oranges, drained
- 1 can (8 oz.) crushed pineapple
- 18 clear plastic cups (9 oz.)

In a large bowl, prepare the pineapple juice concentrate according to package directions. Add orange juice concentrate, water, sugar, lemon juice and fruit. Spoon ¾ cup mixture into each plastic cup. Place cups in a pan and freeze. Remove the cups from the freezer 40-50 minutes before serving.

1 cup: 141 cal., 0 fat (0 sat. fat), 0 chol., 3mg sod., 36g carb. (33g sugars, 1g fiber), 1g pro.

SLOW COOKER

CORN SPOON BREAD

My slow-cooker spoon bread is more moist than corn pudding made in the oven, and the cream cheese is a nice addition. It goes well with Thanksgiving turkey or Christmas ham.
—*Tamara Ellefson, Frederic, WI*

Prep: 15 min. • **Cook:** 3 hours
Makes: 8 servings

- 1   pkg. (8 oz.) cream cheese, softened
- ⅓   cup sugar
- 1   cup 2% milk
- 2   large eggs
- 2   Tbsp. butter, melted
- 1   tsp. salt
- ¼   tsp. ground nutmeg
       Dash pepper
- 2⅓ cups frozen corn, thawed
- 1   can (14¾ oz.) cream-style corn
- 1   pkg. (8½ oz.) cornbread/muffin mix

1. In a large bowl, beat cream cheese and sugar until smooth. Gradually beat in milk. Beat in the eggs, butter, salt, nutmeg and pepper until blended. Stir in corn and cream-style corn. Stir in cornbread mix just until moistened.

2. Pour into a greased 3-qt. slow cooker. Cover and cook on high until the center is almost set, 3-4 hours.

½ cup: 391 cal., 18g fat (10g sat. fat), 100mg chol., 832mg sod., 52g carb. (19g sugars, 2g fiber), 9g pro.

TEST KITCHEN TIP

Spoon bread is a southern side dish. It's soft like pudding and often eaten with a spoon, hence its name. Feel free to add cooked crumbled bacon, chopped green onions or herbs if you want to take it up a notch.

CREAMY PINEAPPLE FLUFF SALAD

Guests of all ages will love this traditional fluff salad, chock-full of pineapple, marshmallows and cherry bits.

—*Janice Hensley, Owingsville, KY*

- -

Takes: 25 min.
Makes: 16 servings

1   pkg. (8 oz.) cream cheese, softened
1   can (14 oz.) sweetened condensed milk
¼   cup lemon juice
2   cans (20 oz.) pineapple tidbits, drained
1½   cups multicolored miniature marshmallows, divided
1   carton (8 oz.) frozen whipped topping, thawed
½   cup chopped nuts
⅓   cup maraschino cherries, chopped

In a large bowl, beat the cream cheese, milk and lemon juice until smooth. Add pineapple and 1 cup miniature marshmallows; fold in whipped topping. Sprinkle with the nuts, cherries and remaining marshmallows. Refrigerate any leftovers.

½ cup: 161 cal., 10g fat (6g sat. fat), 16mg chol., 50mg sod., 17g carb. (12g sugars, 1g fiber), 2g pro.

RANCH POTATO SALAD

I jazz up creamy potato salad with cheese, bacon and ranch salad dressing. My sister asked for the recipe as soon as she tried it.
—*Lynn Breunig, Wind Lake, WI*

Prep: 30 min. + chilling • **Makes:** 8 servings

- 2 lbs. red potatoes
- 1 bottle (8 oz.) ranch salad dressing
- 1 cup shredded cheddar cheese
- 1 pkg. (2.8 oz.) real bacon bits
- ¼ tsp. pepper
  Dash garlic powder

1. Place the potatoes in a large saucepan and cover with water. Bring to a boil. Reduce the heat; cover and simmer until potatoes are tender, 20-25 minutes.

2. In a large bowl, combine the remaining ingredients (dressing will be thick). Drain the potatoes and cut into cubes; add to the dressing and gently toss to coat. Cover and refrigerate for 2 hours or until chilled. Refrigerate leftovers.

1 cup: 316 cal., 22g fat (6g sat. fat), 27mg chol., 649mg sod., 20g carb. (2g sugars, 2g fiber), 9g pro.

READER RAVE

"I wanted to find an easy recipe for a potato salad with no mayo, and I found a keeper with this one! Sometimes I substitute cauliflower for the potatoes— so delish."
—WAGNERLES, TASTEOFHOME.COM

MEXICAN STREET CORN BAKE

We discovered Mexican street corn at a festival. This easy one-pan version saves on prep and cleanup. Every August I freeze a lot of our own fresh sweet corn, and I use that in this recipe, but store-bought corn works just as well.
—*Erin Wright, Wallace, KS*

Prep: 10 min. • **Bake:** 35 min.
Makes: 6 servings

- 6 cups frozen corn (about 30 oz.), thawed and drained
- 1 cup mayonnaise
- 1 tsp. ground chipotle pepper
- ¼ tsp. salt
- ¼ tsp. pepper
- 6 Tbsp. chopped green onions, divided
- ½ cup grated Parmesan cheese
  Lime wedges, optional

1. Preheat oven to 350°. Mix first five ingredients and 4 Tbsp. green onions; transfer to a greased 1½-qt. baking dish. Sprinkle with cheese.

2. Bake, covered, 20 minutes. Uncover; bake until bubbly and lightly browned, 15-20 minutes. Sprinkle with remaining chopped green onions. If desired, serve with lime wedges.

⅔ cup: 391 cal., 30g fat (5g sat. fat), 8mg chol., 423mg sod., 30g carb. (4g sugars, 3g fiber), 6g pro.

start WITH **FROZEN CORN**

HERBED RICE PILAF

This savory side dish has been a family favorite for years. Our daughter, Jennifer, makes it like a pro, which is a huge help for a busy working mom like me. This rice dish is fantastic any time of year, but we particularly enjoy it in the summer with a grilled entree.
—*Jeri Dobrowski, Beach, ND*

- -

Prep: 15 min. • **Cook:** 15 min. + standing
Makes: 6 servings

1	cup uncooked long grain rice
1	cup chopped celery
¾	cup chopped onion
¼	cup butter, cubed
2½	cups water
1	pkg. (2 to 2½ oz.) chicken noodle soup mix
1	tsp. dried thyme
¼	tsp. rubbed sage
¼	tsp. pepper
2	Tbsp. fresh minced parsley
1	Tbsp. chopped pimientos, optional

1. In a large skillet, cook the rice, celery and onion in butter, stirring constantly, until rice is browned. Stir in the next five ingredients; bring to a boil. Reduce the heat; cover and simmer for 15 minutes. Sprinkle with parsley; stir in pimientos if desired.

2. Remove from heat and let stand, covered, for 10 minutes. Fluff with a fork.

¾ cup: 226 cal., 8g fat (5g sat. fat), 23mg chol., 426mg sod., 34g carb. (3g sugars, 2g fiber), 4g pro. **Diabetic exchanges:** 2 starch, 1½ fat.

HOLIDAY BRUSSELS SPROUTS

Turn plain Brussels sprouts into something extra special with peas, celery and bacon. The recipe easily doubles for a crowd.

—*Jodie Beckman, Council Bluffs, IA*

- -

Takes: 25 min. • **Makes:** 6 servings

- 1 pkg. (16 oz.) frozen Brussels sprouts
- 1 pkg. (10 oz.) frozen peas
- 2 Tbsp. butter
- 2 celery ribs, chopped
- 2 bacon strips, cooked and crumbled
- 2 Tbsp. minced fresh chives

1. Cook Brussels sprouts and peas according to package directions; drain.

2. In a large skillet, heat butter over medium-high heat. Add the celery; cook and stir until crisp-tender. Add the Brussels sprouts, peas, bacon and chives; toss to combine.

⅔ cup: 115 cal., 5g fat (3g sat. fat), 12mg chol., 147mg sod., 13g carb. (3g sugars, 5g fiber), 6g pro. **Diabetic exchanges:** 2 vegetable, 1 fat.

BACON-TOMATO SALAD

We love this wonderful salad that tastes like a piled-high BLT without the time, effort or carbs. Plus, you can make it hours ahead of time and keep it in the fridge till serving.
—*Denise Thurman, Columbia, MO*

Takes: 15 min. • **Makes:** 6 servings

- 1 pkg. (12 oz.) iceberg lettuce blend
- 2 cups grape tomatoes, halved
- ¾ cup coleslaw salad dressing
- ¾ cup shredded cheddar cheese
- 12 bacon strips, cooked and crumbled

In a large bowl, combine lettuce blend and tomatoes. Drizzle with dressing; sprinkle with cheese and bacon.

1¼ cups: 268 cal., 20g fat (6g sat. fat), 41mg chol., 621mg sod., 11g carb. (9g sugars, 1g fiber), 10g pro.

"This is such a fantastic salad and so easy. I made it for a small dinner and everyone loved it! I made it exactly as the recipe instructed and wouldn't change a thing. It's one of my new go-to salads!"
—TNICHOLSLCC, TASTEOFHOME.COM

RICH & CREAMY MASHED POTATOES

It's a cinch to jazz up instant mashed potatoes with sour cream and cream cheese, then cook and serve them from a slow cooker. For a special touch, sprinkle with chopped fresh chives, canned french-fried onions or freshly grated Parmesan cheese.
—*Donna Bardocz, Howell, MI*

Prep: 15 min. • **Cook:** 2 hours
Makes: 10 servings

- 3¾ cups boiling water
- 1½ cups 2% milk
- 1 pkg. (8 oz.) cream cheese, softened
- ½ cup butter, cubed
- ½ cup sour cream
- 4 cups mashed potato flakes
- 1 tsp. garlic salt
- ¼ tsp. pepper
  Minced fresh parsley, optional

In a greased 4-qt. slow cooker, whisk boiling water, milk, cream cheese, butter and sour cream until smooth. Stir in the potato flakes, garlic salt and pepper. Cover and cook on low until heated through, 2-3 hours. Sprinkle with parsley if desired.

¾ cup: 299 cal., 20g fat (13g sat. fat), 60mg chol., 390mg sod., 25g carb. (2g sugars, 1g fiber), 6g pro.

CREAMY BLUEBERRY GELATIN SALAD

Plump blueberries and a fluffy topping star in this pretty, refreshing salad that my mom served at every holiday and celebration. Now my grandchildren look forward to sampling it at family gatherings.

—Sharon Hoefert, Greendale, WI

Prep: 30 min. + chilling • **Makes:** 15 servings

- 2 pkg. (3 oz. each) grape gelatin
- 2 cups boiling water
- 1 can (21 oz.) blueberry pie filling
- 1 can (20 oz.) unsweetened crushed pineapple, undrained

TOPPING

- 1 pkg. (8 oz.) cream cheese, softened
- 1 cup sour cream
- ½ cup sugar
- 1 tsp. vanilla extract
- ½ cup chopped walnuts

1. In a large bowl, dissolve gelatin in boiling water. Cool for 10 minutes. Stir in pie filling and pineapple until blended. Transfer to a 13x9-in. dish. Cover and refrigerate until partially set, about 1 hour.

2. For topping, in a small bowl, combine the cream cheese, sour cream, sugar and vanilla. Carefully spread over gelatin; sprinkle with walnuts. Cover and refrigerate until firm.

1 piece: 221 cal., 10g fat (5g sat. fat), 27mg chol., 76mg sod., 29g carb. (26g sugars, 1g fiber), 4g pro.

5 INGREDIENTS | FAST FIX

PESTO PASTA & POTATOES

Although this healthy pasta dish is simple to begin with, the cooking method makes it even simpler—just throw the green beans and pasta into one big pot.
—*Laura Flowers, Moscow, ID*

Takes: 30 min. • **Makes:** 12 servings

1½ lbs. small red potatoes, halved
12 oz. uncooked whole grain spiral pasta
3 cups cut fresh or frozen green beans
1 jar (6½ oz.) prepared pesto
1 cup grated Parmigiano-Reggiano cheese

1. Place potatoes in a large saucepan; add water to cover. Bring to a boil. Reduce heat; cook, uncovered, until tender, 8-10 minutes. Drain; transfer to a large bowl.
2. Meanwhile, cook pasta according to the package directions, adding the green beans during the last 5 minutes of cooking. Drain, reserving ¾ cup pasta water, and add to the potatoes. Toss with the pesto, cheese and enough pasta water to moisten.

¾ cup: 261 cal., 10g fat (3g sat. fat), 11mg chol., 233mg sod., 34g carb. (2g sugars, 5g fiber), 11g pro. **Diabetic exchanges:** 2 starch, 2 fat.

FAST FIX

QUICK BARBECUED BEANS

Here's a simple, classic recipe. This dish has a nice blend of beans, the preparation time is minimal and cooking on the grill adds a new, subtle flavor.
—*Millie Vickery, Lena, IL*

Takes: 25 min. • **Makes:** 5 servings

- 1 can (16 oz.) kidney beans, rinsed and drained
- 1 can (15½ oz.) great northern beans, rinsed and drained
- 1 can (15 oz.) pork and beans
- ½ cup barbecue sauce
- 2 Tbsp. brown sugar
- 2 tsp. prepared mustard

1. In an ungreased 8-in. square disposable foil pan, combine all ingredients.
2. Grill, covered, over medium heat until heated through, 15-20 minutes, stirring occasionally.

¾ cup: 264 cal., 2g fat (0 sat. fat), 0 chol., 877mg sod., 51g carb. (15g sugars, 13g fiber), 14g pro.

FAST FIX

TURKEY RAMEN NOODLE SALAD

My husband and I make this ramen noodle salad together. When we bring it to potlucks, we pack the ramen and almonds separately and toss in the nuts in right before it's time to dish up. They stay nice and crunchy that way.
—*Kristen Pallant, Big Arm, MT*

Takes: 20 min. • **Makes:** 6 servings

- ⅓ cup white wine vinegar
- ¼ cup canola oil
- 3 Tbsp. sugar
- ½ tsp. pepper
- 2 pkg. (3 oz. each) Oriental ramen noodles
- 1 pkg. (14 oz.) coleslaw mix
- 1 lb. sliced deli turkey, chopped
- ½ cup sliced almonds, toasted
- ¼ cup sesame seeds
    Thinly sliced green onions, optional

1. In a small bowl, whisk vinegar, oil, sugar, pepper and contents of ramen noodle seasoning packets until blended.
2. Break noodles into small pieces; place in a large bowl. Add coleslaw mix and turkey. Drizzle with dressing; toss to coat. Sprinkle with almonds and sesame seeds. If desired, top with green onions. Serve immediately.
Note: To toast nuts, bake in a shallow pan in a 350° oven for 5-10 minutes or cook in a skillet over low heat until nuts are lightly browned, stirring occasionally.

1⅔ cups: 406 cal., 22g fat (4g sat. fat), 27mg chol., 1222mg sod., 32g carb. (10g sugars, 4g fiber), 21g pro.

MACARONI COLESLAW

My friend Peggy brought this coleslaw to one
of our picnics, and everyone liked it so much,
we all had to have the recipe.
—*Sandra Matteson, Westhope, ND*

Prep: 25 min. + chilling
Makes: 16 servings

- 1 pkg. (7 oz.) ring macaroni or ditalini
- 1 pkg. (14 oz.) coleslaw mix
- 2 medium onions, finely chopped
- 2 celery ribs, finely chopped
- 1 medium cucumber, finely chopped
- 1 medium green pepper, finely chopped
- 1 can (8 oz.) whole water chestnuts,
  drained and chopped

DRESSING
- 1½ cups Miracle Whip Light
- ⅓ cup sugar
- ¼ cup cider vinegar
- ½ tsp. salt
- ¼ tsp. pepper

1. Cook the macaroni according to package
directions; drain and rinse pasta in cold water.
Transfer to a large bowl; add coleslaw mix,
onions, celery, cucumber, green pepper and
water chestnuts.

2. In a small bowl, whisk the dressing
ingredients. Pour over salad; toss to coat.
Cover and refrigerate for at least 1 hour.

¾ cup: 150 cal., 5g fat (1g sat. fat), 6mg chol.,
286mg sod., 24g carb. (12g sugars, 2g fiber),
3g pro. **Diabetic exchanges:** 1 starch,
1 vegetable, 1 fat.

DID YOU KNOW?

The word "coleslaw" is derived
from the Dutch word koolsla,
literally translated as cabbage
salad. The term has evolved to
refer to many types of crunchy,
shredded-vegetable salads that
hold up well after being dressed.

LAYERED CORNBREAD SALAD

When the garden comes in, we harvest the veggies and layer them with cornbread and sweet relish for this snappy salad. Everyone wants seconds.
—*Rebecca Clark, Warrior, AL*

Prep: 45 min. + chilling
Makes: 14 servings

- 1 pkg. (8½ oz.) cornbread/muffin mix
- 1 cup mayonnaise
- ½ cup sweet pickle relish
- 2 cans (15 oz. each) pinto beans, rinsed and drained
- 4 medium tomatoes, chopped
- 1 medium green pepper, chopped
- 1 medium onion, chopped
- 10 bacon strips, cooked and crumbled

1. Preheat oven to 400°. Prepare cornbread batter according to package directions. Pour into a greased 8-in. square baking pan. Bake until a toothpick inserted in center comes out clean, 15-20 minutes. Cool completely in pan on a wire rack.

2. Coarsely crumble cornbread into a large bowl. In a small bowl, mix the mayonnaise and relish.

3. In a 3-qt. trifle bowl or glass bowl, layer a third of the cornbread and half of each of the following: beans, tomatoes, pepper, onion, bacon and the mayonnaise mixture. Repeat layers. Top with remaining cornbread. Refrigerate salad, covered, for 2-4 hours before serving.

¾ cup: 299 cal., 18g fat (3g sat. fat), 26mg chol., 491mg sod., 27g carb. (9g sugars, 4g fiber), 7g pro.

CONNIE'S TORTELLINI SALAD

Make this substantial salad for a party or potluck or just to enjoy whenever you have a craving for tortellini. We bring this along for long, leisurely weekends at the lake.
—*Connie Eaton, Pittsburgh, PA*

Takes: 30 min.
Makes: 16 servings

- 1 pkg. (13 oz.) dried cheese tortellini
- 1 medium zucchini, halved and sliced
- 1 cup Italian salad dressing
- 1 pint grape tomatoes
- 1 can (14 oz.) water-packed artichoke hearts, rinsed, drained and quartered
- 1 jar (11.1 oz.) pitted Greek olives, drained
- 1 carton (8 oz.) miniature fresh mozzarella cheese balls, drained

In a large saucepan, cook tortellini according to package directions. Drain; transfer to a large bowl. Immediately add zucchini and dressing; toss to coat. Stir in the remaining ingredients. Serve warm or refrigerate and serve cold.

¾ cup: 260 cal., 17g fat (5g sat. fat), 28mg chol., 856mg sod., 19g carb. (2g sugars, 2g fiber), 7g pro.

SAUSAGE DRESSING

I relied on this slow-cooker dressing recipe one Thanksgiving when there was no room left in my oven. The results were fantastic. Even family members who don't usually eat stuffing had some.
—*Mary Kendall, Appleton, WI*

Prep: 20 min. • **Cook:** 3 hours
Makes: 10 servings

- 1 lb. bulk pork sausage
- 1 large onion, chopped
- 2 celery ribs, chopped
- 1 can (14½ oz.) chicken broth
- 2 large eggs, lightly beaten
- ¼ cup butter, melted
- 1½ tsp. rubbed sage
- ½ tsp. pepper
- 1 pkg. (14 oz.) seasoned stuffing cubes (about 9 cups)
- 1 large tart apple, chopped
- 1 cup chopped walnuts or pecans

1. In a large skillet, cook and crumble sausage with onion and celery over medium heat until sausage is no longer pink, 5-7 minutes. Using a slotted spoon, transfer sausage mixture to a greased 5-qt. slow cooker.

2. Stir in broth, eggs, melted butter, sage and pepper. Add remaining ingredients; mix lightly to combine.

3. Cook, covered, on low until a thermometer inserted in center reads 165°, for 3-4 hours, stirring once.

⅔ cup: 412 cal., 25g fat (7g sat. fat), 75mg chol., 1080mg sod., 37g carb. (5g sugars, 4g fiber), 13g pro.

CREAMY COLESLAW

For me, this is the best coleslaw recipe because a package of shredded cabbage and carrots really cuts down on prep time. This is wonderful for potlucks or to serve to your family on a busy weeknight.
—*Renee Endress, Galva, IL*

- -

Takes: 10 min. • **Makes:** 6 servings

1	pkg. (14 oz.) coleslaw mix
¾	cup mayonnaise
⅓	cup sour cream
¼	cup sugar
¾	tsp. seasoned salt
½	tsp. ground mustard
¼	tsp. celery salt

Place coleslaw mix in a large bowl. In a small bowl, combine the remaining ingredients; stir until blended. Pour over coleslaw mix and toss to coat. Refrigerate until serving.

¾ cup: 283 cal., 24g fat (5g sat. fat), 19mg chol., 431mg sod., 13g carb. (11g sugars, 2g fiber), 1g pro.

TEST KITCHEN TIP

For a change of pace, try this recipe with broccoli slaw mix. Greek yogurt can be used instead of sour cream for less fat and more protein. If you like your coleslaw tart, add ¼ cup vinegar or lemon juice or maybe even a julienned Granny Smith apple.

CRUNCHY SPINACH CASSEROLE
Our holidays would not be the same without this family tradition. My mother made it every Thanksgiving when I was growing up; now I make it every Christmas as well. We triple the recipe because the kids can't get enough.
—*Sharon Scaletta, Johnstown, PA*

Prep: 15 min. • **Bake:** 35 min.
Makes: 4 servings

- ½ cup butter, divided
- 2 celery ribs, finely chopped
- 1 small onion, finely chopped
- 2 pkg. (10 oz. each) frozen chopped spinach, thawed and squeezed dry
- 1 can (10¾ oz.) condensed cream of mushroom soup, undiluted
- 2 cups cubed bread (½ in.)

1. Preheat oven to 350°. In a large skillet, heat ¼ cup butter over medium heat. Add the celery and onion; cook and stir until tender, 4-5 minutes. Stir in spinach and soup.
2. Transfer to a 1½-qt. round baking dish. In a small saucepan, melt remaining butter over medium heat. Stir in bread cubes. Sprinkle over top. Bake until bubbly and bread cubes are golden brown, 35-40 minutes.
¾ cup: 369 cal., 29g fat (15g sat. fat), 64mg chol., 974mg sod., 23g carb. (4g sugars, 7g fiber), 8g pro.

CHILI CORNBREAD SALAD

A co-worker brought this wonderful dish to a potluck several years ago. I scooped up one of the recipes she left next to the pan. Now I make it for get-togethers and, like her, supply copies of the recipe.
—*Kelly Newsom, Jenks, OK*

Prep: 20 min. + chilling
Bake: 20 min. + cooling • **Makes:** 15 servings

- 1 pkg. (8½ oz.) cornbread/muffin mix
- 1 can (4 oz.) chopped green chiles, undrained
- ⅛ tsp. ground cumin
- ⅛ tsp. dried oregano
  Pinch rubbed sage
- 1 cup mayonnaise
- 1 cup sour cream
- 1 envelope ranch salad dressing mix
- 2 cans (15 oz. each) pinto beans, rinsed and drained
- 2 cans (15¼ oz. each) whole kernel corn, drained
- 3 medium tomatoes, chopped
- 1 cup chopped green pepper
- 1 cup chopped green onions
- 10 bacon strips, cooked and crumbled
- 2 cups shredded cheddar cheese

1. Prepare cornbread batter according to the package directions. Stir in the chiles, cumin, oregano and sage. Spread in a greased 8-in. square baking pan. Bake at 400° until a toothpick inserted in the center comes out clean, 20-25 minutes. Cool.

2. In a small bowl, combine mayonnaise, sour cream and dressing mix; set aside. Crumble half of the cornbread into a 13x9-in. dish. Layer with half of the beans, mayonnaise mixture, corn, tomatoes, green pepper, onions, bacon and cheese. Repeat layers (dish will be very full). Cover and refrigerate for 2 hours.

1 serving: 383 cal., 24g fat (8g sat. fat), 39mg chol., 839mg sod., 30g carb. (9g sugars, 5g fiber), 12g pro.

READER RAVE

"I recently made this recipe for a church function. I made it in a trifle bowl. It was so pretty and I received many compliments on it. My trifle bowl was empty at the end of the function. I will be making this again."
—NICHOLLETTE, TASTEOFHOME.COM

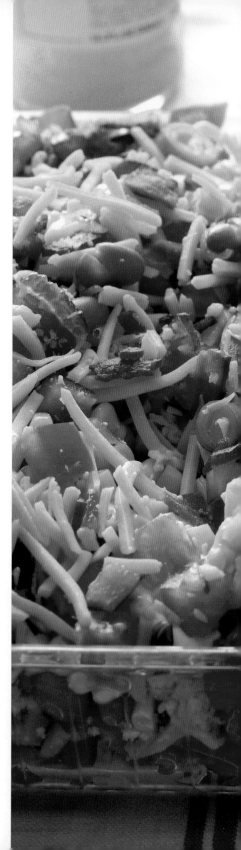

STRAWBERRY-CHICKEN SALAD WITH BUTTERED PECANS

Having lived in several states in the South, I grew an affinity for pecans. I toss them into recipes for a little added flavor and crunch. Fresh berries and other nuts round out this refreshing salad.

—Lisa Varner, El Paso, TX

Takes: 15 min. • **Makes:** 6 servings

- 2 **Tbsp. butter**
- 1 **cup pecan halves**
- ¼ **tsp. salt**
- ⅛ **tsp. pepper**

DRESSING

- 2 **Tbsp. balsamic vinegar**
- 2 **Tbsp. olive oil**
- 1 **Tbsp. sugar**
- 1 **Tbsp. orange juice**
- ⅛ **tsp. pepper**

SALAD

- 1 **pkg. (5 oz.) spring mix salad greens**
- ¾ **lb. sliced rotisserie chicken breast**
- 1 **cup sliced fresh strawberries**
- 1 **cup shredded Swiss cheese**
  Salad croutons, optional

1. In a large heavy skillet, melt butter. Add the pecans; cook over medium heat until the nuts are toasted, about 4 minutes. Stir in the salt and pepper.

2. In a small bowl, whisk dressing ingredients until blended. To assemble the salad, in a large bowl, combine salad greens, chicken, strawberries and cheese. Drizzle with the dressing; toss to coat. Serve with buttered pecans and, if desired, croutons.

1 serving: 392 cal., 30g fat (8g sat. fat), 77mg chol., 210mg sod., 10g carb. (6g sugars, 3g fiber), 24g pro.

CREAMY RANCHIFIED POTATOES

My daughter-in-law gave me this recipe and, over the years, I have adjusted it to our tastes. It's so nice to come home from work to a hot, tasty potato dish that's ready to serve.
—*Jane Whittaker, Pensacola, FL*

Prep: 15 min. • **Cook:** 6 hours
Makes: 8 servings

- 2 lbs. small red potatoes, quartered
- 1 cup cubed fully cooked ham
- 1 can (10¾ oz.) condensed cream of potato soup, undiluted
- 1 carton (8 oz.) spreadable chive and onion cream cheese
- 3 Tbsp. minced chives
- 1 envelope ranch salad dressing mix
- 1 tsp. pepper
- 6 oz. pepper jack cheese, grated

In a 4-qt. slow cooker, combine first seven ingredients. Cook, covered, on low until potatoes are tender, 6-8 hours. Top with cheese; stir to combine.

¾ cup: 297 cal., 15g fat (8g sat. fat), 53mg chol., 933mg sod., 28g carb. (2g sugars, 3g fiber), 14g pro.

TEST KITCHEN TIP

Feel free to use any type of grated cheese if you're not a fan of pepper jack. You can also substitute fully cooked cubed chicken or turkey for the ham.

START WITH **PACKAGE OF RICE PILAF MIX**

MUSHROOMS & PEAS RICE PILAF

You can add just about anything to a basic rice pilaf. Here, peas and baby portobello mushrooms boost the flavor and texture.
—*Stacy Mullens, Gresham, OR*

Takes: 25 min. • **Makes:** 6 servings

- 1 pkg. (6.6 oz.) rice pilaf mix with toasted almonds
- 1 Tbsp. butter
- 1½ cups fresh or frozen peas
- 1 cup sliced baby portobello mushrooms

1. Prepare the rice pilaf according to the package directions.
2. In a large skillet, heat butter over medium heat. Add peas and mushrooms; cook and stir until tender, 6-8 minutes. Stir in rice.

⅔ cup: 177 cal., 6g fat (2g sat. fat), 10mg chol., 352mg sod., 28g carb. (3g sugars, 3g fiber), 5g pro. **Diabetic exchanges:** 2 starch, ½ fat.

"This is my kind of go-to recipe on busy nights. It goes together quickly, and my family really likes it. I plan to make this again and again"

—SHORTBREADLOVER, TASTEOFHOME.COM

MINTY PINEAPPLE FRUIT SALAD

Minced fresh mint adds bright flavor to this easy, quick and low-fat pineapple salad. You can give it a berry twist by using blueberries and raspberries in place of the grapes, but don't forget the secret dressing ingredient—the lemonade!
—*Janie Colle, Hutchinson, KS*

Takes: 15 min. • **Makes:** 8 servings

- 4 cups cubed fresh pineapple
- 2 cups sliced fresh strawberries
- 1 cup green grapes
- 3 Tbsp. thawed lemonade concentrate
- 2 Tbsp. honey
- 1 Tbsp. minced fresh mint

Place fruit in a large bowl. In another bowl, mix remaining ingredients; stir gently into fruit. Refrigerate, covered, until serving.

¾ cup: 99 cal., 0 fat (0 sat. fat), 0 chol., 4mg sod., 26g carb. (21g sugars, 2g fiber), 1g pro. **Diabetic exchanges:** 1½ fruit, ½ starch.

CORN & BROCCOLI IN CHEESE SAUCE

This veggie side dish is one of my standbys. My daughter adds leftover ham to make it extra hearty. The best part is it's made in the slow cooker, saving you space in the oven.
—*Joyce Johnson, Uniontown, OH*

- -

Prep: 10 min. • **Cook:** 3 hours
Makes: 8 servings

- 1 pkg. (16 oz.) frozen corn, thawed
- 1 pkg. (16 oz.) frozen broccoli florets, thawed
- 4 oz. reduced-fat process cheese (Velveeta), cubed
- ½ cup shredded cheddar cheese
- 1 can (10¼ oz.) reduced-fat reduced-sodium condensed cream of chicken soup, undiluted
- ¼ cup fat-free milk

1. In a 4-qt. slow cooker, combine the corn, broccoli and cheeses. In a small bowl, combine soup and milk; pour over the vegetable mixture.
2. Cover and cook on low until heated through, 3-4 hours. Stir before serving.
¾ cup: 148 cal., 5g fat (3g sat. fat), 16mg chol., 409mg sod., 21g carb. (4g sugars, 3g fiber), 8g pro. **Diabetic exchanges:** 1 starch, 1 medium-fat meat.

RAMEN NOODLE SALAD

With an added crunch from ramen noodles and sunflower seeds, plus a sweet, glossy dressing, this bright and lively salad is a definite crowd-pleaser!
—*Beverly Sprague, Baltimore, MD*

Takes: 25 min. • **Makes:** 16 servings

- ½ cup sugar
- ½ cup canola oil
- ¼ cup cider vinegar
- 1½ tsp. soy sauce
- ¼ tsp. salt
- 2 pkg. (3 oz. each) ramen noodles
- 2 Tbsp. butter
- 1 bunch romaine, torn (7 cups)
- 1 bunch broccoli, cut into florets (4 cups)
- 6 green onions, chopped
- ½ cup sunflower kernels

1. Whisk together the first five ingredients. Refrigerate, covered, until serving.

2. Discard seasoning packet from noodles or save for another use. Break noodles into small pieces. In a large skillet, heat the butter over medium-high heat. Add noodles; saute until golden brown.

3. Combine romaine, broccoli, onions, sunflower kernels and noodles. Just before serving, whisk dressing and pour over salad; toss to coat.

¾ cup: 189 cal., 13g fat (3g sat. fat), 4mg chol., 144mg sod., 17g carb. (7g sugars, 2g fiber), 4g pro.

DELUXE HASH BROWN CASSEROLE

My son-in-law gave me the recipe for this hash brown casserole, which my kids say is addictive. It's also an amazing make-ahead dish for when you need to prep ahead.
—*Amy Oswalt, Burr, NE*

- -

Prep: 10 min. • **Bake:** 50 min.
Makes: 12 servings

- 1½ cups sour cream onion dip
- 1 can (10¾ oz.) condensed cream of chicken soup, undiluted
- 1 envelope ranch salad dressing mix
- 1 tsp. onion powder
- 1 tsp. garlic powder
- ½ tsp. pepper
- 1 pkg. (30 oz.) frozen shredded hash brown potatoes, thawed
- 2 cups shredded cheddar cheese
- ½ cup crumbled cooked bacon

READER RAVE

"Made this for a church potluck and it was one of the first dishes finished. I added more cheese and crumbled bacon to the top during the last 10 minutes of baking. Definitely a keeper."
—CHERI, TASTEOFHOME.COM

Preheat oven to 375°. In a large bowl, mix the first six ingredients; stir in potatoes, cheese and bacon. Transfer the mixture to a greased 13x9-in. baking dish. Bake until golden brown, 50-60 minutes.

Freeze option: Cover and freeze unbaked casserole. To use, partially thaw in refrigerator overnight. Remove the casserole from the refrigerator 30 minutes before baking. Preheat the oven to 375°. Bake casserole as directed until top is golden brown and a thermometer inserted in center reads 165°, increasing time to 1¼-1½ hours.

⅔ cup: 273 cal., 17g fat (6g sat. fat), 36mg chol., 838mg sod., 20g carb. (2g sugars, 2g fiber), 10g pro.

NUTTY BROCCOLI SLAW

My daughter gave me the recipe for this delightful salad. The sweet dressing nicely coats a crisp blend of broccoli slaw mix, onions, almonds and sunflower kernels. Crushed ramen noodles provide even more crunch. It's a smash hit wherever I take it.

—*Dora Mae Clapsaddle, Kensington, OH*

- -

Takes: 15 min. • **Makes:** 16 servings

- 1 pkg. (3 oz.) chicken ramen noodles
- 1 pkg. (16 oz.) broccoli coleslaw mix
- 2 cups sliced green onions (about 2 bunches)
- 1½ cups broccoli florets
- 1 can (6 oz.) ripe olives, drained and halved
- 1 cup sunflower kernels, toasted
- ½ cup slivered almonds, toasted
- ½ cup sugar
- ½ cup cider vinegar
- ½ cup olive oil

1. Set aside the noodle seasoning packet; crush the noodles and place in a large bowl. Add the slaw mix, onions, broccoli, olives, sunflower kernels and almonds.

2. In a jar with a tight-fitting lid, combine the sugar, vinegar, oil and contents of seasoning packet; shake well. Drizzle over salad and toss to coat. Serve immediately.

¾ cup: 206 cal., 15g fat (2g sat. fat), 0 chol., 248mg sod., 16g carb. (9g sugars, 3g fiber), 4g pro.

TEST KITCHEN TIP

Shave a few calories from this slaw by reducing the vinegar and olive oil from ½ cup each to ⅓ cup. Add 1 teaspoon each minced garlic and ginger plus 1 tablespoon toasted sesame oil for an Asian-inspired twist to the dressing. If you prefer a more neutral flavor, use canola oil in place of olive oil.

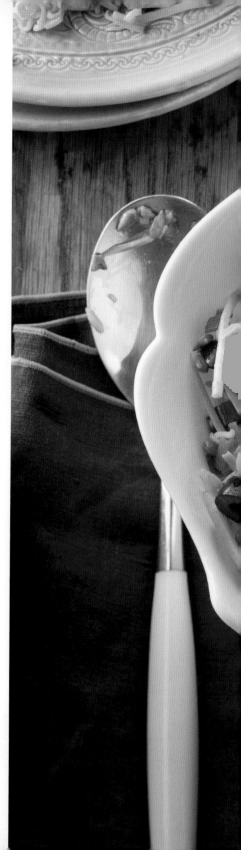

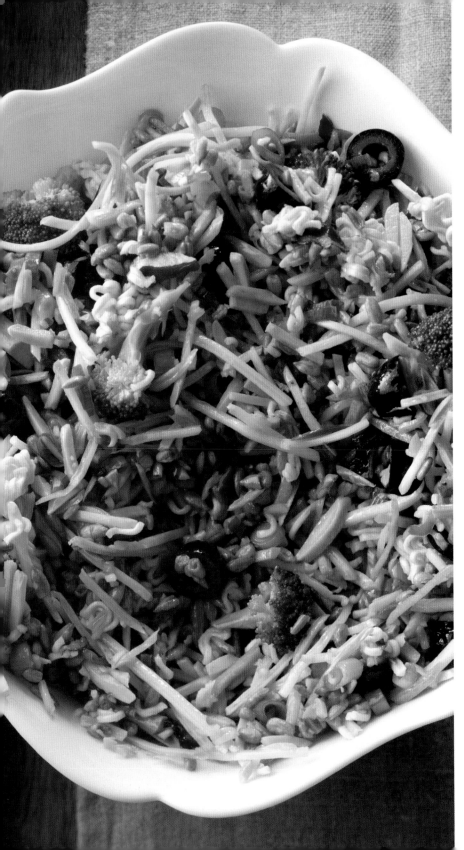

5 INGREDIENTS | FAST FIX

FLUFFY GREEN GRAPE SALAD

I received this recipe from a cousin-in-law at a family reunion. Since then, I've brought it to many gatherings. It can also be enjoyed as a fruity dessert.
—*Kelli Giffen, Barrie, ON*

Takes: 20 min. • **Makes:** 12 servings

- 2 cans (8 oz. each) crushed pineapple, undrained
- 1 pkg. (3.4 oz.) instant pistachio pudding mix
- 1 carton (12 oz.) frozen whipped topping, thawed
- 2 cups halved green grapes

In a large bowl, combine the pineapple and pudding mix; mix well. Cover and refrigerate for 10 minutes. Fold in the whipped topping and grapes. Refrigerate until serving.

½ cup: 160 cal., 5g fat (5g sat. fat), 0 chol., 119mg sod., 25g carb. (23g sugars, 1g fiber), 0 pro.

CHEESY BACON RANCH POTATO STUFFING

Every family seems to have a favorite stuffing recipe. We've been making this one for years. It's so delicious no gravy is required!
—*Sandra Dombek, Camillus, NY*

Prep: 25 min. • **Bake:** 40 min.
Makes: 16 servings

- 3⅓ cups cubed potato dinner rolls, divided
- ⅔ envelope ranch salad dressing mix
- 6 cups mashed potatoes (with added milk and butter)
- 2 medium celery ribs, finely chopped
- 1 cup sliced baby portobello mushrooms
- 5 bacon strips, cooked and crumbled
- 1⅓ cups shredded Monterey Jack cheese
  Chopped green onions, optional

1. Preheat oven to 350°. On an ungreased 15x10x1-in. baking pan, bake cubed rolls until toasted, 7-10 minutes. Meanwhile, stir the ranch dressing mix into mashed potatoes.
2. Fold in 2 cups cubed rolls, chopped celery, mushrooms and bacon. Transfer to a greased 13x9-in. baking dish; top with the remaining cubed rolls. Place the pan on a baking sheet. Bake, uncovered, 35 minutes. Sprinkle with cheese; bake until cheese is melted and top is golden brown, 5-10 minutes longer. If desired, top with green onions.
¾ cup: 156 cal., 7g fat (4g sat. fat), 20mg chol., 473mg sod., 17g carb. (2g sugars, 1g fiber), 5g pro.

TEST KITCHEN TIP

Here's a handy method for make-ahead mashed potatoes: Make a big batch of homemade mashed potatoes and freeze individual servings in muffin cups. Once frozen, pop them out and store in freezer containers. During the week, pull out as many servings as needed and heat them in the microwave.

CRANBERRY PINEAPPLE SALAD

Impress dinner guests with this delightfully different take on traditional cranberry sauce. The nuts add a tasty crunch.
—*Dorothy Angley, Carver, MA*

Prep: 15 min. + chilling • **Makes:** 12 servings

- 1¾ cups boiling water
- 2 pkg. (3 oz. each) raspberry gelatin
- 1 can (14 oz.) jellied cranberry sauce
- 1 can (8 oz.) crushed pineapple, undrained
- ¾ cup orange juice
- 1 Tbsp. lemon juice
- ½ cup chopped walnuts
  Lettuce leaves, optional
  Miracle Whip, optional

Add boiling water to raspberry gelatin; stir until dissolved, about 2 minutes. Stir in the cranberry sauce. Add pineapple, orange juice and lemon juice. Refrigerate until thickened, about 30 minutes. Stir in nuts. Pour into an 11x7-in. dish. Refrigerate until set. Cut into 12 squares; if desired, serve each with a lettuce leaf and a dollop of Miracle Whip.
1 piece: 149 cal., 3g fat (0 sat. fat), 0 chol., 49mg sod., 30g carb. (25g sugars, 1g fiber), 2g pro.

POUTINE

The ultimate in French-Canadian comfort food, poutine commonly features french fries topped with cheese curds and gravy. This side dish is quick to fix with frozen potatoes and packaged gravy, but it has all the traditional comfort you'd expect.
—*Shelisa Terry, Henderson, NV*

Takes: 30 min. • **Makes:** 4 servings

- 4 cups frozen french-fried potatoes
- 1 envelope brown gravy mix
- ¼ tsp. pepper
- ½ cup white cheddar cheese curds or cubed white cheddar cheese

1. Prepare french-fried potatoes according to package directions.
2. Meanwhile, prepare gravy mix according to package directions. Stir in pepper. Place fries on a serving plate; top with the cheese curds and gravy.

1 serving: 244 cal., 13g fat (4g sat. fat), 17mg chol., 465mg sod., 26g carb. (2g sugars, 2g fiber), 7g pro.

SLOW-COOKER ITALIAN MUSHROOMS

I make these mushrooms for all of our big family gatherings, and everyone wants to know what the secret ingredients are that make them so good. They're a star as a side dish, and leftovers go well with steaks, a roast or your favorite entree.
—*Becky Schmitz, Fond du Lac, WI*

- -

Prep: 10 min. • **Cook:** 5 hours
Makes: 8 servings

3	lbs. medium fresh mushrooms
¾	cup butter, melted
¼	cup Italian salad dressing
3	Tbsp. chicken bouillon granules
1	envelope zesty Italian salad dressing mix
½	tsp. onion powder
½	tsp. dried oregano
½	tsp. Worcestershire sauce

Place mushrooms in a 6-qt. slow cooker. Mix the remaining ingredients; pour over mushrooms. Cook, covered, on low until mushrooms are tender, 5-6 hours. Serve with a slotted spoon.

½ cup: 221 cal., 19g fat (11g sat. fat), 46mg chol., 1394mg sod., 9g carb. (2g sugars, 0 fiber), 4g pro.

FREEZE IT

FAVORITE CHEESY POTATOES

My family loves these potatoes. I make a large batch in disposable pans and serve them at all our get-togethers. They're wonderful for holidays or even a special occasion brunch.
—*Brenda Smith, Curran, MI*

- -

Prep: 30 min. • **Bake:** 45 min.
Makes: 12 servings

- 3½ lbs. potatoes (about 7 medium), peeled and cut into ¾-in. cubes
- 1 can (10½ oz.) condensed cream of potato soup, undiluted
- 1 cup French onion dip
- ¾ cup 2% milk
- ⅔ cup sour cream
- 1 tsp. minced fresh parsley
- ¼ tsp. salt
- ¼ tsp. pepper
- 1 pkg. (16 oz.) process cheese (Velveeta), cubed
  Additional minced fresh parsley

1. Preheat oven to 350°. Place potatoes in a Dutch oven; add water to cover. Bring to a boil. Reduce heat; cook, uncovered, until tender, 8-12 minutes. Drain. Cool slightly.

2. In a large bowl, mix soup, onion dip, milk, sour cream, parsley, salt and pepper; gently fold in potatoes and cheese. Transfer to a greased 13x9-in. baking dish.

3. Bake, covered, 30 minutes. Uncover; bake until heated through and cheese is melted, 15-20 minutes longer. Just before serving, stir to combine; sprinkle with additional parsley. (Potatoes will thicken upon standing.)

Freeze option: Cover and freeze unbaked casserole. To use, partially thaw in refrigerator overnight. Remove the casserole from the refrigerator 30 minutes before baking. Preheat oven to 350°. Cover with foil; bake as directed until heated through and a thermometer inserted in center reads 165°, increasing covered time to 1¼-1½ hours. Uncover; bake until lightly browned, 15-20 minutes longer. Just before serving, stir to combine. If desired, sprinkle with additional parsley.

½ cup: 294 cal., 16g fat (10g sat. fat), 42mg chol., 813mg sod., 26g carb. (6g sugars, 2g fiber), 10g pro.

TEST KITCHEN TIP

Generally, three medium russet potatoes or eight to 10 small new white potatoes equal 1 pound. If you usually purchase the same type of potatoes, weigh them in the produce section of your store so you know what 1 pound of your favorite variety is.

CRANBERRY SALAD

Dried cranberries and diced apple drizzled with a fresh cranberry vinaigrette give this salad a subtle twist. It's perfect for a special holiday menu or to enjoy on a weeknight with your favorite entree.
—Taste of Home *Test Kitchen*

- -

Takes: 20 min. • **Makes:** 10 servings

- 1 pkg. (10 oz.) mixed salad greens
- 1 medium red apple, diced
- 1 medium green apple, diced
- 1 cup shredded Parmesan cheese
- ½ cup dried cranberries
- ½ cup slivered almonds, toasted

DRESSING

- 1 cup fresh cranberries
- ½ cup sugar
- ½ cup cider vinegar
- ¼ cup thawed apple juice concentrate
- 1 tsp. salt
- 1 tsp. ground mustard
- 1 tsp. grated onion
- 1 cup canola oil

Combine the first six ingredients. To make dressing, pulse next seven ingredients in a blender, covered, until well mixed. While processing, gradually add the oil in a steady stream. Drizzle desired amount of dressing over salad; toss to coat. Refrigerate any leftover dressing.

Note: To toast nuts, bake in a shallow pan in a 350° oven for 5-10 minutes or cook in a skillet over low heat until nuts are lightly browned, stirring occasionally.

1 serving: 367 cal., 28g fat (3g sat. fat), 6mg chol., 398mg sod., 28g carb. (22g sugars, 3g fiber), 5g pro.

start WITH
PACKAGE OF MIXED SALAD GREENS

PINA COLADA CARROT SALAD

This carrot salad with pina colada yogurt, green grapes and macadamia nuts rocks a tropical vibe. Just mix and chill out.

—*Emily Tyra, Traverse City, MI*

Takes: 10 min. • **Makes:** 4 servings

- 1   pkg. (10 oz.) julienned carrots
- 1   cup green grapes, halved
- ¾   cup pina colada yogurt
- ⅓   cup salted dry roasted macadamia nuts, chopped
    Lemon wedges

In a large bowl, combine carrots, grapes, pina colada yogurt and macadamia nuts; toss to coat. Squeeze lemon wedges over salad before serving.

¾ cup: 184 cal., 9g fat (2g sat. fat), 2mg chol., 157mg sod., 24g carb. (19g sugars, 3g fiber), 3g pro. **Diabetic exchanges:** 1½ fat, 1 starch, 1 vegetable.

CUCUMBER SHELL SALAD

Ranch dressing is the mild coating for this pleasant pasta salad chock-full of crunchy cucumber, onion and green peas.

—*Paula Ishii, Ralston, NE*

Prep: 20 min. + chilling • **Makes:** 16 servings

- 1   pkg. (16 oz.) medium pasta shells
- 1   pkg. (16 oz.) frozen peas, thawed
- 1   medium cucumber, halved and sliced
- 1   small red onion, chopped
- 1   cup ranch salad dressing

Cook pasta according to package directions; drain and rinse in cold water. In a large bowl, combine the pasta, peas, cucumber and onion. Add dressing; toss to coat. Cover and chill at least 2 hours before serving.

¾ cup: 165 cal., 1g fat (0 sat. fat), 0 chol., 210mg sod., 33g carb. (0 sugars, 3g fiber), 6g pro. **Diabetic exchanges:** 2 starch.

SOUTHWESTERN
FISH TACOS, PAGE 235

CHAPTER 5

Easy Meals

Turn to these recipes for quick, simple
dinners the whole family will love.

TURKEY & CORNBREAD STUFFING RELLENOS

Give your Thanksgiving leftovers a Mexican vibe with these zesty rellenos. To adjust the heat, just add more or fewer peppers, or more or less adobo sauce.

—*Christine Friesenhahn, Boerne, TX*

- -

Prep: 30 min. + standing • **Cook:** 5 min.
Makes: 6 servings

- 6 **large poblano peppers (about 1½ lbs.)**
- 1½ **cups chopped cooked turkey**
- 1½ **cups cooked cornbread stuffing**
- 2 **pkg. (8½ oz. each) cornbread/muffin mix**
- 1 **carton (8 oz.) egg substitute**
  Oil for deep-fat frying
- 1 **can (14 oz.) whole-berry cranberry sauce**
- 1 **chipotle pepper in adobo sauce plus 1 Tbsp. adobo sauce**

1. Place poblano peppers on a broiler pan. Broil 4 in. from heat until skins blister, about 5 minutes. With tongs, rotate peppers a quarter turn. Broil and rotate until all sides are blistered and blackened. Immediately place peppers in a large bowl; let stand, covered, 10 minutes.

2. Peel off and discard charred skin. Cut and discard tops from peppers; remove seeds. In a small bowl, combine turkey and stuffing. Fill peppers with turkey mixture. Place the corn muffin mix and egg substitute in separate shallow bowls. Roll stuffed peppers in corn muffin mix, then in egg substitute, then again in corn muffin mix.

3. In an electric skillet, heat ½ in. of oil to 375°. Fry stuffed peppers, a few at a time, until browned, 2-4 minutes on each side. Drain on paper towels.

4. Place cranberry sauce, chipotle pepper and adobo sauce in a blender; cover and process until blended, 10 seconds. Serve with peppers.

1 serving: 592 cal., 33g fat (4g sat. fat), 36mg chol., 632mg sod., 60g carb. (26g sugars, 5g fiber), 17g pro.

SLOW COOKER | FREEZE IT

SAUCY CHICKEN & TORTELLINI

This heartwarming dish is something I threw together years ago for my oldest daughter. When she's having a rough day, I put on the slow cooker and prepare this special recipe.
—*Mary Morgan, Dallas, TX*

- -

Prep: 10 min. • **Cook:** 6¼ hours
Makes: 8 servings

1½	**lbs. boneless skinless chicken breasts, cut into 1-in. cubes**
½	**lb. sliced fresh mushrooms**
1	**large onion, chopped**
1	**medium sweet red pepper, cut into ½-in. pieces**
1	**medium green pepper, cut into ½-in. pieces**
1	**can (2¼ oz.) sliced ripe olives, drained**
1	**jar (24 oz.) marinara sauce**
1	**jar (15 oz.) Alfredo sauce**
2	**pkg. (9 oz. each) refrigerated cheese tortellini**
	Grated Parmesan cheese, optional
	Torn fresh basil, optional

1. In a 5-qt. slow cooker, combine first seven ingredients. Cook, covered, on low until chicken is tender, 6-8 hours.

2. Stir in the Alfredo sauce and tortellini. Cook, covered, until the tortellini is tender, 15-20 minutes. If desired, top with Parmesan cheese and basil.

Freeze option: Freeze cooled, cooked mixture in freezer containers. To use, partially thaw in refrigerator overnight. Microwave, covered, on high, in a microwave-safe dish until heated through, stirring gently; add water if necessary.

1¼ cups: 437 cal., 15g fat (7g sat. fat), 91mg chol., 922mg sod., 44g carb. (8g sugars, 5g fiber), 31g pro.

PIZZA MACARONI & CHEESE

My grandma made this for us once during a visit and I never forgot just how good it was. Since my kids love anything with pepperoni and cheese, I bake it so they can enjoy it as much as I did.

—*Juli Meyers, Hinesville, GA*

- -

Prep: 30 min. • **Bake:** 25 min.
Makes: 12 servings

2 pkg. (14 oz. each) deluxe macaroni
   and cheese dinner mix
½ cup sour cream
1 can (14½ oz.) petite diced
   tomatoes, drained

1 can (15 oz.) pizza sauce
1 small green pepper, chopped
1 small sweet red pepper, chopped
2 cups shredded Italian cheese blend
2 oz. sliced pepperoni

1. Preheat oven to 350°. Cook macaroni according to package directions for al dente. Drain; return to pan. Stir in the contents of cheese packets and sour cream. Transfer to a greased 13x9-in. baking dish.

2. In a small bowl, combine tomatoes and pizza sauce; drop by spoonfuls over macaroni. Top with peppers, cheese and pepperoni. Bake, uncovered, until bubbly, 25-30 minutes.

1 cup: 340 cal., 14g fat (7g sat. fat), 37mg chol., 927mg sod., 37g carb. (5g sugars, 3g fiber), 14g pro.

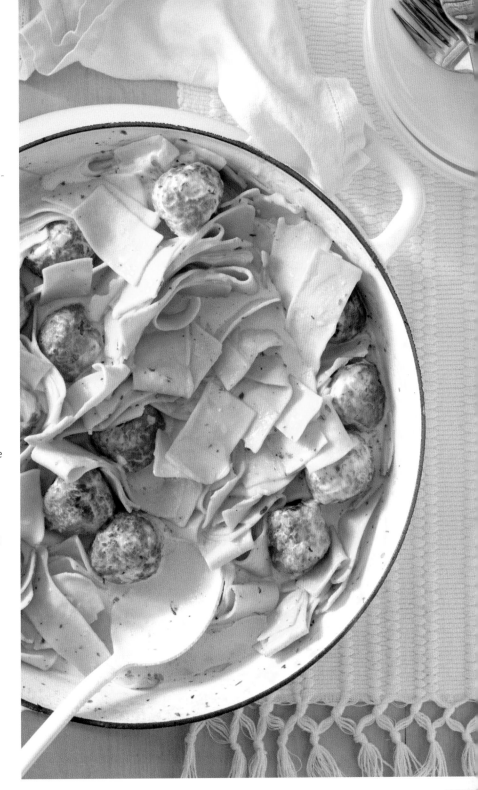

FAST FIX

EASY MEATBALL STROGANOFF

This recipe has fed not only my own family, but many neighborhood kids! They come running when I make this supper. It's one of those things you throw together after work on a busy day because you know it works.
—*Julie May, Hattiesburg, MS*

- -

Takes: 30 min. • **Makes:** 4 servings

3	cups uncooked egg noodles
1	Tbsp. olive oil
1	pkg. (12 oz.) frozen fully cooked Italian meatballs, thawed
1½	cups beef broth
1	tsp. dried parsley flakes
¾	tsp. dried basil
½	tsp. salt
½	tsp. dried oregano
¼	tsp. pepper
1	cup heavy whipping cream
¾	cup sour cream

1. Cook egg noodles according to package directions for al dente; drain.

2. Meanwhile, in a large skillet, heat oil over medium-high heat. Brown meatballs; remove from pan. Add broth, stirring to loosen the browned bits from pan. Add the seasonings. Bring to a boil; cook until liquid is reduced to ½ cup, 5-7 minutes.

3. Add meatballs, noodles and cream. Bring to a boil. Reduce heat; simmer, covered, until slightly thickened, 3-5 minutes. Stir in sour cream; heat through.

1 serving: 717 cal., 57g fat (30g sat. fat), 172mg chol., 1291mg sod., 31g carb. (5g sugars, 2g fiber), 20g pro.

BREADED PORK TENDERLOIN

Meat is a hard sell with my teenage daughter, unless I make it look like a restaurant dish. Drizzle ranch dressing or barbecue sauce on top, and it's a home run.

—Donna Carney, New Lexington, OH

- -

Takes: 30 min. • **Makes:** 4 servings

- 1 pork tenderloin (1 lb.)
- ⅓ cup all-purpose flour
- ⅓ cup cornbread/muffin mix
- ½ tsp. salt
- ¼ tsp. pepper
- 1 large egg, beaten
- 4 Tbsp. canola oil
  Ranch or barbecue sauce, optional

1. Cut pork crosswise into ½-in. slices. In a shallow bowl, mix flour, muffin mix, salt and pepper. Place egg in a separate shallow bowl. Dip pork in egg, then in flour mixture, patting to help coating adhere.

2. In a large skillet, heat 2 Tbsp. oil over medium heat. Add half of the pork; cook until a thermometer reads 145°, 3-4 minutes on each side. Drain on paper towels. Wipe skillet clean; repeat with remaining oil and pork. If desired, serve with sauce.

3 oz. cooked pork: 338 cal., 20g fat (3g sat. fat), 110mg chol., 327mg sod., 12g carb. (2g sugars, 1g fiber), 26g pro.

CHEESEBURGER SKILLET DINNER

This skillet dinner is quick, and the leftovers—if there are any—can be reheated to make a second meal as tasty as the first.

—*Karen Grimes, Stephens City, VA*

Takes: 25 min. • **Makes:** 6 servings

- 1 pkg. (7¼ oz.) macaroni and cheese
- 1 lb. ground turkey or beef
- ½ cup chopped onion
- 1 pkg. (16 oz.) frozen mixed vegetables
- ⅓ cup ketchup
- ¼ cup water
- ½ tsp. prepared mustard
- ¼ tsp. garlic powder
- ¾ cup shredded cheddar cheese
  Salt and pepper to taste

1. Prepare macaroni and cheese according to package directions.

2. Meanwhile, in a large skillet, brown the turkey or beef with the onion; drain. Stir in the vegetables, ketchup, water, mustard and garlic powder. Cook until the vegetables are crisp-tender, about 10 minutes. Add cheddar cheese and stir until melted. Mix in macaroni and cheese. Season with salt and pepper.

1 cup: 436 cal., 20g fat (10g sat. fat), 87mg chol., 679mg sod., 24g carb. (10g sugars, 4g fiber), 25g pro.

CHICKEN CHILE RELLENOS CASSEROLE

My husband likes Mexican food and hearty casseroles, so I decided to combine the two. This chicken with poblanos and chiles always satisfies our south-of-the border cravings.
—*Erica Ingram, Lakewood, OH*

Prep: 20 min. • **Bake:** 35 min. + standing
Makes: 8 servings

- 2 Tbsp. butter
- 2 poblano peppers, seeded and coarsely chopped
- 1 small onion, finely chopped
- 2 Tbsp. all-purpose flour
- 1 tsp. ground cumin
- 1 tsp. smoked paprika
- ¼ tsp. salt
- ⅔ cup 2% milk
- 1 pkg. (8 oz.) cream cheese, cubed
- 2 cups shredded pepper jack cheese
- 2 cups coarsely shredded rotisserie chicken
- 1 can (4 oz.) chopped green chiles
- 2 pkg. (8½ oz. each) cornbread/muffin mix

1. Preheat oven to 350°. In a large skillet, heat butter over medium-high heat. Add peppers and onion; cook and stir until the peppers are tender, 4-6 minutes.

2. Stir in flour and seasonings until blended; gradually stir in milk. Bring to a boil, stirring constantly; cook and stir until thickened, about 1 minute. Stir in cream cheese until blended. Add pepper jack, chicken and green chiles; heat through, stirring to combine. Transfer to a greased 11x7-in. baking dish.

3. Prepare cornbread batter according to package directions. Spread over chicken mixture. Bake, uncovered, until golden brown and a toothpick inserted in topping comes out clean, 35-40 minutes or. Let stand for 10 minutes before serving.

1 serving: 610 cal., 34g fat (16g sat. fat), 151mg chol., 987mg sod., 51g carb. (16g sugars, 5g fiber), 27g pro.

---

5 INGREDIENTS | FAST FIX

CHEESY SUMMER SQUASH FLATBREADS

When you want a meatless meal with Mediterranean style, these flatbreads smothered with squash, hummus and mozzarella deliver the goods.
—*Matthew Hass, Ellison Bay, WI*

Takes: 30 min. • **Makes:** 4 servings

- 3 small yellow summer squash, sliced ¼ in. thick
- 1 Tbsp. olive oil
- ½ tsp. salt
- 2 cups fresh baby spinach, coarsely chopped
- 2 naan flatbreads
- ⅓ cup roasted red pepper hummus
- 1 carton (8 oz.) fresh mozzarella cheese pearls
  Pepper

1. Preheat oven to 425°. Toss squash with oil and salt; spread evenly in a 15x10x1-in. baking pan. Roast squash until tender, 8-10 minutes. Transfer to a bowl; stir in spinach.

2. Place naan flatbreads on a baking sheet; spread with hummus. Top with the squash mixture and cheese. Bake on a lower oven rack just until cheese is melted, 4-6 minutes. Sprinkle with pepper.

½ topped flatbread: 332 cal., 20g fat (9g sat. fat), 47mg chol., 737mg sod., 24g carb. (7g sugars, 3g fiber), 15g pro.

PULLED PORK GRILLED CHEESE

My family combined two of our favorite things: grilled cheese sandwiches and pulled pork. This recipe is super fast and easy when you use store-bought pulled pork.
—*Crystal Jo Bruns, Iliff, CO*

- -

Takes: 30 min. • **Makes:** 4 servings

- 1   carton (16 oz.) refrigerated fully cooked barbecued shredded pork
- 1   garlic clove, minced
- 8   slices country white bread
- 6   oz. sliced Manchego cheese or 8 slices Monterey Jack cheese
- 1   small red onion, thinly sliced
- ¼   cup mayonnaise

1. Heat shredded pork according to package directions. Stir in garlic. Layer four slices of bread with cheese, onion, pork mixture and remaining bread. Spread the outsides of sandwiches with mayonnaise.

2. In a large nonstick skillet, toast sandwiches in batches over medium-low heat until the bread is golden brown and cheese is melted, 2-3 minutes per side.

1 sandwich: 605 cal., 29g fat (13g sat. fat), 74mg chol., 1406mg sod., 53g carb. (22g sugars, 2g fiber), 29g pro.

start WITH
REFRIGERATED SHREDDED PORK

WEEKDAY BEEF STEW

A flaky puff pastry biscuit adds comfort to an easy weeknight beef stew. Make a salad and call your crowd to the table.

—*Daniel Anderson, Kenosha, WI*

Takes: 30 min. • **Makes:** 4 servings

- 1 sheet frozen puff pastry, thawed
- 1 pkg. (15 oz.) refrigerated beef roast au jus
- 2 cans (14½ oz. each) diced tomatoes, undrained
- 1 pkg. (16 oz.) frozen vegetables for stew
- ¾ tsp. pepper
- 2 Tbsp. cornstarch
- 1¼ cups water

1. Preheat oven to 400°. Unfold puff pastry. Using a 4-in. round cookie cutter, cut out four circles. Place 2 in. apart on a greased baking sheet. Bake pastry circles until golden brown, 14-16 minutes.

2. Meanwhile, shred beef with two forks; transfer to a large saucepan. Add tomatoes, vegetables and pepper; bring to a boil. In a small bowl, mix cornstarch and water until smooth; stir into beef mixture. Return to a boil, stirring constantly; cook and stir until thickened, 1-2 minutes.

3. Ladle stew into four bowls; top each with a pastry round.

1½ cups with 1 pastry round: 604 cal., 25g fat (8g sat. fat), 73mg chol., 960mg sod., 65g carb. (10g sugars, 9g fiber), 32g pro.

CHICKEN POTPIE GALETTE WITH CHEDDAR-THYME CRUST

Give traditional chicken potpie an open-faced spin with this rustic galette. The rich filling and flaky cheddar crust make it so homey.
—*Elisabeth Larsen, Pleasant Grove, UT*

Prep: 45 min. + chilling
Bake: 30 min. + cooling • **Makes:** 8 servings

- 1¼ cups all-purpose flour
- ½ cup shredded sharp cheddar cheese
- 2 Tbsp. minced fresh thyme
- ¼ tsp. salt
- ½ cup cold butter, cubed
- ¼ cup ice water

FILLING
- 3 Tbsp. butter
- 2 large carrots, sliced
- 1 celery rib, diced
- 1 small onion, diced
- 8 oz. sliced fresh mushrooms
- 3 cups julienned Swiss chard
- 3 garlic cloves, minced
- 1 cup chicken broth
- 3 Tbsp. all-purpose flour
- ½ tsp. salt
- ¼ tsp. pepper
- 2 cups shredded cooked chicken
- ½ tsp. minced fresh oregano
- 2 Tbsp. minced fresh parsley

1. Combine flour, cheese, thyme and salt; cut in the butter until crumbly. Gradually add ice water, tossing with a fork until dough holds together when pressed. Shape into a disk; refrigerate 1 hour.
2. For filling, melt butter in a large saucepan over medium-high heat. Add the carrots, celery and onion; cook and stir until slightly softened, 5-7 minutes. Add mushrooms; cook 3 minutes longer. Add the Swiss chard and garlic; cook until wilted, 2-3 minutes.
3. Whisk together the broth, flour, salt and pepper; slowly pour over vegetables, stirring constantly. Cook until thickened, 2-3 minutes. Stir in chicken and oregano.
4. Preheat oven to 400°. On a floured sheet of parchment paper, roll dough into a 12-in. circle. Transfer to a baking sheet. Spoon filling over pastry to within 2 in. of edge. Fold pastry edge over filling, pleating as you go, leaving center uncovered. Bake on a lower oven rack until crust is golden brown and filling bubbly, 30-35 minutes. Cool 15 minutes before slicing. Sprinkle with parsley.
1 piece: 342 cal., 21g fat (12g sat. fat), 81mg chol., 594mg sod., 22g carb. (2g sugars, 2g fiber), 16g pro.

FAST FIX
GARLIC TILAPIA WITH MUSHROOM RISOTTO

Boxed risotto makes it quick; mushrooms, shallots and cheese make it tasty. Serve the risotto alongside seasoned fish for a healthy weeknight supper in a hurry.
—*Lynn Moretti, Oconomowoc, WI*

Takes: 30 min. • **Makes:** 4 servings

- 1 pkg. (5½ oz.) Parmesan risotto mix
- 1 cup sliced fresh mushrooms
- ¼ cup chopped shallots
- 1½ lbs. tilapia fillets
- 1½ tsp. seafood seasoning
- 4 Tbsp. butter, divided
- 3 garlic cloves, sliced
- ¼ cup grated Parmesan cheese

1. Cook risotto according to package directions, adding mushrooms and shallots with the water.
2. Meanwhile, sprinkle tilapia with seafood seasoning. In a large nonstick skillet, heat 2 Tbsp. butter over medium heat. In batches, cook tilapia with garlic until fish just begins to flake easily with a fork, about 5 minutes, turning fillets halfway through cooking.
3. Stir cheese and remaining butter into risotto; remove from heat. Serve with tilapia.
1 serving: 432 cal., 18g fat (10g sat. fat), 118mg chol., 964mg sod., 32g carb. (3g sugars, 1g fiber), 39g pro.

FAST FIX
QUICK TACOS AL PASTOR

My husband and I tried pork and pineapple tacos at a truck stand in Hawaii. They were so tasty, I decided to make my own version at home.
—*Lori McLain, Denton, TX*

Takes: 25 min.
Makes: 4 servings (8 tacos)

- 1 pkg. (15 oz.) refrigerated pork roast au jus
- 1 cup well-drained unsweetened pineapple chunks, divided
- 1 Tbsp. canola oil
- ½ cup enchilada sauce
- 8 corn tortillas (6 in.), warmed
- ½ cup finely chopped onion
- ¼ cup chopped fresh cilantro
  Optional ingredients: crumbled queso fresco, salsa verde and lime wedges

1. Coarsely shred pork, reserving juices. In a small bowl, crush half of the pineapple with a fork.
2. In a large nonstick skillet, heat oil over medium-high heat. Add whole pineapple chunks; cook until lightly browned, turning occasionally, 2-3 minutes. Remove from pan.
3. Add the enchilada sauce and crushed pineapple to same skillet; stir in pork and reserved juices. Cook over medium-high heat until liquid is evaporated, 4-6 minutes, stirring occasionally.
4. Serve in tortillas with pineapple chunks, onion and cilantro. If desired, top with cheese and salsa, and serve with lime wedges.
2 tacos: 317 cal., 11g fat (3g sat. fat), 57mg chol., 573mg sod., 36g carb. (12g sugars, 5g fiber), 24g pro. **Diabetic exchanges:** 3 lean meat, 2 starch, 1 fat.

HONEY CHICKEN STIR-FRY

I'm a busy mom, so I like meals that can be ready in as little time as possible. This tasty all-in-one stir-fry with a hint of sweetness from honey is a big timesaver.
—*Caroline Sperry, Allentown, MI*

Takes: 30 min. • **Makes:** 4 servings

- 2 tsp. cornstarch
- 1 Tbsp. cold water
- 3 tsp. olive oil, divided
- 1 lb. boneless skinless chicken breasts, cut into 1-in. pieces
- 1 garlic clove, minced
- 3 Tbsp. honey
- 2 Tbsp. reduced-sodium soy sauce
- ⅛ tsp. salt
- ⅛ tsp. pepper
- 1 pkg. (16 oz.) frozen broccoli stir-fry vegetable blend
  Hot cooked rice, optional

1. Mix cornstarch and water until smooth. In a large nonstick skillet, heat 2 tsp. oil over medium-high heat; stir-fry chicken and garlic 1 minute. Add the honey, soy sauce, salt and pepper; cook and stir until the chicken is no longer pink, 2-3 minutes. Remove from pan.

2. In same pan, stir-fry vegetable blend in remaining oil just until tender, 4-5 minutes. Return chicken to pan. Stir the cornstarch mixture and add to pan; bring to a boil. Cook and stir until thickened, about 1 minute. Serve with rice if desired.

1 cup stir-fry: 249 cal., 6g fat (1g sat. fat), 63mg chol., 455mg sod., 21g carb. (15g sugars, 3g fiber), 25g pro. **Diabetic exchanges:** 3 lean meat, 2 vegetable, ½ starch.

TEST KITCHEN TIP

Select a skillet or wok large enough to accommodate the volume of food you'll be stir-frying. If the food is crowded in the pan, it will steam. Stir-fry food in batches if necessary.

BLACKENED CATFISH WITH MANGO AVOCADO SALSA

A delightful and delicious rub dresses up catfish. Assemble the salsa while you're waiting for the flavors in the fish to blend. My family thinks this is marvelous.
—*Laura Fisher, Westfield, MA*

Prep: 20 min. + chilling • **Cook:** 10 min.
Makes: 4 servings (2 cups salsa)

- 2 tsp. dried oregano
- 2 tsp. ground cumin
- 2 tsp. paprika
- 2¼ tsp. pepper, divided
- ¾ tsp. salt, divided
- 4 catfish fillets (6 oz. each)
- 1 medium mango, peeled and cubed
- 1 medium ripe avocado, peeled and cubed
- ⅓ cup finely chopped red onion
- 2 Tbsp. minced fresh cilantro
- 2 Tbsp. lime juice
- 2 tsp. olive oil

1. Combine the oregano, cumin, paprika, 2 tsp. pepper and ½ tsp. salt; rub over fillets. Refrigerate for at least 30 minutes.
2. Meanwhile, in a small bowl, combine the mango, avocado, red onion, cilantro, lime juice and remaining salt and pepper. Chill until serving.
3. In a large cast-iron skillet, cook fillets in oil over medium heat until fish flakes easily with a fork, 5-7 minutes on each side. Serve with the salsa.

1 fillet with ½ cup salsa: 376 cal., 22g fat (4g sat. fat), 80mg chol., 541mg sod., 17g carb. (9g sugars, 6g fiber), 28g pro. **Diabetic exchanges:** 5 lean meat, 1 starch, ½ fat.

JERK CHICKEN WITH TROPICAL COUSCOUS

Caribbean cuisine brightens up our weeknights thanks to its bold colors and flavors. Done in less than 30 minutes, this chicken is one of my go-to easy meals.

—*Jeanne Holt, Mendota Heights, MN*

Takes: 25 min. • **Makes:** 4 servings

1	can (15.25 oz.) mixed tropical fruit
1	lb. boneless skinless chicken breasts, cut into 2½-in. strips
3	tsp. Caribbean jerk seasoning
1	Tbsp. olive oil
½	cup chopped sweet red pepper
1	Tbsp. finely chopped seeded jalapeno pepper
⅓	cup thinly sliced green onions (green portion only)
1½	cups reduced-sodium chicken broth
3	Tbsp. chopped fresh cilantro, divided
1	Tbsp. lime juice
¼	tsp. salt
1	cup uncooked whole wheat couscous Lime wedges

1. Drain mixed fruit, reserving ¼ cup syrup. Chop fruit.

2. Toss chicken with jerk seasoning. In a large skillet, heat oil over medium-high heat; saute chicken until no longer pink, 4-5 minutes. Remove from pan, reserving drippings.

3. In same pan, saute peppers and green onions in drippings 2 minutes. Add broth, 1 Tbsp. cilantro, lime juice, salt, reserved syrup and chopped fruit; bring to a boil. Stir in couscous; reduce heat to low. Place the chicken on top; cook, covered, until liquid is absorbed and chicken is heated through, 3-4 minutes. Sprinkle with remaining cilantro. Serve with lime wedges.

1½ cups: 411 cal., 7g fat (1g sat. fat), 63mg chol., 628mg sod., 57g carb. (19g sugars, 7g fiber), 31g pro.

ITALIAN CRUMB-CRUSTED BEEF ROAST

Italian-style panko crumbs and seasoning give this roast beef a special touch. It's an effortless weeknight meal, so you can put more energy into relaxing.

—*Maria Regakis, Saugus, MA*

Prep: 10 min. • **Bake:** 1¾ hours + standing
Makes: 8 servings

- 1   beef sirloin tip roast (3 lbs.)
- ¼   tsp. salt
- ¾   cup Italian-style panko (Japanese) bread crumbs
- ¼   cup mayonnaise
- 3   Tbsp. dried minced onion
- ½   tsp. Italian seasoning
- ¼   tsp. pepper

1. Preheat oven to 325°. Place roast on a rack in a shallow roasting pan; sprinkle with salt. In a small bowl, mix remaining ingredients; press onto top and sides of roast.

2. Roast until the meat reaches desired doneness (for medium-rare, a thermometer should read 135°; medium, 140°; medium well, 145°), 1¾-2¼ hours. Remove the roast from oven; tent with foil. Let roast stand for 10 minutes before slicing.

5 oz. cooked beef: 319 cal., 15g fat (3g sat. fat), 111mg chol., 311mg sod., 7g carb. (0 sugars, 0 fiber), 35g pro. **Diabetic exchanges:** 5 lean meat, 1 fat, ½ starch.

MINI SAUSAGE PIES

The simple ingredients and family-friendly flavor of these little sausage cups make them a dinner favorite in our house. The fact that every person gets his or her own pie makes them even better!

—*Kerry Dingwall, Wilmington, NC*

Prep: 35 min. • **Bake:** 30 min.
Makes: 1 dozen

- 1 pkg. (17.3 oz.) frozen puff pastry, thawed
- 1 lb. bulk sage pork sausage
- 6 green onions, chopped
- ½ cup chopped dried apricots
- ¼ tsp. pepper
- ⅛ tsp. ground nutmeg
- 1 large egg, lightly beaten

1. Preheat oven to 375°. On a lightly floured surface, unfold pastry sheets; roll each into a 16x12-in. rectangle. Using a floured cutter, cut twelve 4-in. circles from one sheet; press onto bottoms and up sides of ungreased muffin cups. Using a floured cutter, cut twelve 3½-in. circles from remaining sheet.

2. Mix sausage, green onions, apricots and spices lightly but thoroughly. Place ¼ cup mixture into each pastry cup. Brush edges of smaller pastry circles with egg; place over pies, pressing edges to seal. Brush with egg. Cut slits in top.

3. Bake sausage pies until golden brown and a thermometer inserted in filling reads 160°, 30-35 minutes. Cool for 5 minutes before removing from pan to a wire rack.

Freeze option: Cool baked pies and freeze in freezer containers. To use, partially thaw pies in refrigerator overnight. Reheat on a baking sheet in a preheated 350° oven until heated through, 14-17 minutes.

2 mini pies: 551 cal., 36g fat (10g sat. fat), 82mg chol., 784mg sod., 42g carb. (5g sugars, 5g fiber), 16g pro.

MEDITERRANEAN BULGUR BOWL

Bowls are all the rage, and this one doesn't disappoint. For a twist, try an Italian version with pesto, mozzarella, tomatoes, spinach and basil.

—*Renata Smith, Brookline, MA*

- -

Takes: 30 min. • **Makes:** 4 servings

- 1 cup bulgur
- ½ tsp. ground cumin
- ¼ tsp. salt
- 2 cups water
- 1 can (15 oz.) garbanzo beans or chickpeas, rinsed and drained
- 6 oz. fresh baby spinach (about 8 cups)
- 2 cups cherry tomatoes, halved
- 1 small red onion, halved and thinly sliced
- ½ cup crumbled feta cheese
- ¼ cup hummus
- 2 Tbsp. chopped fresh mint
- 2 Tbsp. lemon juice

1. In a 6-qt. stockpot, combine the first four ingredients; bring to a boil. Reduce the heat; simmer, covered, until tender, 10-12 minutes. Stir in garbanzo beans; heat through.

2. Remove from heat; stir in the spinach. Let stand, covered, until spinach is wilted, about 5 minutes. Stir in the remaining ingredients. Serve warm or refrigerate and serve cold.

2 cups: 311 cal., 7g fat (2g sat. fat), 8mg chol., 521mg sod., 52g carb. (6g sugars, 12g fiber), 14g pro.

HEALTH TIP

With the spinach, tomatoes and feta cheese, this healthy dish supplies enough vitamin A to reach the daily recommendation.

BBQ CHICKEN & APPLE BREAD PUDDING

To me, bread pudding is the epitome of comfort food and it's simply too good to reserve only for dessert. This sweet-and-savory twist on the classic is a delicious new way to enjoy an old favorite.
—*Shauna Havey, Roy, UT*

Prep: 45 min. + cooling • **Bake:** 35 min.
Makes: 8 servings

- 1 pkg. (8½ oz.) cornbread/muffin mix
- 6 Tbsp. butter, divided
- 1 large sweet onion, thinly sliced
- ⅔ cup barbecue sauce, divided
- 2 cups diced cooked chicken
- 2 large eggs, beaten
- 1 cup half-and-half cream
- 1 tsp. salt
- ½ tsp. pepper
- 1¼ cups shredded Monterey Jack cheese
- 1 small green apple, peeled and diced
  Minced chives

1. Prepare cornbread according to package directions and bake using a greased and floured 8-in. square baking pan. Cool. Reduce oven setting to 375°. Meanwhile, in a small skillet, heat 2 Tbsp. butter over medium heat. Add onion; cook and stir until softened. Reduce heat to medium-low; cook until deep golden brown and caramelized, 30-40 minutes. Remove from the heat and set aside.
2. Pour ¼ cup barbecue sauce over chicken; toss to coat.
3. Cube cornbread. Microwave remaining butter, covered, on high until melted, about 30 seconds. Whisk in eggs, cream, salt and pepper. Add caramelized onions. Pour egg mixture over cornbread cubes. Add chicken, cheese and apples. Toss gently to combine.
4. Pour mixture into a greased 8-in. square or 1½-qt. baking dish; bake until bubbly and the top is golden brown, 35 minutes. Drizzle the reserved barbecue sauce over top of bread pudding. Sprinkle with chives.
1 serving: 465 cal., 25g fat (13g sat. fat), 156mg chol., 1028mg sod., 37g carb. (19g sugars, 3g fiber), 21g pro.

FAST FIX

SOUTHWESTERN FISH TACOS

These bright tacos take me on an instant trip to sunny Southern California. This recipe has been on my family's most-requested list for many years.
—*Joan Hallford, North Richland Hills, TX*

Takes: 20 min. • **Makes:** 2 servings (4 tacos)

- ¼ cup mayonnaise
- ¼ cup sour cream
- 2 Tbsp. minced fresh cilantro
- 4 tsp. taco seasoning
- ½ lb. cod or haddock fillets, cut into 1-in. pieces
- 1 Tbsp. lemon juice
- 1 Tbsp. canola oil
- 4 taco shells
  Optional ingredients: shredded lettuce, chopped tomato and lime wedges

1. For sauce, mix mayonnaise, sour cream, cilantro and 2 tsp. taco seasoning. In another bowl, toss the cod with lemon juice and the remaining taco seasoning.
2. In a skillet, heat oil over medium-high heat; saute cod just until it begins to flake easily with a fork, 4-6 minutes (fish may break apart as it cooks). Spoon into taco shells; serve with sauce and remaining ingredients as desired.
2 tacos: 506 cal., 38g fat (8g sat. fat), 52mg chol., 852mg sod., 20g carb. (1g sugars, 1g fiber), 20g pro.

HEALTH TIP

Switch to reduced-fat mayo and sour cream for the sauce and you will save more than 100 calories and 10 grams of fat per serving.

ASPARAGUS NICOISE SALAD

I've used my Nicoise as both an appetizer and a main-dish salad, and it's a winner every time I put it on the table. Here's to a colorful and healthy make-ahead dish.

—*Jan Meyer, St. Paul, MN*

- -

Takes: 20 min. • **Makes:** 4 servings

- 1 lb. small red potatoes (about 10), halved
- 1 lb. fresh asparagus, trimmed and halved crosswise
- 3 pouches (2½ oz. each) albacore white tuna in water
- ½ cup pitted Greek olives, halved, optional
- ½ cup zesty Italian salad dressing

1. Place potatoes in a large saucepan; add water to cover by 2 in. Bring to a boil. Reduce heat; cook, uncovered, until the potatoes are tender, 10-12 minutes, adding the asparagus during the last 2-4 minutes of cooking. Drain the potatoes and asparagus; immediately drop into ice water.

2. To serve, drain potatoes and asparagus; pat dry and divide among four plates. Add tuna and, if desired, olives. Drizzle with the salad dressing.

1 serving: 233 cal., 8g fat (0 sat. fat), 22mg chol., 583mg sod., 23g carb. (4g sugars, 3g fiber), 16g pro. **Diabetic exchanges:** 2 lean meat, 1½ starch, 1½ fat, 1 vegetable.

CHICKEN ZUCCHINI CASSEROLE

A co-worker shared this recipe that was originally her grandmother's. When I make it, I use pre-cooked chicken from the grocery store and fresh zucchini my neighbor gives me from his garden.
—*Bev Dutro, Dayton, OH*

Prep: 20 min. • **Bake:** 45 min.
Makes: 6 servings

- 1 pkg. (6 oz.) stuffing mix
- ¾ cup butter, melted
- 3 cups diced zucchini
- 2 cups cubed cooked chicken breast
- 1 can (10¾ oz.) condensed cream of chicken soup, undiluted
- 1 medium carrot, shredded
- ½ cup chopped onion
- ½ cup sour cream

1. In a large bowl, combine stuffing mix and butter. Set aside ½ cup for topping. Add the zucchini, chicken, soup, carrot, onion and sour cream to the remaining stuffing mixture.
2. Transfer to a greased 11x7-in. baking dish. Sprinkle with reserved stuffing mixture. Bake, uncovered, at 350° until golden brown and bubbly, 40-45 minutes.

1 cup: 481 cal., 31g fat (18g sat. fat), 115mg chol., 1174mg sod., 27g carb. (6g sugars, 2g fiber), 21g pro.

READER RAVE

"I made this using a package of low-sodium stuffing mix. The results were incredible. It was quick, easy and oh, so tasty! I will definitely make it again. It could easily be doubled for a larger family or for leftovers."
—BOBBIE PERRY, TASTEOFHOME.COM

LOADED CHICKEN CARBONARA CUPS

Spaghetti cups with a chicken carbonara twist make for a tasty and fun family dinner.
—*Jeanne Holt, Mendota Heights, MN*

Prep: 30 min. • **Bake:** 15 min.
Makes: 1 dozen

- 4 oz. uncooked whole wheat spaghetti
- 1 large egg, lightly beaten
- 5 oz. frozen chopped spinach, thawed and squeezed dry (about ½ cup)
- ½ cup 2% cottage cheese
- ½ cup shredded Parmesan cheese, divided
- ¼ tsp. lemon-pepper seasoning
- 6 bacon strips, cooked and crumbled, divided
- ½ cup reduced-fat reduced-sodium condensed cream of chicken soup, undiluted
- ¼ cup reduced-fat spreadable chive and onion cream cheese
- 1 cup chopped cooked chicken breast
- ⅓ cup shredded part-skim mozzarella cheese
- ¼ cup finely chopped oil-packed sun-dried tomatoes

1. Preheat oven to 350°. In a saucepan, cook spaghetti according to package directions; drain, reserving ⅓ cup pasta water.
2. In a large bowl, mix egg, spinach, cottage cheese, ¼ cup Parmesan cheese, lemon pepper and half of the bacon. Add spaghetti; toss to combine. Divide among 12 greased muffin cups. Using a greased tablespoon, make an indentation in the center of each.
3. In a large bowl, whisk together soup, cream cheese and reserved pasta water. Stir in the chicken, mozzarella cheese and tomatoes; spoon into cups. Sprinkle with the remaining bacon and Parmesan cheese.
4. Bake until set, about 15 minutes. Cool for 5 minutes before removing from pan.
2 pasta cups: 266 cal., 12g fat (5g sat. fat), 74mg chol., 553mg sod., 20g carb. (4g sugars, 3g fiber), 21g pro. **Diabetic exchanges:** 2 lean meat, 1½ fat, 1 starch.

MAKEOVER SWISS CHICKEN SUPREME

Enjoy this lighter take on a classic. My saucy version has 560 fewer calories, 81 percent less fat and nearly 75 percent less sodium.
—*Stephanie Bell, Kaysville, UT*

Prep: 15 min. • **Bake:** 30 min.
Makes: 4 servings

- 4 boneless skinless chicken breast halves (4 oz. each)
- 1 Tbsp. dried minced onion
- ½ tsp. garlic powder
- ¼ tsp. salt
- ⅛ tsp. pepper
- 4 slices (¾ oz. each) reduced-fat Swiss cheese
- 1 can (10¾ oz.) reduced-fat reduced-sodium condensed cream of chicken soup, undiluted
- ⅓ cup reduced-fat sour cream
- ½ cup fat-free milk
- ⅓ cup crushed reduced-fat Ritz crackers (about 8 crackers)
- 1 tsp. butter, melted

1. Place the chicken in a 13x9-in. baking dish coated with cooking spray. Sprinkle with the minced onion, garlic powder, salt and pepper. Top each with a slice of cheese.
2. In a small bowl, combine the soup, sour cream and milk; pour over chicken. Toss the cracker crumbs and butter; sprinkle over chicken. Bake, uncovered, at 350° until a thermometer reads 170°, 30-40 minutes.
1 chicken breast half : 291 cal., 11g fat (5g sat. fat), 89mg chol., 587mg sod., 14g carb. (5g sugars, 0 fiber), 34g pro. **Diabetic exchanges:** 3 lean meat, 1 starch, 1 fat.

SPICY RICE CASSEROLE

Stir up pork sausage, wild rice and jalapeno for a quick weeknight dish. It's delicious with cornbread and easy to make ahead and reheat for a potluck contribution.
—*Debbie Terenzini-Wilkerson, Lusby, MD*

- -

Takes: 30 min. • **Makes:** 4 servings

- 1 lb. mild bulk pork sausage
- 1 tsp. ground cumin
- ½ tsp. garlic powder
- 2 medium onions, chopped
- 2 medium green peppers, chopped
- 2 tsp. reduced-sodium beef bouillon granules
- 2 cups boiling water
- 1 to 2 jalapeno peppers, finely minced and seeded
- 1 pkg. (6.20 oz.) fast-cooking long grain and wild rice mix

1. In a large skillet, cook sausage, cumin and garlic powder over medium heat until meat is no longer pink; drain. Add onions and green peppers; saute until crisp-tender.

2. Dissolve bouillon in water; add to skillet. Stir in the jalapeno, rice and rice seasoning packet; bring to a boil. Reduce heat and simmer, uncovered, until water is absorbed, 5-10 minutes.

Note: Wear disposable gloves when cutting hot peppers; the oils can burn skin. Avoid touching your face.

1½ cups: 473 cal., 25g fat (8g sat. fat), 61mg chol., 1365mg sod., 45g carb. (5g sugars, 1g fiber), 18g pro.

FAST FIX

ASIAN CHICKEN CRUNCH WRAPS

My kids love all kinds of wraps and Asian foods. This is an easy recipe that works for everyone in our house.
—*Mary Lou Timpson, Colorado City, AZ*

- -

Takes: 25 min. • **Makes:** 4 servings

8	frozen breaded chicken tenders (about 10 oz.)
2	cups coleslaw mix
½	cup sweet chili sauce
2	green onions, chopped
2	Tbsp. chopped fresh cilantro
1	tsp. soy sauce
4	flour tortillas (8 in.), warmed
½	cup dry roasted peanuts, chopped

1. Bake chicken tenders according to package directions. Meanwhile, in a large bowl, toss coleslaw mix with chili sauce, green onions, cilantro and soy sauce.
2. Arrange chicken down the center of each tortilla; top with the coleslaw mixture and peanuts. Fold sides of tortillas over filling and roll up. Cut each diagonally in half.
1 wrap: 519 cal., 21g fat (3g sat. fat), 13mg chol., 1250mg sod., 66g carb. (19g sugars, 7g fiber), 19g pro.

FAST FIX

GARLIC SALMON LINGUINE

This garlicky pasta is so nice to make on busy weeknights because I usually have everything I need on hand. I serve mine with asparagus, rolls and fruit.
—*Theresa Hagan, Glendale, AZ*

- -

Takes: 20 min. • **Makes:** 6 servings

1	pkg. (16 oz.) linguine
⅓	cup olive oil
3	garlic cloves, minced
1	can (14¾ oz.) salmon, drained, bones and skin removed
¾	cup chicken broth
¼	cup minced fresh parsley
½	tsp. salt
⅛	tsp. cayenne pepper

1. Cook linguine according to the package directions; drain.
2. Meanwhile, in a large skillet, heat oil over medium heat. Add garlic; cook and stir until tender, about 1 minute (do not allow to brown). Stir in the remaining ingredients; heat through. Add the linguine; toss gently to combine.
1 serving: 489 cal., 19g fat (3g sat. fat), 31mg chol., 693mg sod., 56g carb. (3g sugars, 3g fiber), 25g pro.

5 INGREDIENTS | FAST FIX

MANGO & GRILLED CHICKEN SALAD

We live in the South, and this fruity chicken salad is a weeknight standout, especially on hot days. I buy salad greens and add veggies for color and crunch.
—*Sherry Little, Sherwood, AR*

Takes: 25 min. • **Makes:** 4 servings

- 1 lb. chicken tenderloins
- ½ tsp. salt
- ¼ tsp. pepper

SALAD

- 6 cups torn mixed salad greens
- ¼ cup raspberry or balsamic vinaigrette
- 1 medium mango, peeled and cubed
- 1 cup fresh sugar snap peas, halved lengthwise

1. Toss chicken tenderloins with salt and pepper. Moisten a paper towel with cooking oil; using long-handled tongs, rub on grill rack to coat lightly. Grill chicken, covered, over medium heat or broil 4 in. from heat until no longer pink, 3-4 minutes on each side. Cut chicken into 1-in. pieces.

2. Divide greens among four plates; drizzle with vinaigrette. Top with chicken, mango and peas; serve immediately.

1 serving: 210 cal., 2g fat (0 sat. fat), 56mg chol., 447mg sod., 22g carb. (16g sugars, 4g fiber), 30g pro. **Diabetic exchanges:** 3 lean meat, 2 vegetable, ½ starch, ½ fat.

TEST KITCHEN TIP

When buying mangoes, look for those with unblemished green to yellow skin tinged with red. Ripe mangoes will feel firm when gently pressed and have a sweet, fruity aroma.

SLOW COOKER

TANDOORI CHICKEN PANINI

The tandoori-style spices in this chicken give it a bold flavor that's so hard to resist. It tastes incredible tucked between pieces of naan, then grilled for an Indian-inspired sandwich.
—*Yasmin Arif, Manassas, VA*

Prep: 25 min. • **Cook:** 3 hours
Makes: 6 servings

- 1½ lbs. boneless skinless chicken breasts
- ¼ cup reduced-sodium chicken broth
- 2 garlic cloves, minced
- 2 tsp. minced fresh gingerroot
- 1 tsp. paprika
- ¼ tsp. salt
- ¼ to ½ tsp. cayenne pepper
- ¼ tsp. ground turmeric
- 6 green onions, chopped
- 6 Tbsp. chutney
- 6 naan flatbreads

1. Place first eight ingredients in a 3-qt. slow cooker. Cook, covered, on low until chicken is tender, 3-4 hours.

2. Shred chicken with two forks. Stir in the green onions.

3. Spread chutney over one side of each naan. Top chutney side of three naan with chicken mixture; top with remaining naan, chutney side down.

4. Cook sandwiches on a panini maker or indoor grill until golden brown, 6-8 minutes. To serve, cut each sandwich in half.

½ sandwich: 351 cal., 6g fat (2g sat. fat), 68mg chol., 830mg sod., 44g carb. (12g sugars, 2g fiber), 27g pro. **Diabetic exchanges:** 3 starch, 3 lean meat.

CHICKEN & WAFFLES

My first experience with chicken and waffles sent my taste buds into orbit. I first made the dish into appetizers, but we all love them as a main course, too.

—*Lisa Renshaw, Kansas City, MO*

Takes: 25 min. • **Makes:** 4 servings

- 12 **frozen crispy chicken strips (about 18 oz.)**
- ½ **cup honey**
- 2 **tsp. hot pepper sauce**
- 8 **frozen waffles, toasted**

1. Bake chicken strips according to package directions. Meanwhile, in a small bowl, mix honey and pepper sauce.

2. Cut chicken into bite-sized pieces; serve on waffles. Drizzle with honey mixture.

1 serving: 643 cal., 22g fat (3g sat. fat), 32mg chol., 958mg sod., 93g carb. (39g sugars, 6g fiber), 21g pro.

READER RAVE

"Easy to put together, I used leftover take-out chicken. The honey/hot pepper sauce is what really makes this dish—I used Sriracha sauce."

—JMARTINELLI13, TASTEOFHOME.COM

FAST FIX

LEMONY TORTELLINI BACON SALAD

Summer meals shouldn't be complicated. We love this simple salad on warm nights. Adding a glass of iced tea or lemonade on the side is just right.

—*Samantha Vicars, Kenosha, WI*

- -

Takes: 20 min. • **Makes:** 4 servings

- 2 cups frozen cheese tortellini (about 8 oz.)
- 4 cups fresh broccoli florets
- ¾ cup mayonnaise
- 1 Tbsp. balsamic vinegar
- 2 tsp. lemon juice
- ¾ tsp. dried oregano
- ¼ tsp. salt
- 1 pkg. (5 oz.) spring mix salad greens
- 4 bacon strips, cooked and crumbled

1. In a large saucepan, cook the tortellini according to package directions, adding broccoli during the last 5 minutes of cooking. Meanwhile, in a small bowl, mix mayonnaise, vinegar, lemon juice, oregano and salt.

2. Drain tortellini and broccoli; gently rinse with cold water. Transfer to a large bowl. Add dressing; toss to coat. Serve over the salad greens; sprinkle with bacon.

1 cup salad with 2 cups greens: 484 cal., 40g fat (7g sat. fat), 32mg chol., 693mg sod., 21g carb. (3g sugars, 4g fiber), 11g pro.

5 INGREDIENTS

RAVIOLI LASAGNA

When you taste this casserole, you might think it came from a complicated, from-scratch recipe. You'll be pleasantly surprised to learn it starts with frozen ravioli and has only four other ingredients.

—*Patricia Smith, Asheboro, NC*

- -

Prep: 25 min. • **Bake:** 40 min.
Makes: 8 servings

- 1 lb. ground beef
- 1 jar (28 oz.) spaghetti sauce
- 1 pkg. (25 oz.) frozen sausage or cheese ravioli
- 1½ cups shredded part-skim mozzarella cheese
  Minced fresh basil

1. In a large skillet, cook beef over medium heat until no longer pink; drain. In a greased 2½-qt. baking dish, layer a third of the spaghetti sauce, half of the ravioli and beef, and ½ cup cheese; repeat layers. Top with remaining sauce and cheese.
2. Cover and bake at 400° until heated through, 40-45 minutes. Top with basil.

1 cup: 438 cal., 18g fat (7g sat. fat), 77mg chol., 1178mg sod., 42g carb. (7g sugars, 5g fiber), 26g pro.

READER RAVE

"Super easy and really tasty. I used pepperoni instead of beef. Easy to adapt with different meat and different ravioli fillings. This will be a regular at our table!"
—LETTUCELEAF, TASTEOFHOME.COM

ITALIAN WEDDING SOUP SUPPER

Classic Italian wedding soup is a marriage of meatballs, pasta and veggies in a flavorful broth. My family loves it, so I created a stick-to-your-ribs skillet version you can eat with a fork.

—Patricia Harmon, Baden, PA

Prep: 25 min. • **Cook:** 15 min.
Makes: 6 servings

- 2 cups small pasta shells
- ½ lb. boneless skinless chicken breasts, cut into ¾-in. cubes
- 2 Tbsp. olive oil, divided
- 1 medium onion, chopped
- 1 medium carrot, finely chopped
- 1 celery rib, chopped
- 1 pkg. (12 oz.) frozen fully cooked Italian meatballs, thawed
- 1 can (10¾ oz.) reduced-fat reduced-sodium condensed cream of chicken soup, undiluted
- 1 pkg. (10 oz.) frozen chopped spinach, thawed and squeezed dry
- 1 cup reduced-sodium chicken broth
- 2 tsp. minced fresh thyme or ½ tsp. dried thyme
- ½ tsp. salt
- ⅛ tsp. pepper
- ¾ cup shredded Asiago cheese

1. Cook pasta according to the package directions. Meanwhile, in a large skillet, saute chicken in 1 Tbsp. oil until no longer pink; remove and keep warm.
2. In the same skillet, saute the onion, carrot and celery in remaining oil until tender. Add the meatballs, soup, spinach, broth, thyme, salt, pepper and reserved chicken; cover and cook until heated through, 4-6 minutes.
3. Drain pasta; stir into skillet. Sprinkle with Asiago cheese.
1⅓ cups: 473 cal., 24g fat (10g sat. fat), 63mg chol., 1006mg sod., 38g carb. (7g sugars, 4g fiber), 28g pro.

LASAGNA CUPS

I love lasagna and garlic bread, so it only made sense to put them together in these fun little cups. Have one as an appetizer, or two for a meal.

—Angelique Douglas, Maryville, IL

Prep: 40 min. • **Bake:** 15 min.
Makes: 16 lasagna cups

- 3 individual lasagna noodles
- ½ lb. ground turkey or beef
- 1 cup meatless pasta sauce
- ⅓ cup 2% cottage cheese
- ¼ tsp. garlic powder
- 2 tubes (8 oz. each) refrigerated crescent rolls
- 2 cups shredded Italian cheese blend or cheddar cheese
- 1 cup grape tomatoes, halved

1. Preheat oven to 375°. Cook lasagna noodles according to package directions. Drain and rinse with water; cut each noodle into six squares.
2. In a large skillet, cook and crumble turkey over medium heat until no longer pink, 5-7 minutes. Stir in sauce, cottage cheese and garlic powder; bring to a boil. Remove from heat.
3. Unroll both tubes of crescent dough; separate each into eight triangles. Press each triangle onto bottom and up sides of a greased muffin cup. Layer each with 1 Tbsp. cheese, one noodle piece and 1 rounded Tbsp. meat sauce (discard extra noodle pieces). Sprinkle with remaining cheese.
4. Bake on a lower oven rack until crust is golden brown, 15-20 minutes. Let stand 5 minutes before removing from pan. Top with tomatoes.
2 lasagna cups: 412 cal., 21g fat (9g sat. fat), 39mg chol., 839mg sod., 34g carb. (7g sugars, 1g fiber), 18g pro.

SPICY SHREDDED BEEF SANDWICHES

If you like your shredded beef with a little kick, then this recipe is for you. For an even zestier version of this recipe, add another jar of jalapenos or use hot peppers instead of the pepperoncini.

—*Kristen Langmeier, Faribault, MN*

- -

Prep: 15 min. • **Cook:** 8 hours
Makes: 12 servings

- 1 **boneless beef chuck roast (4 to 5 lbs.)**
- 2 **medium onions, coarsely chopped**
- 1 **jar (16 oz.) sliced pepperoncini, undrained**
- 1 **jar (8 oz.) pickled jalapeno slices, drained**
- 1 **bottle (12 oz.) beer or nonalcoholic beer**
- 1 **envelope onion soup mix**
- 5 **garlic cloves, minced**
- ½ **tsp. pepper**
- 12 **kaiser rolls, split**
- 12 **slices provolone cheese**

1. Cut roast in half; place in a 4- or 5-qt. slow cooker. Add the onions, pepperoncini, jalapenos, beer, soup mix, garlic and pepper.
2. Cover and cook on low until meat is tender, 8-10 hours.
3. Remove meat. Skim fat from cooking liquid. When cool enough to handle, shred meat with two forks and return to slow cooker; heat through. Serve ½ cup meat mixture on each roll with a slice of cheese.
Note: Look for pepperoncini (pickled peppers) in the pickle and olive section of your grocery store.
1 sandwich: 534 cal., 23g fat (9g sat. fat), 113mg chol., 1187mg sod., 38g carb. (3g sugars, 3g fiber), 41g pro.

CRUNCHY ASIAN CHICKEN SALAD

I love this crunchy, citrusy salad. One day I had my husband drive an hour to the nearest Applebee's restaurant just so I could eat it! That's when I decided to come up with my own version that's a great stand-in for the original. I'm happy and my husband is, too!
—*Mandy Bird, Holbrook, ID*

Takes: 25 min. • **Makes:** 4 servings

- 4 frozen breaded chicken tenders (about 8 oz.)
- ⅓ cup mayonnaise
- 3 Tbsp. honey
- 2 Tbsp. rice vinegar
- 1½ tsp. Dijon mustard
- ¼ tsp. sesame oil
- 1 pkg. (10 oz.) hearts of romaine salad mix
- 1 pkg. (14 oz.) coleslaw mix
- ¼ cup crispy chow mein noodles
- ⅓ cup sliced almonds, toasted

1. Cook chicken tenders according to package directions. Meanwhile, whisk together mayonnaise, honey, vinegar, mustard and sesame oil.

2. To serve, place romaine and coleslaw mixes in a large bowl; toss with dressing. Divide among four plates. Cut chicken into bite-sized pieces; place over salads. Sprinkle with noodles and almonds.

Note: To toast nuts, bake in a shallow pan in a 350° oven for 5-10 minutes or cook in a skillet over low heat until nuts are lightly browned, stirring occasionally.

1 serving: 419 cal., 25g fat (3g sat. fat), 11mg chol., 602mg sod., 42g carb. (20g sugars, 7g fiber), 12g pro.

GARLIC SPAGHETTI SQUASH WITH MEAT SAUCE

I have reduced grains and other starches in my diet due to health reasons, so I was looking for satisfying meals that don't use pasta or potatoes. When I was tinkering with this recipe, I discovered that spaghetti squash is fun to experiment with and eat.
—*Becky Ruff, McGregor, IA*

Prep: 15 min. • **Bake:** 45 min.
Makes: 4 servings

- 1 medium spaghetti squash (about 4 lbs.)
- 1 lb. lean ground beef (90% lean)
- 2 cups sliced fresh mushrooms
- 4 garlic cloves, minced, divided
- 4 plum tomatoes, chopped
- 2 cups pasta sauce
- ½ tsp. pepper, divided
- 1 Tbsp. olive oil
- ¼ tsp. salt
  Grated Parmesan cheese, optional

1. Preheat oven to 375°. Cut the squash lengthwise in half; remove and discard seeds. Place squash in a 13x9-in. baking pan, cut side down; add ½ in. hot water. Bake, uncovered, 40 minutes. Drain water from the pan; turn squash cut side up. Bake until the squash is tender, 5-10 minutes longer.
2. In a large skillet, cook beef and mushrooms over medium heat until beef is no longer pink, 6-8 minutes, breaking beef into crumbles; drain. Add half of the garlic; cook and stir 1 minute. Stir in the tomatoes, pasta sauce and ¼ tsp. pepper; bring to a boil. Reduce heat; simmer, uncovered, 15-20 minutes.
3. When squash is cool enough to handle, use a fork to separate strands. In a large skillet, heat oil over medium heat. Add remaining garlic; cook and stir 1 minute. Stir in squash, salt and remaining pepper; heat through. Serve with meat sauce and, if desired, cheese.
1¼ cups squash with 1 cup meat sauce: 443 cal., 17g fat (5g sat. fat), 71mg chol., 770mg sod., 49g carb. (12g sugars, 11g fiber), 29g pro. **Diabetic exchanges:** 3 starch, 3 lean meat, 1 vegetable, ½ fat.

HEARTY MAC & CHEESE

Whether it's a cold winter night or a rainy summer day, this quick and easy comfort food is sure to satisfy! And it's a fun way to jazz up boxed macaroni mix.
—*Carol Wohlgemuth, Riding Mountain, MB*

Prep: 15 min. • **Cook:** 25 min.
Makes: 6 servings

- 1 pkg. (7¼ oz.) macaroni and cheese dinner mix
- 1 lb. ground beef
- 3 Tbsp. chopped onion
- 2 Tbsp. chopped green pepper
- 1 can (10¾ oz.) condensed tomato soup, undiluted
- 2 Tbsp. water
- 2 Tbsp. ketchup
- 2 tsp. prepared mustard
- 1 tsp. seasoned salt
- 1 tsp. chili powder
- ½ tsp. dried oregano
- ¼ tsp. ground cumin
- ¼ tsp. pepper
- 1 cup frozen corn, thawed
- 1 cup shredded cheddar cheese
- ¼ cup butter, cubed
- ¼ cup 2% milk

1. Cook the macaroni and cheese dinner mix according to the package directions; set the cheese packet aside. Meanwhile, in a large skillet, cook the beef, onion and green pepper over medium heat until meat is no longer pink and vegetables are tender; drain.
2. Add the soup, water, ketchup, mustard and seasonings. Bring to a boil. Reduce the heat; simmer, uncovered, for 4 minutes.
3. Drain macaroni; add to beef mixture. Add corn, cheese, contents of reserved cheese packet, butter and milk. Cook and stir until cheese and butter are melted.
1 cup: 480 cal., 24g fat (13g sat. fat), 92mg chol., 1253mg sod., 39g carb. (12g sugars, 2g fiber), 25g pro.

ROASTED VEGGIE STRUDEL

Roasted Brussels sprouts and potatoes go well with bacon and Brie in my shortcut strudel. I leave the potato skin on for extra flavor and texture.

—*Carole Holt, Mendota Heights, MN*

- -

Prep: 40 min. + cooling • **Bake:** 20 min.
Makes: 4 servings

- 2 cups Brussels sprouts, quartered
- 1 small Yukon Gold potato, cut into ½-in. cubes
- 1 Tbsp. olive oil
- ½ tsp. garlic pepper blend
- ¼ tsp. salt
- ⅓ cup julienned oil-packed sun-dried tomatoes
- 2 green onions, chopped
- 1 tube (8 oz.) refrigerated crescent rolls
- 4 oz. Brie cheese, cut into ½-in. cubes
- 5 bacon strips, cooked and crumbled
- 1 large egg
- 3 Tbsp. pine nuts

1. Preheat oven to 425°. Toss the first five ingredients; spread in a greased 15x10x1-in. pan. Roast until tender, about 15 minutes, stirring once.

2. Drain tomatoes, reserving 1 Tbsp. oil for egg wash. Add tomatoes and green onions to roasted vegetables; cool. Reduce the oven setting to 350°.

3. On a lightly floured surface, unroll crescent dough into one long rectangle; pinch to seal perforations. Roll the dough into a 14x9-in. rectangle; transfer to a large baking sheet. Stir cheese and bacon into vegetables; spoon lengthwise down center third of rectangle. On each long side, cut 1-in. strips at an angle to within ½ in. of filling. Fold one strip from each side over filling, pinching ends to join; repeat. Seal ends of braid.

4. Whisk together egg and reserved oil; brush over strudel. Sprinkle with pine nuts. Bake until golden brown, 20-25 minutes.

1 piece: 532 cal., 35g fat (12g sat. fat), 62mg chol., 1035mg sod., 36g carb. (6g sugars, 3g fiber), 18g pro.

TURKEY LO MEIN

I substituted turkey for pork in this classic Chinese recipe. It was a hit at our church potluck, and my husband and two children love it, too.

—Leigh Lundy, York, NE

- -

Takes: 30 min. • **Makes:** 6 servings

1 lb. lean ground turkey
2 medium carrots, thinly sliced
1 medium onion, chopped
½ tsp. garlic powder
2 pkg. (3 oz. each) ramen noodles
1½ cups water
6 cups shredded cabbage
1 cup frozen peas, thawed
¼ cup reduced-sodium soy sauce

1. In a large skillet, cook and crumble turkey with carrots, onion and garlic powder over medium-high heat until meat is no longer pink, 5-7 minutes.

2. Break up noodles and add to skillet; stir in contents of seasoning packets and water. Bring to a boil. Reduce heat; simmer, covered, 3-5 minutes. Add the remaining ingredients; cook and stir until cabbage is crisp-tender, 1-3 minutes.

1⅓ cups: 297 cal., 11g fat (4g sat. fat), 52mg chol., 580mg sod., 29g carb. (3g sugars, 4g fiber), 21g pro. **Diabetic exchanges:** 2 starch, 2 lean meat.

ONE-SKILLET PORK CHOP SUPPER

My husband, Clark, and I reserve this recipe for Sundays after the grandkids have gone home and we're too tired to prepare a big meal. It's comforting and quick.
—*Kathy Thompson, Port Orange, FL*

Prep: 10 min. • **Cook:** 30 min.
Makes: 4 servings

- 1 Tbsp. butter
- 4 pork loin chops (½ in. thick and 7 oz. each)
- 3 medium red potatoes, cut into small wedges
- 3 medium carrots, cut into ½-in. slices, or 2 cups fresh baby carrots
- 1 medium onion, cut into wedges
- 1 can (10¾ oz.) condensed cream of mushroom soup, undiluted
- ¼ cup water
  Cracked black pepper and chopped fresh parsley, optional

1. In a large cast-iron or other heavy skillet, heat butter over medium heat. Brown the pork chops on both sides; remove from pan, reserving drippings.
2. In same pan, saute vegetables in drippings until lightly browned. Whisk together soup and water; stir into vegetables. Bring to a boil. Reduce heat; simmer, covered, just until the vegetables are tender, 15-20 minutes.
3. Add chops; cook, covered, until a thermometer inserted in pork reads 145°. Remove from heat; let stand 5 minutes. If desired, sprinkle with pepper and parsley.
1 serving: 390 cal., 15g fat (6g sat. fat), 97mg chol., 700mg sod., 28g carb. (6g sugars, 4g fiber), 33g pro.

SOUTHWEST-STYLE SHEPHERD'S PIE

I was born in Montreal and lived in New England and the Southwest, so I've merged these influences into recipes like this hearty shepherd's pie made with turkey, corn and green chiles.

—*Lynn Price, Millville, MA*

- -

Prep: 20 min. • **Bake:** 25 min.
Makes: 6 servings

- 1¼ lbs. lean ground turkey
- 1 small onion, chopped
- 2 garlic cloves, minced
- ½ tsp. salt, divided
- 1 can (14¾ oz.) cream-style corn
- 1 can (4 oz.) chopped green chiles
- 1 to 2 Tbsp. chipotle hot pepper sauce, optional
- 2⅔ cups water
- 2 Tbsp. butter
- 2 Tbsp. half-and-half cream
- ½ tsp. pepper
- 2 cups mashed potato flakes

1. Preheat oven to 425°. In a large skillet, cook turkey, onion, garlic and ¼ tsp. salt over medium heat until turkey is no longer pink and onion is tender, 8-10 minutes, breaking up turkey into crumbles. Stir in corn, green chiles and, if desired, pepper sauce. Transfer to a greased 8-in. square baking dish.

2. Meanwhile, in a saucepan, bring water, butter, cream, pepper and remaining salt to a boil. Remove from heat. Stir in the potato flakes. Spoon over turkey mixture, spreading to cover. Bake until bubbly and potatoes are light brown, 25-30 minutes.

1 cup: 312 cal., 12g fat (5g sat. fat), 78mg chol., 583mg sod., 31g carb. (4g sugars, 3g fiber), 22g pro. **Diabetic exchanges:** 3 lean meat, 2 starch, 1 fat.

FAST FIX | FREEZE IT
DAD'S FAVORITE BARBECUE MEAT LOAVES

It warms my heart to serve dishes that make my loved ones happy. This recipe does that, and then some.

—*Leta Winters, Johnson City, TN*

- -

Takes: 30 min. • **Makes:** 4 servings

- 1 large egg, lightly beaten
- ½ cup stuffing mix, crushed
- 3 Tbsp. 2% milk
- 2 Tbsp. grated Parmesan cheese
- 1 Tbsp. plus ¼ cup barbecue sauce, divided
- 1 lb. ground beef

1. Preheat oven to 425°. In a large bowl, combine egg, stuffing mix, milk, cheese and 1 Tbsp. barbecue sauce. Add beef; mix lightly but thoroughly. Shape into four 4x2-in. loaves in a foil-lined 15x10x1-in. baking pan.

2. Bake until a thermometer reads 160°, 15-20 minutes. Spread with remaining barbecue sauce before serving.

Freeze option: Individually wrap cooled meat loaves in plastic and foil, then freeze. To use, partially thaw the meat loaves in refrigerator overnight. Unwrap loaves; reheat in a greased 15x10x1-in. baking pan in a preheated 350° oven until heated through and a thermometer inserted in center reads 165°. Top each with 1 Tbsp. barbecue sauce before serving.

1 mini meat loaf: 305 cal., 16g fat (6g sat. fat), 120mg chol., 449mg sod., 15g carb. (8g sugars, 1g fiber), 24g pro.

READER RAVE

"Good stuff. I used stovetop herb stuffing. No need to add extra spices, but you can if you want. I usually add some chopped onion, a tablespoon of Worcestershire sauce and tablespoon of Asian chili paste for spice. This is an easy and versatile dinner."

—CORWIN44, TASTEOFHOME.COM

SPINACH FETA TURNOVERS

These quick and easy turnovers are a favorite
with my wife. They are delicious and will melt
in your mouth.

—*David Baruch, Weston, FL*

Takes: 30 min. • **Makes:** 4 servings

- 2 **large eggs**
- 1 **pkg. (10 oz.) frozen leaf spinach,
  thawed, squeezed dry and chopped**
- ¾ **cup crumbled feta cheese**
- 2 **garlic cloves, minced**
- ¼ **tsp. pepper**
- 1 **tube (13.8 oz.) refrigerated
  pizza crust
  Refrigerated tzatziki sauce, optional**

1. In a bowl, whisk eggs; set aside 1 Tbsp..
Combine the spinach, feta cheese, garlic,
pepper and remaining beaten eggs.
2. Unroll pizza crust; roll into a 12-in. square.
Cut into four 3-in. squares. Top each square
with about ⅓ cup spinach mixture. Fold into
a triangle and pinch edges to seal. Cut slits in
top; brush with reserved egg.
3. Place on a greased baking sheet. Bake at
425° until golden brown, 10-12 minutes. If
desired, serve with tzatziki sauce.
1 turnover: 361 cal., 9g fat (4g sat. fat),
104mg chol., 936mg sod., 51g carb. (7g
sugars, 4g fiber), 17g pro.

EASY CHICKEN TAMALE PIE

All you need are some simple ingredients from the pantry to put this slow cooker meal together. I love the fact I can go fishing while it cooks.

—*Peter Halferty, Corpus Christi, TX*

Prep: 20 min. • **Cook:** 7 hours
Makes: 8 servings

- 1 lb. ground chicken
- 1 tsp. ground cumin
- 1 tsp. chili powder
- ½ tsp. salt
- ¼ tsp. pepper
- 1 can (15 oz.) black beans, rinsed and drained
- 1 can (14½ oz.) diced tomatoes, undrained
- 1 can (11 oz.) whole kernel corn, drained
- 1 can (10 oz.) enchilada sauce
- 2 green onions, chopped
- ¼ cup minced fresh cilantro
- 1 pkg. (8½ oz.) cornbread/muffin mix
- 2 large eggs, lightly beaten
- 1 cup shredded Mexican cheese blend
  Optional toppings: sour cream, salsa and minced fresh cilantro

1. In a large skillet, cook chicken over medium heat until no longer pink, 6-8 minutes, breaking into crumbles. Stir in seasonings.
2. Transfer to a 4-qt. slow cooker. Stir in beans, tomatoes, corn, enchilada sauce, green onions and cilantro. Cook, covered, on low until heated through, 6-8 hours.
3. In a small bowl, combine the muffin mix and eggs; spoon over the chicken mixture. Cook, covered, on low until a toothpick inserted in corn bread layer comes out clean, 1-1½ hours longer.
4. Sprinkle with cheese; let stand, covered, 5 minutes. If desired, serve with toppings.
1 serving: 359 cal., 14g fat (5g sat. fat), 110mg chol., 1021mg sod., 40g carb. (11g sugars, 5g fiber), 20g pro.

EASY CHEDDAR CHICKEN POTPIE

My kids love chicken potpie, and I really like that this is so quick and easy to put together with frozen veggies and store-bought gravy. To make it even simpler, my friend and I decided to top it with a biscuit crust instead of homemade pastry. It's delicious!
—*Linda Drees, Palestine, TX*

Prep: 20 min. • **Bake:** 25 min.
Makes: 6 servings

- 1   pkg. (16 oz.) frozen vegetables for stew, thawed and coarsely chopped
- 1   jar (12 oz.) chicken gravy
- 2   cups shredded cheddar cheese
- 2   cups cubed cooked chicken
- 2   cups biscuit/baking mix
- 1   tsp. minced fresh or ¼ tsp. dried thyme
- 2   large eggs, room temperature
- ¼   cup 2% milk

1. Combine vegetables and gravy in a large saucepan. Bring to a boil. Reduce heat; stir in cheese and chicken. Cook and stir until the cheese is melted. Pour into a greased 2-qt. round or 11x7-in. baking dish.

2. Combine biscuit mix and thyme in a small bowl. In another bowl, whisk eggs and milk; stir into dry ingredients just until moistened. Drop by tablespoonfuls over chicken mixture; spread gently.

3. Bake, uncovered, at 375° until golden brown, 23-27 minutes. Let stand for 5 minutes before serving.

1 serving: 481 cal., 22g fat (10g sat. fat), 146mg chol., 977mg sod., 41g carb. (3g sugars, 2g fiber), 29g pro.

Start WITH **FROZEN VEGETABLES**

TURKEY SALSA BOWLS WITH TORTILLA WEDGES

I used this recipe when I taught Junior Chef classes at my church. The children loved designing their own salsa bowls using whole grains, colorful veggies and lean protein. It was a fun way to teach them that food can be both delicious and nutritious!
—*Jean Gottfried, Upper Sandusky, OH*

Prep: 15 min. • **Cook:** 25 min.
Makes: 8 servings

- 1 lb. lean ground turkey
- ½ cup chopped sweet pepper
- ¼ cup thinly sliced celery
- 2 green onions, chopped
- 1 jar (16 oz.) medium salsa
- 1 can (16 oz.) kidney beans, rinsed and drained
- 1 cup uncooked instant brown rice
- 1 cup water
- 4 whole wheat tortillas (8 in.)
- 1 Tbsp. canola oil
- 8 cups torn romaine (about 1 head)
  Optional toppings: chopped tomatoes, sliced ripe olives, cubed avocado, shredded cheddar cheese and chopped green onions

1. Preheat oven to 400°. In a large skillet, cook and crumble turkey with pepper, celery and green onions over medium-high heat until no longer pink, 5-7 minutes. Stir in salsa, beans, rice and water; bring to a boil. Reduce heat; simmer, covered, until the liquid is absorbed, about 15 minutes.

2. Brush both sides of tortillas with oil; cut each into eight wedges. Arrange in a single layer on a baking sheet. Bake until lightly browned, 8-10 minutes.

3. To serve, divide lettuce among eight bowls; top with turkey mixture. Serve with tortilla wedges and toppings as desired.

1 serving: 279 cal., 7g fat (1g sat. fat), 39mg chol., 423mg sod., 36g carb. (4g sugars, 6g fiber), 18g pro. **Diabetic exchanges:** 2 starch, 2 lean meat, 1 vegetable.

SLOW COOKER
GREEN CHILI CHOPS WITH SWEET POTATOES

It takes only a few minutes to combine these ingredients in a slow cooker, and you'll have a filling, healthy dinner waiting for you at the end of the day. We serve it with fresh-baked garlic bread.

—*Marina Ashworth, Denver, CO*

Prep: 20 min. • **Cook:** 6 hours
Makes: 4 servings

- 3 medium sweet potatoes, peeled and cut into ½-in. slices
- 1 large onion, chopped
- 1 large green pepper, coarsely chopped
- 1½ cups frozen corn
- ½ tsp. salt
- ¼ tsp. pepper
- 4 boneless pork loin chops (6 oz. each)
- 1 can (10 oz.) mild green enchilada sauce
- ½ cup sour cream
- 2 Tbsp. reduced-sodium teriyaki sauce

1. In a 6-qt. slow cooker, combine sweet potatoes, onion, green pepper, corn, salt and pepper. Top with pork chops. In a small bowl, mix enchilada sauce, sour cream and teriyaki sauce; pour over meat.

2. Cook, covered, on low until meat is tender, 6-8 hours.

1 serving: 495 cal., 17g fat (7g sat. fat), 102mg chol., 909mg sod., 45g carb. (16g sugars, 5g fiber), 39g pro.

SKINNY COBB SALAD

This version of Cobb salad has all the taste and creaminess with half the fat and calories.
—*Taylor Kiser, Brandon, FL*

Takes: 25 min. • **Makes:** 4 servings

- ¼ cup fat-free plain Greek yogurt
- 2 Tbsp. reduced-fat ranch salad dressing
- 1 to 2 tsp. cold water

SALAD

- 3 cups coleslaw mix
- 3 cups chopped lettuce
- 1 large apple, chopped
- ½ cup crumbled reduced-fat feta or blue cheese
- 1 cup cubed cooked chicken breast
- 2 green onions, chopped
- 4 turkey bacon strips, chopped and cooked
- 1 can (15 oz.) garbanzo beans or chickpeas, rinsed and drained
- 1 small ripe avocado, peeled and cubed

1. Mix yogurt and dressing; thin with water as desired. Toss coleslaw mix with lettuce; divide among four plates.

2. Arrange the remaining ingredients in rows over top. Drizzle with yogurt mixture.

1 serving: 324 cal., 13g fat (3g sat. fat), 48mg chol., 646mg sod., 31g carb. (11g sugars, 9g fiber), 23g pro. **Diabetic exchanges:** 2 lean meat, 2 fat, 1½ starch, 1 vegetable.

TEST KITCHEN TIP

The easiest avocados to peel and slice are those that are ripe yet firm. Cut the avocado in half lengthwise. Twist the halves in opposite directions to separate. Carefully tap the seed with the blade of a sharp knife. Rotate the knife to loosen the seed and lift it out. To remove peel, scoop out the flesh from each half with a large metal spoon, staying close to the peel. Slice; dip slices in lemon juice to prevent browning.

TORTELLINI BAKE

Summer in New Hampshire brings plenty of fresh zucchini and squash. One year I had such a surplus from my garden that I was searching for different ways to use it. That's when I came up with this recipe. Serve it as a side dish or on its own as a light meal.

—*Donald Roberts, Amherst, NH*

Prep: 20 min. • **Bake:** 20 min.
Makes: 8 servings

- 1   pkg. (10 oz.) refrigerated cheese tortellini
- 1   Tbsp. olive oil
- 1   small zucchini, diced
- 1   yellow squash, diced
- 1   onion, diced
- 1   sweet red pepper, diced
- 1   tsp. dried basil
- ½   tsp. pepper
- ½   tsp. salt
- 1   cup shredded part-skim mozzarella cheese
- 1   cup half-and-half cream

1. Cook tortellini according to the package directions. Meanwhile, heat oil in a skillet; cook zucchini, squash, onion, red pepper and seasonings until vegetables are crisp-tender.
2. Drain tortellini; combine with vegetable mixture, mozzarella and cream in a 1½-qt. baking dish.
3. Bake, uncovered, at 375° until heated through, about 20 minutes.

¾ cup: 219 cal., 10g fat (5g sat. fat), 38mg chol., 362mg sod., 22g carb. (5g sugars, 2g fiber), 10g pro.
Freeze option: Cool unbaked casserole; cover and freeze. To use, partially thaw in refrigerator overnight. Remove casserole from refrigerator 30 minutes before baking. Preheat oven to 375°. Bake casserole as directed, increasing time as needed to heat through and for a thermometer inserted in center to read 165°.

GRILLED SAUSAGE-BASIL PIZZAS

These easy little pizzas are a wonderful change of pace from the classic cookout menu. Let everybody go crazy with a variety of toppings.

—*Lisa Speer, Palm Beach, FL*

Takes: 30 min. • **Makes:** 4 servings

- 4   Italian sausage links (4 oz. each)
- 4   naan flatbreads or whole pita breads
- ¼   cup olive oil
- 1   cup tomato basil pasta sauce
- 2   cups shredded part-skim mozzarella cheese
- ½   cup grated Parmesan cheese
- ½   cup thinly sliced fresh basil

1. Grill the sausages, covered, over medium heat until a thermometer reads 160°, 10-12 minutes, turning occasionally. Cut into ¼-in. slices.
2. Brush both sides of flatbreads with oil. Grill flatbreads, covered, over medium heat until bottoms are lightly browned, 2-3 minutes.
3. Remove from grill. Layer grilled sides with sauce, sausage, cheeses and basil. Return to grill; cook, covered, until cheese is melted, 2-3 minutes longer.

1 pizza: 808 cal., 56g fat (19g sat. fat), 112mg chol., 1996mg sod., 41g carb. (9g sugars, 3g fiber), 34g pro.

READER RAVE

"Really good! We used turkey Italian sausage links and I added some sliced red onion to the toppings as well. I also used fresh mozzarella and they tasted so good and were very filling!"

—GRAMMY DEBBIE, TASTEOFHOME.COM

TASTY TURKEY SKILLET

I use boxed rice and pasta mixes as the bases for a variety of quick meals. This colorful dish is super simple to cook on the stovetop using fried rice mix, tender turkey and convenient frozen vegetables.

—*Betty Kleberger, Florissant, MO*

Prep: 10 min. • **Cook:** 35 min.
Makes: 4 servings

- 1   lb. turkey breast tenderloins, cut into ¼-in. strips
- 1   pkg. (6.2 oz.) fried rice mix
- 1   Tbsp. butter
- 2   cups water
- ⅛   tsp. cayenne pepper
- 1½ cups frozen corn, thawed
- 1   cup frozen broccoli cuts, thawed
- 2   Tbsp. chopped sweet red pepper, optional

1. In a skillet coated with cooking spray, cook turkey over medium heat until no longer pink; drain. Remove turkey and keep warm.

2. Set aside seasoning packet from rice. In the same skillet, saute rice in butter until lightly browned. Stir in the water, cayenne and contents of seasoning packet.

3. Bring to a boil. Reduce heat; cover and simmer for 15 minutes. Stir in the corn, broccoli, red pepper if desired and turkey. Return to a boil. reduce heat; cover and simmer until the rice and vegetables are tender, 6-8 minutes.

1¼ cups: 351 cal., 6g fat (2g sat. fat), 53mg chol., 971mg sod., 43g carb. (4g sugars, 4g fiber), 35g pro.

SAUSAGE & SPINACH CALZONES

These comforting calzones are perfect for quick meals—or even a midnight snack. My nurse co-workers always ask me to make them when it's my turn to bring in lunch.
—*Kourtney Williams, Mechanicsville, VA*

Takes: 30 min. • **Makes:** 4 servings

- ½ lb. bulk Italian sausage
- 3 cups fresh baby spinach
- 1 tube (13.8 oz.) refrigerated pizza crust
- ¾ cup shredded part-skim mozzarella cheese
- ½ cup part-skim ricotta cheese
- ¼ tsp. pepper
- Pizza sauce, optional

1. Preheat oven to 400°. In a large skillet, cook and crumble sausage over medium heat until no longer pink, 4-6 minutes; drain. Add spinach; cook and stir until wilted. Remove from heat.

2. On a lightly floured surface, unroll and pat dough into a 15x11-in. rectangle. Cut into four rectangles. Sprinkle the mozzarella cheese on one half of each rectangle to within 1 in. of the edges.

3. Stir the ricotta cheese and pepper into the sausage mixture; spoon over the mozzarella cheese. Fold the dough over filling; press edges with a fork to seal. Place on a greased baking sheet.

4. Bake until calzones are light golden brown, 10-15 minutes. If desired, serve calzones with pizza sauce.

Freeze option: Freeze cooled calzones in an airtight freezer container. To use, microwave on high until heated through.

1 calzone: 489 cal., 22g fat (9g sat. fat), 54mg chol., 1242mg sod., 51g carb. (7g sugars, 2g fiber), 23g pro.

HAZELNUT CAKE
SQUARES, PAGE 282

CHAPTER 6

Sweet &
Simple Finales

Here's hoping you saved room for dessert, because
with these delicacies, we saved the best for last!

APPLE CINNAMON CAKE

This cake is equally good for breakfast or dessert, so be sure to not eat all of it after dinner! It's easy to make, super moist on the inside and has a crispy, cinnamon-rich crunch on the outside.

—*Marideane Maxwell, Albany, GA*

- -

Prep: 15 min. • **Bake:** 40 min. + cooling
Makes: 12 servings

- 1 pkg. yellow cake mix (regular size)
- 1 can (21 oz.) apple pie filling
- 4 large eggs, room temperature
- ⅔ cup canola oil
- 6 Tbsp. cinnamon sugar

GLAZE

- 1 cup confectioners' sugar
- ¼ tsp. ground cinnamon
- 1 to 2 Tbsp. water

1. Preheat oven to 350°. Grease and flour a 10-in. fluted tube pan. Combine cake mix, pie filling, eggs and oil; beat on low speed 30 seconds. Beat on medium 2 minutes. Pour half of the batter into prepared pan. Sprinkle with 3 Tbsp. cinnamon sugar. Add remaining cake mix; top with remaining cinnamon sugar.
2. Bake until a toothpick inserted in center comes out clean, 40-45 minutes. Cool in pan 10 minutes before removing to a wire rack to cool completely. Mix confectioners' sugar, cinnamon and enough water to reach desired consistency. Spoon glaze over cake, allowing some to flow over sides.
Note: For easier removal of cakes, use solid shortening to grease plain and fluted tube pans.
1 slice: 292 cal., 15g fat (2g sat. fat), 62mg chol., 328mg sod., 62g carb. (40g sugars, 1g fiber), 3g pro.

start WITH
YELLOW CAKE MIX

FREEZER STRAWBERRY SHORTBREAD DESSERT

When I'm planning party menus, I appreciate recipes I can make in advance. This dessert can be prepped and frozen up to two weeks before serving.

—*Cassie Alexander, Muncie, IN*

- -

Prep: 25 min. + freezing • **Makes:** 15 servings

- 1¼ cups crushed pretzels
- ¼ cup sugar
- ½ cup butter, melted

FILLING

- 1 can (14 oz.) sweetened condensed milk
- ½ cup thawed non-alcoholic strawberry daiquiri mix
- 1 pkg. (8 oz.) cream cheese, softened
- 1 container (16 oz.) frozen sweetened sliced strawberries, thawed
- 1 carton (8 oz.) frozen whipped topping, thawed

SAUCE

- 1 container (16 oz.) frozen sweetened sliced strawberries, thawed and undrained

1. In a small bowl, combine the pretzels, sugar and butter. Press onto the bottom of a greased 11x7-in. dish. Refrigerate for 30 minutes.

2. For filling, in a large bowl, combine milk and daiquiri mix. Beat in cream cheese until smooth. Stir in strawberries; fold in whipped topping. Pour over crust (dish will be full). Freeze for 4 hours before serving.

3. For sauce, puree thawed undrained strawberries in a food processor or blender. Strain through a fine sieve. Drizzle over top.

1 piece: 349 cal., 17g fat (11g sat. fat), 41mg chol., 240mg sod., 48g carb. (40g sugars, 1g fiber), 4g pro.

LEMONADE ICEBOX PIE

Here is the dessert that comes to mind when I put together my favorite summer meal. High and fluffy, this refreshing pie has a creamy smooth consistency and a definite lemonade flavor that we really appreciate.

—*Cheryl Wilt, Eglon, WV*

- -

Prep: 15 min. + chilling • **Makes:** 8 servings

- 1 pkg. (8 oz.) cream cheese, softened
- 1 can (14 oz.) sweetened condensed milk
- ¾ cup thawed lemonade concentrate
- 1 carton (8 oz.) frozen whipped topping, thawed
  Yellow food coloring, optional
- 1 graham cracker crust (9 in.)

In a large bowl, beat cream cheese and milk until smooth. Beat in lemonade concentrate. Fold in whipped topping and, if desired, food coloring. Pour mixture into crust. Cover and refrigerate until set.

1 piece: 491 cal., 24g fat (15g sat. fat), 48mg chol., 269mg sod., 61g carb. (52g sugars, 0 fiber), 7g pro.

READER RAVE

"I made this pie on one of the hottest weekends of the year. Its cool, creamy texture and sweet lemonade flavor created the perfect dessert to help us beat the heat."

—PAGERD, TASTEOFHOME.COM

APPLE PIE A LA MODE

I was planning a dinner party and wanted a dessert that wowed. My caramel apple ice cream pie certainly does the trick. Now it's a family favorite.

—*Trisha Kruse, Eagle, ID*

- -

Prep: 15 min. + freezing • **Makes:** 8 servings

- 1 can (21 oz.) apple pie filling
- 1 graham cracker crust (9 in.)
- 2 cups butter pecan ice cream, softened if necessary
- 1 jar (12 oz.) hot caramel ice cream topping
- ¼ cup chopped pecans, toasted

1. Spread half of the pie filling over crust. Top with half of the ice cream; freeze 30 minutes. Drizzle with half of the caramel topping; layer with remaining pie filling. Freeze 30 minutes. Scoop remaining ice cream over top. Freeze, covered, until firm.

2. Remove from freezer 30 minutes before serving. In a microwave, warm remaining caramel topping. Serve pie with warm caramel topping; sprinkle with pecans.

Note: To toast nuts, bake in a shallow pan in a 350° oven for 5-10 minutes or cook in a skillet over low heat until nuts are lightly browned, stirring occasionally.

1 piece: 398 cal., 14g fat (4g sat. fat), 13mg chol., 357mg sod., 69g carb. (59g sugars, 2g fiber), 3g pro.

5 INGREDIENTS

CHOCOLATE PEANUT BUTTER CHIP COOKIES

It's a snap to make a batch of tasty cookies with this recipe. My husband and son gobble them up.
—*Mary Pulyer, Port St. Lucie, FL*

Prep: 10 min. • **Bake:** 10 min./batch
Makes: 4 dozen

- 1 pkg. devil's food cake mix (regular size)
- 2 large eggs, room temperature
- ⅓ cup canola oil
- 1 pkg. (10 oz.) peanut butter chips

1. In a bowl, beat cake mix, eggs and oil (batter will be very stiff). Stir in chips.
2. Roll into 1-in. balls. Place on lightly greased baking sheets; flatten slightly. Bake at 350° until a slight indentation remains when lightly touched, about 10 minutes. Cool on pans for 2 minutes before removing to wire racks.

2 cookies: 184 cal., 9g fat (3g sat. fat), 18mg chol., 205mg sod., 22g carb. (12g sugars, 2g fiber), 4g pro.

BERRY DREAM CAKE

I use cherry gelatin to give a boxed cake mix an eye-appealing marbled effect. Top it with your favorite fruit.

—*Margaret McNeil, Germantown, TN*

- -

Prep: 15 min. + chilling
Bake: 30 min. + chilling • **Makes:** 15 servings

- 1 **pkg. white cake mix (regular size)**
- 1½ **cups boiling water**
- 1 **pkg. (3 oz.) cherry gelatin**
- 1 **pkg. (8 oz.) cream cheese, softened**
- 2 **cups whipped topping**
- 4 **cups fresh strawberries, coarsely chopped**

1. Prepare and bake the cake mix batter according to package directions, using a greased 13x9-in. baking pan.

2. In a small bowl, add boiling water to gelatin; stir 2 minutes to completely dissolve. Cool cake on a wire rack 3-5 minutes. Using a wooden skewer, pierce holes in top of cake to within 1 in. of edge, twisting skewer gently to make slightly larger holes. Gradually pour gelatin over cake, being careful to fill each hole. Cool 15 minutes. Refrigerate, covered, 30 minutes.

3. In a large bowl, beat cream cheese until fluffy. Fold in whipped topping. Carefully spread over cake. Top with strawberries. Cover and refrigerate for at least 2 hours before serving.

1 piece: 306 cal., 16g fat (6g sat. fat), 54mg chol., 315mg sod., 37g carb. (22g sugars, 1g fiber), 5g pro.

CARIBBEAN BREAD PUDDING

A completely unexpected dessert from the slow cooker, this bread pudding is moist and sweet with plump, juicy raisins and wonderful tropical flavors of pineapple and coconut.

—*Elizabeth Doss, California City, CA*

- -

Prep: 30 min. • **Cook:** 4 hours
Makes: 16 servings

- 1 **cup raisins**
- 1 **can (8 oz.) crushed pineapple, undrained**
- 2 **large firm bananas, halved**
- 1 **can (12 oz.) evaporated milk**
- 1 **can (10 oz.) frozen non-alcoholic pina colada mix**
- 1 **can (6 oz.) unsweetened pineapple juice**
- 3 **large eggs, room temperature**
- ½ **cup cream of coconut**
- ¼ **cup light rum, optional**
- 1 **loaf (1 lb.) French bread, cut into 1-in. cubes**
  Whipped cream and maraschino cherries, optional

1. In a small bowl, combine the raisins and pineapple; set aside. In a blender, combine the bananas, milk, pina colada mix, pineapple juice, eggs, cream of coconut and, if desired, rum. Cover and process until smooth.

2. Place two-thirds of the bread in a greased 6-qt. slow cooker. Top with 1 cup of the raisin mixture. Layer with the remaining bread and raisin mixture. Pour banana mixture into the slow cooker. Cover and cook on low until a knife inserted in the center comes out clean, 4-5 hours. Serve warm, with whipped cream and cherries if desired.

¾ cup: 245 cal., 4g fat (3g sat. fat), 7mg chol., 215mg sod., 46g carb. (27g sugars, 2g fiber), 5g pro.

LEMON BERRY DUMP CAKE

This sweet-tart cake recipe is so much fun to make with my grandkids. They love just dumping it all in and watching it magically become a pretty, delicious dessert.
—*Nancy Heishman, Las Vegas, NV*

Prep: 10 min. • **Bake:** 45 min. + cooling
Makes: 15 servings (3 cups lemon topping)

- 6 cups fresh or frozen blueberries
- 1 tsp. ground cinnamon
- ¾ cup butter, melted
- 1 pkg. lemon cake mix (regular size)

TOPPING

- 2 containers (6 oz. each) lemon yogurt
- 1 container (8 oz.) frozen whipped topping, thawed
- ½ cup marshmallow creme
- ⅓ cup lemon curd
  Additional blueberries, optional

1. Preheat oven to 350°. Toss the blueberries with cinnamon; spread into a greased 13x9-in. baking dish. Drizzle with half of the melted butter. Sprinkle with cake mix; drizzle with remaining butter.
2. Bake until golden brown and fruit is bubbly, 45-55 minutes. Cool on a wire rack.
3. Beat together yogurt, whipped topping, marshmallow creme and lemon curd. Serve dump cake with the yogurt mixture and, if desired, additional blueberries.

1 serving: 340 cal., 15g fat (9g sat. fat), 31mg chol., 297mg sod., 48g carb. (33g sugars, 1g fiber), 3g pro.

PEANUT BUTTER ROCKY ROAD CHEESECAKE

My classic chocolate and peanut butter pairing updates a tried-and-true cheesecake filling to pure creamy, crunchy bliss.
—*Jacyn Siebert, San Francisco, CA*

Prep: 30 min. • **Bake:** 55 min. + chilling
Makes: 16 servings

- 2 cups graham cracker crumbs
- ½ cup butter, melted
- ¼ cup sugar

FILLING

- 4 pkg. (8 oz. each) cream cheese, softened
- 1½ cups sugar
- 3 Tbsp. vanilla extract
- ⅛ tsp. salt
- 4 large eggs, room temperature, lightly beaten

TOPPING

- 2 Tbsp. creamy peanut butter
- 2 Tbsp. honey
- 1 jar (7 oz.) marshmallow creme
- ½ cup hot fudge ice cream topping, warmed slightly
- ½ cup chopped salted peanuts

1. Preheat oven to 325°. Mix cracker crumbs, butter and sugar; press onto bottom and 1 in. up sides of a greased 9-in. springform pan.
2. In a large bowl, beat the cream cheese and sugar until smooth. Beat in the vanilla and salt. Add the eggs; beat on low speed just until blended. Pour into crust. Place on a baking sheet.
3. Bake cheesecake until center is almost set, 55-60 minutes. Cool on a wire rack for 10 minutes. Loosen sides from pan with a knife. Cool 1 hour longer. Refrigerate the cheesecake overnight, covering when completely cooled.
4. Remove rim from pan. In a microwave, warm peanut butter and honey; mix until smooth. Drop spoonfuls of marshmallow creme, fudge topping and peanut butter mixture alternately over top of cheesecake. Swirl together using a toothpick or skewer. Sprinkle with peanuts.

1 slice: 533 cal., 32g fat (17g sat. fat), 119mg chol., 363mg sod., 52g carb. (42g sugars, 1g fiber), 8g pro.

TEST KITCHEN TIP

To prevent cracks in a cheesecake, avoid overbeating after adding the eggs—beat on low just until blended. Gently fold in by hand any additional ingredients like chocolate chips. Don't overbake. When done, the edges should be puffed; the center set but still soft. The center will firm upon cooling. Finally, cool your cheesecake on a rack at room temperature for 1 hour before refrigerating. Refrigerate for 3 hours, uncovered, or until thoroughly chilled. Then you can cover and continue to refrigerate overnight or up to 2 days.

STRAWBERRY-BANANA PUDDING CAKE

This luscious pink pudding cake is so easy to put together. Top it with ice cream and fresh fruit, and you'll have one very happy family.
—*Nadine Mesch, Mount Healthy, OH*

- -

Prep: 15 min. • **Cook:** 3½ hours + standing
Makes: 10 servings

- 1   **pkg. strawberry cake mix (regular size)**
- 1   **pkg. (3.4 oz.) instant banana cream pudding mix**
- 2   **cups plain Greek yogurt**
- 4   **large eggs, room temperature**
- 1   **cup water**
- ¾   **cup canola oil**
- 2   **Tbsp. minced fresh basil**
- 1   **cup white baking chips**
     Optional toppings: vanilla ice cream, sliced bananas, sliced strawberries and fresh basil

1. In a large bowl, combine the first six ingredients; beat on low speed 30 seconds. Beat on medium 2 minutes; stir in basil. Transfer to a greased 5-qt. slow cooker. Cook, covered, on low until edges of cake are golden brown (center will be moist), 3½ to 4 hours.

2. Remove slow cooker insert; sprinkle cake with baking chips. Let cake stand, uncovered, 10 minutes before serving. Serve cake with toppings as desired.

1 serving: 373 cal., 29g fat (8g sat. fat), 90mg chol., 239mg sod., 23g carb. (21g sugars, 0 fiber), 5g pro.

DAY AFTER THANKSGIVING COOKIES

Use your leftover cranberry sauce and pumpkin to bake some cookies. I've used jellied and whole-berry cranberry sauce.
—*Heather Bates, Athens, ME*

Prep: 25 min. + chilling
Bake: 15 min./batch + cooling
Makes: about 6 dozen

- 1   cup butter, softened
- 1   cup sugar
- 1   cup packed brown sugar
- ¾   cup canned pumpkin pie filling
- ½   cup whole-berry cranberry sauce
- 1   large egg, room temperature
- 2   tsp. vanilla extract
- 2½ cups all-purpose flour
- 1½ cups quick-cooking oats
- 2   tsp. ground cinnamon
- 1   tsp. baking soda
- ½   tsp. salt
- ½   tsp. ground nutmeg
- ¼   tsp. ground cloves
- 1   cup white baking chips
- 1   cup semisweet chocolate chips

1. In a large bowl, cream butter and sugars until light and fluffy. Beat in pumpkin pie filling, cranberry sauce, egg and vanilla. In another large bowl, whisk the flour, oats, cinnamon, baking soda, salt, nutmeg and cloves; gradually beat into creamed mixture. Stir in chips. Refrigerate, covered, until firm, about 2 hours.

2. Preheat oven to 350°. Drop dough by rounded tablespoonfuls 2 in. apart onto ungreased baking sheets. Bake until edges are golden brown, 15-18 minutes. Cool on pans 5 minutes; remove from pans to wire racks to cool completely.

1 cookie: 98 cal., 4g fat (3g sat. fat), 10mg chol., 63mg sod., 15g carb. (10g sugars, 1g fiber), 1g pro.

EASY FOUR-LAYER CHOCOLATE DESSERT

I grew up on these nutty, chocolaty layered treats. Now I make them for both my mom and myself, since I know she loves them, too.
—*Kristen Stecklein, Waukesha, WI*

Prep: 25 min. • **Bake:** 15 min. + cooling
Makes: 15 servings

- 1 **cup all-purpose flour**
- ½ **cup cold butter**
- 1 **cup chopped walnuts, toasted, divided**
- 1 **pkg. (8 oz.) cream cheese, softened**
- 1 **cup confectioners' sugar**
- 2 **cartons (8 oz. each) frozen whipped topping, thawed, divided**
- 2½ **cups 2% milk**
- 2 **pkg. (3.9 oz. each) instant chocolate pudding mix**
- 1 **cup semisweet chocolate chunks**
  Chocolate syrup

1. Preheat oven to 350°. Place flour in a small bowl; cut in butter until crumbly. Stir in ½ cup walnuts. Press onto bottom of an ungreased 13x9-in. baking dish. Bake until light golden brown, 12-15 minutes. Cool completely on a wire rack.

2. In a small bowl, beat cream cheese and confectioners' sugar until smooth; fold in one carton whipped topping. Spread over crust. In a large bowl, whisk milk and pudding mix 2 minutes. Gently spread over cream cheese layer. Top with remaining whipped topping. Sprinkle with chocolate chunks and remaining walnuts. Refrigerate until cold.

3. Cut into bars. Just before serving, drizzle with chocolate syrup.

Note: To toast nuts, bake in a shallow pan in a 350° oven for 5-10 minutes or cook in a skillet over low heat until nuts are lightly browned, stirring occasionally.

1 piece: 434 cal., 26g fat (15g sat. fat), 36mg chol., 195mg sod., 46g carb. (27g sugars, 2g fiber), 5g pro.

NUTELLA HAND PIES

These pint-size Nutella hand pies made with puff pastry just might be too good to share. We promise you'll have grateful recipients if you do, but don't let that stop you from saving a few for yourself!
—Taste of Home *Test Kitchen*

- -

Takes: 30 min. • **Makes:** 9 servings

1   **large egg**
1   **Tbsp. water**
1   **sheet frozen puff pastry, thawed**
3   **Tbsp. Nutella**
1   **to 2 tsp. grated orange zest**
ICING
⅓   **cup confectioners' sugar**
½   **tsp. orange juice**
⅛   **tsp. grated orange zest**
    Additional Nutella, optional

1. Preheat oven to 400°. In a small bowl, whisk egg with water.
2. Unfold puff pastry; cut into nine squares. Place 1 tsp. Nutella in center of each; sprinkle with orange zest. Brush edges of pastry with egg mixture. Fold one corner over filling to form a triangle; press edges to seal. Transfer to an ungreased baking sheet.
3. Bake until golden brown and pastry has cooked through, 17-20 minutes. Cool slightly.
4. In a small bowl, mix confectioners' sugar, orange juice and orange zest; drizzle over pies. If desired, warm additional Nutella in a microwave and drizzle over tops.
1 hand pie: 190 cal., 10g fat (2g sat. fat), 21mg chol., 100mg sod., 24g carb. (8g sugars, 2g fiber), 3g pro.

BERRY, LEMON & DOUGHNUT HOLE TRIFLE

I whipped up this impressive dessert for my son and his friends in only a few minutes. It's been a favorite in our house ever since.
—*Ellen Riley, Murfreesboro, TN*

Takes: 25 min. • **Makes:** 10 servings

- 2 cups cold 2% milk
- 1 pkg. (3.4 oz.) instant lemon pudding mix
- 1 carton (8 oz.) frozen whipped topping, thawed and divided
- 16 to 32 plain doughnut holes
- 3 cups fresh strawberries, halved
- 2 cups fresh blueberries

1. Whisk milk and pudding mix for 2 minutes. Let stand for 2 minutes or until soft-set. Fold in 2½ cups whipped topping; set aside.

2. Place half of doughnut holes in a 3-qt. trifle bowl; spread half of pudding mixture over the top. Top with half of the strawberries and blueberries. Repeat layers. Top with the remaining whipped topping. Chill until serving.

1 cup: 250 cal., 11g fat (7g sat. fat), 6mg chol., 250mg sod., 33g carb. (24g sugars, 2g fiber), 3g pro.

TROPICAL CRANBERRY COBBLER

The sunny island flavors of pineapple and orange go so well with the tart cranberries in this Hawaiian-inspired dessert. A scoop of vanilla ice cream makes it a creamy treat.

—*Jeanne Holt, Mendota Heights, MN*

- -

Prep: 20 min. • **Cook:** 4 hours + standing
Makes: 12 servings

2	cups fresh or frozen cranberries, thawed
1	can (20 oz.) unsweetened pineapple tidbits, drained
¾	cup sweetened shredded coconut
¾	cup orange marmalade
½	cup packed light brown sugar
6	Tbsp. butter, melted

TOPPING

1	pkg. yellow cake mix (regular size)
1	pkg. (3.4 oz.) instant coconut cream pudding mix
4	large eggs, room temperature
¾	cup pineapple-orange juice
½	cup butter, melted
¼	cup packed light brown sugar
1	tsp. vanilla extract
	Whipped cream, optional
¼	cup sweetened shredded coconut, toasted

1. In a greased 6-qt. oval slow cooker, layer cranberries, pineapple and ¾ cup coconut. In a bowl, mix marmalade, brown sugar and melted butter; spoon evenly over fruit.

2. In a large bowl, combine the first seven topping ingredients; beat on low speed 1 minute. Beat on medium 2 minutes. Pour over filling.

3. Cook, covered, on low until top springs back when lightly touched, about 4 hours. Turn off slow cooker. Remove insert; let stand 15 minutes before serving. If desired, serve with whipped cream. Sprinkle with toasted shredded coconut.

1 serving: 514 cal., 22g fat (13g sat. fat), 98mg chol., 508mg sod., 78g carb. (59g sugars, 2g fiber), 5g pro.

TEST KITCHEN TIP

This dessert is a cross between a cobbler, dump cake and upside-down cake, with a substantial cake layer. Adding a package of pudding mix makes the cake layer tender and moist. Be sure to look for instant pudding mix, not cook-and-serve. If you don't have pineapple-orange juice on hand, use apple, grape, plain orange or pineapple juice. Most of the pineapple flavor in this dish comes from the fruit layer.

CARAMEL FUDGE CHEESECAKE

I combined several recipes to satisfy both the chocolate lovers and cheesecake fans in my family. With a fudge brownie crust, crunchy pecans and a gooey layer of caramel, this gem of a dessert is hard to resist.

—*Brenda Ruse, Truro, NS*

Prep: 30 min. • **Bake:** 35 min. + chilling
Makes: 12 servings

- 1 pkg. fudge brownie mix (8-in. square pan size)
- 1 pkg. (14 oz.) caramels
- ¼ cup evaporated milk
- 1¼ cups coarsely chopped pecans
- 2 pkg. (8 oz. each) cream cheese, softened
- ½ cup sugar
- 2 large eggs, room temperature, lightly beaten
- 2 oz. unsweetened chocolate, melted and cooled

1. Prepare brownie batter according to package directions. Spread into a greased 9-in. springform pan. Place on a baking sheet. Bake at 350° for 20 minutes. Place pan on a wire rack for 10 minutes (leave oven on).
2. Meanwhile, in a microwave-safe bowl, melt caramels with milk. Pour over brownie crust; sprinkle with pecans.
3. In a large bowl, beat cream cheese and sugar until light and fluffy. Add eggs; beat on low speed just until combined. Stir in melted chocolate. Pour over pecans. Return pan to baking sheet.
4. Bake until center of cheesecake is almost set, 35-40 minutes. Cool on a wire rack for 10 minutes. Run a knife around edge of pan to loosen; cool 1 hour longer. Refrigerate overnight, covering when completely cooled. Remove sides of pan.
1 piece: 635 cal., 38g fat (13g sat. fat), 90mg chol., 369mg sod., 69g carb. (51g sugars, 3g fiber), 10g pro.

SHOWN ON PAGE 266

HAZELNUT CAKE SQUARES

Whenever one of my daughters is asked to bring a dish to a church function, a birthday party or any special occasion, they ask me for this recipe. It is so easy to prepare because it starts with a cake mix. It doesn't need icing, so it is perfect for bake sales, too.

—*Brenda Melancon, McComb, MS*

Prep: 10 min. • **Bake:** 25 min. + cooling
Makes: 15 servings

- 1 pkg. yellow cake mix (regular size)
- 3 large eggs, room temperature
- ⅔ cup water
- ⅔ cup Nutella
- ¼ cup canola oil
- ½ cup semisweet chocolate chips
- ½ cup chopped hazelnuts, toasted
- ½ cup brickle toffee bits, optional
  Confectioners' sugar, optional

1. Preheat oven to 350°. Grease a 13x9-in. baking pan.
2. In a large bowl, combine cake mix, eggs, water, Nutella and oil; beat on low speed 30 seconds. Beat on medium 2 minutes. Fold in chocolate chips, hazelnuts and, if desired, toffee bits. Transfer to prepared pan. Bake until a toothpick inserted in center comes out clean, 25-30 minutes.
3. Cool completely in pan on a wire rack. Dust with confectioners' sugar if desired.
1 piece: 280 cal., 14g fat (3g sat. fat), 37mg chol., 245mg sod., 38g carb. (24g sugars, 2g fiber), 4g pro.

5 INGREDIENTS

SHORTCUT COCONUT-PECAN CHOCOLATE TASSIES

You can garnish these cookies with pecan halves or a couple of chocolate chips before baking, or drizzle them with a little melted chocolate after taking them out of the oven.

—*Deb Villenauve, Krakow, WI*

Prep: 25 min. • **Bake:** 10 min./batch + cooling
Makes: about 3 dozen

- 1 pkg. chocolate cake mix (regular size)
- ½ cup quick-cooking oats
- 1 large egg, room temperature, lightly beaten
- 6 Tbsp. butter, melted and cooled slightly
- ¾ cup coconut-pecan frosting
  Pecan halves or melted semisweet chocolate, optional

1. Preheat oven to 350°. Mix cake mix and oats; stir in egg and melted butter. Shape mixture into 1-in. balls. Press onto bottom and up sides of greased mini-muffin cups.
2. Bake just until set, 8-10 minutes. Cool slightly before removing to wire racks; cool completely.
3. Top each with about 1 tsp. frosting. If desired, top with pecans or drizzle with melted chocolate.
1 tassie: 94 cal., 4g fat (2g sat. fat), 10mg chol., 105mg sod., 13g carb. (8g sugars, 1g fiber), 1g pro.

TEST KITCHEN TIP

It can be tricky to tell when the cake cups are done baking. Once set, they'll look more matte than glossy. If you're a fan of German chocolate cake, you'll love these little bite-sized versions.

OLD-FASHIONED OATMEAL RAISIN COOKIES

I've been making these cookies for nearly 30 years. The spice cake mix provides a delicious backdrop to the oat and raisins. They are an all-time favorite with my family.
—*Nancy Horton, Greenbrier, TN*

Prep: 10 min. • **Bake:** 10 min./batch
Makes: 7 dozen

- ¾ cup canola oil
- ¼ cup packed brown sugar
- 2 large eggs, room temperature
- ½ cup 2% milk
- 1 pkg. spice cake mix (regular size)
- 2 cups old-fashioned oats
- 2½ cups raisins
- 1 cup chopped pecans

1. In a large bowl, beat oil and brown sugar until blended. Beat in the eggs, then milk. Combine cake mix and oats; gradually add to brown sugar mixture and mix well. Fold in raisins and pecans.

2. Drop by tablespoonfuls 2 in. apart onto greased baking sheets. Bake at 350° until golden brown, 10-12 minutes. Cool for 1 minute before removing to wire racks.

1 cookie: 79 cal., 4g fat (1g sat. fat), 7mg chol., 50mg sod., 10g carb. (6g sugars, 1g fiber), 1g pro.

MISSISSIPPI MUD PIE

This southern favorite is one we can never get enough of. My grandmother, mother and aunts always made this dessert for parties and picnics. Now I make it for my own crew because it's so easy and everyone loves it!
—*Elizabeth Williston, Thibodaux, LA*

Prep: 30 min. • **Bake:** 15 min. + cooling
Makes: 12 servings

- 1 cup all-purpose flour
- 1 cup chopped pecans
- ½ cup butter, softened
- 1 pkg. (5.9 oz.) instant chocolate pudding mix
- 1 pkg. (8 oz.) cream cheese, softened
- 1 cup confectioners' sugar
- 1 container (16 oz.) frozen whipped topping, thawed, divided
  Toasted chopped pecans and chocolate curls, optional

1. Preheat oven to 350°. In a large bowl, beat flour, pecans and butter until blended. Press into the bottom of a 13x9-in. baking dish. Bake until golden brown, about 15 minutes. Remove to a wire rack; cool completely.

2. Make chocolate pudding according to package directions; let stand for 5 minutes. In a bowl, beat cream cheese and sugar until smooth; fold in 1 cup whipped topping. Spread cream cheese mixture over cooled crust. Spread pudding over cream cheese layer; top with remaining whipped topping. If desired, top with additional pecans and chocolate curls.

1 piece: 466 cal., 29g fat (17g sat. fat), 46mg chol., 214mg sod., 44g carb. (28g sugars, 2g fiber), 5g pro.

SLOW-COOKER CHERRY BUCKLE

I saw this recipe on a cooking show and came up with my own version. When the sweet aroma of this homey dessert drifts around the house, it's hard not to take a peek inside.

—*Sherri Melotik, Oak Creek, WI*

Prep: 10 min. • **Cook:** 3 hours
Makes: 8 servings

    2   cans (15 oz. each) sliced
        pears, drained
    1   can (21 oz.) cherry pie filling
    ¼   tsp. almond extract
    1   pkg. yellow cake mix (regular size)
    ¼   cup old-fashioned oats
    ¼   cup sliced almonds
    1   Tbsp. brown sugar
    ½   cup butter, melted
        Vanilla ice cream, optional

1. In a greased 5-qt. slow cooker, combine pears and pie filling; stir in extract. In a large bowl, combine cake mix, oats, almonds and brown sugar; stir in melted butter. Sprinkle over fruit.

2. Cook, covered, on low until topping is golden brown, 3-4 hours. If desired, serve with ice cream.

1 serving: 324 cal., 13g fat (8g sat. fat), 31mg chol., 152mg sod., 49g carb. (24g sugars, 2g fiber), 1g pro.

COFFEE ICE CREAM COOKIE CUPS

My siblings and I love ice cream, so I invented this fun dessert for my sister's birthday party. Everyone asked for more. I've also tried it with peanut butter cookie dough and other ice creams flavors, but I like this combination of ingredients the best.

—*Marcus Dooley, Red Oak, TX*

Prep: 30 min. • **Bake:** 15 min. + freezing
Makes: 12 servings

1 tube (16½ oz.) refrigerated chocolate chip cookie dough
2 cups coffee ice cream
Whipped cream and chocolate syrup
⅓ cup English toffee bits or almond brickle chips

1. Preheat oven to 350°. Let dough stand at room temperature 5-10 minutes to soften. Cut into 12 slices; press onto bottoms and up the sides of greased muffin cups.

2. Bake until golden brown, 12-14 minutes. Cool slightly on a wire rack. Spoon ice cream into each cup. Cover and freeze until firm, 1-2 hours.

3. Remove cups from pan. Garnish with the whipped cream and chocolate syrup. Sprinkle with toffee bits.

1 serving: 255 cal., 13g fat (5g sat. fat), 20mg chol., 131mg sod., 33g carb. (24g sugars, 1g fiber), 2g pro.

BANANA CREAM CHOCOLATE TRUFFLES

A stash of ripe bananas and my curious imagination were the spark behind these truffles. The outcome blew my family and friends away. I don't even particularly like bananas, but I could eat these all day long.
—*Michele Lassuy, Orlando, FL*

Prep: 35 min. + freezing
Makes: about 4 dozen

- 1 pkg. (14.3 oz.) Golden Oreo cookies
- 1 pkg. (8 oz.) cream cheese, softened
- 2 tsp. banana extract
- ⅓ cup mashed ripe banana
- 1 lb. milk chocolate candy coating, melted
  Dried banana chips, coarsely crushed

1. Pulse cookies in a food processor until fine crumbs form. In a bowl, beat cream cheese and extract until blended. Beat in banana. Stir in cookie crumbs. Freeze, covered, until firm enough to shape, about 2 hours.
2. Shape mixture into 1-in. balls. Dip cookie balls in candy coating; place balls on waxed paper-lined baking sheets. Top immediately with banana chips.
3. Refrigerate until set, about 30 minutes. Store coated truffles in a covered container in the refrigerator.

1 truffle: 110 cal., 6g fat (4g sat. fat), 5mg chol., 45mg sod., 13g carb. (9g sugars, 0 fiber), 1g pro.

TEST KITCHEN TIP

To easily coat the truffles, use two forks to dip and turn them in the chocolate candy coating. To crush the banana chips, place them in a zip-top plastic bag and pound them with a meat mallet or rolling pin until broken.

FROZEN PEANUT BUTTER & CHOCOLATE TERRINE

Here's a dessert that can be made ahead of time and stored in the freezer. The layers of banana, chocolate and peanut butter give it an awesome "wow" factor. It cuts nicely, too.
—*Jennifer Jackson, Keller, TX*

Prep: 30 min. + freezing • **Makes:** 12 servings

- 15 **Nutter Butter cookies, crushed (about 2 cups), divided**
- 1 **carton (16 oz.) mascarpone cheese**
- 1 **cup sugar**
- 2 **tsp. vanilla extract**
- 1 **carton (8 oz.) frozen whipped topping, thawed**
- 1 **medium banana, sliced**
- 1 **cup semisweet chocolate chips, melted and cooled slightly**
- 1 **Tbsp. baking cocoa**
- 1 **cup chunky peanut butter**

1. Line a 9x5-in. loaf pan with plastic wrap, letting edges extend up all sides. Sprinkle with a third of the crushed cookies.

2. In a large bowl, mix mascarpone cheese, sugar and vanilla; fold in whipped topping. Divide mixture evenly among three bowls.

3. To one portion of cheese mixture, fold in sliced banana; add to loaf pan, spreading evenly. Repeat cookie layer. To second portion, stir in the melted chocolate and cocoa; add to the loaf pan. Sprinkle with the remaining cookies. To third portion, stir in peanut butter. Spread over top of terrine.

4. Freeze, covered, until firm, at least 5 hours. To serve, invert terrine onto a platter; remove plastic wrap. Cut into slices.

1 slice: 568 cal., 39g fat (18g sat. fat), 47mg chol., 190mg sod., 49g carb. (38g sugars, 3g fiber), 10g pro.

5 INGREDIENTS

LEMON-BERRY ICE CREAM PIE

I love the combination of fresh strawberries and lemon curd in this ice cream pie. It's so refreshing, especially in an easy make-ahead dessert like this.

—*Roxanne Chan, Albany, CA*

Prep: 15 min. + freezing • **Makes:** 8 servings

- 1 **pint strawberry ice cream, softened**
- 1 **graham cracker crust (9 in.)**
- 1 **cup lemon curd**
- 2 **cups frozen whipped topping, thawed**
- 1 **pint fresh strawberries, halved**

1. Spoon ice cream into pie crust; freeze 2 hours or until firm.

2. Spread lemon curd over ice cream; top with whipped topping. Freeze, covered, 4 hours or until firm.

3. Remove from freezer 10 minutes before serving. Serve with strawberries.

1 piece: 370 cal., 13g fat (7g sat. fat), 40mg chol., 171mg sod., 58g carb. (40g sugars, 1g fiber), 2g pro.

READER RAVE

"This was quick, easy and refreshing in the hot summertime. I used vanilla ice cream and blueberries, and everybody loved it."

—MATTELIZ, TASTEOFHOME.COM

CAKE & BERRY CAMPFIRE COBBLER

This warm cobbler is one of our favorite ways to end a busy day of fishing, hiking, swimming or rafting. It's yummy with ice cream—and so easy to make!
—*June Dress, Meridian, ID*

Prep: 10 min. • **Grill:** 30 min.
Makes: 12 servings

2	cans (21 oz. each) raspberry pie filling
1	pkg. yellow cake mix (regular size)
1¼	cups water
½	cup canola oil
	Vanilla ice cream, optional

1. Prepare grill or campfire for low heat, using 16-20 charcoal briquettes or large wood chips.
2. Line an ovenproof Dutch oven with heavy-duty aluminum foil; add pie filling. In a large bowl, combine the cake mix, water and oil. Spread over pie filling.
3. Cover Dutch oven. When briquettes or wood chips are covered with white ash, place Dutch oven directly on top of 8-10 of them. Using long-handled tongs, place remaining briquettes on pan cover.
4. Cook until filling is bubbly and a toothpick inserted in the topping comes out clean, 30-40 minutes. To check for doneness, use the tongs to carefully lift the cover. Serve with ice cream if desired.
Note: This recipe does not use eggs.
1 serving: 342 cal., 12g fat (2g sat. fat), 0 chol., 322mg sod., 57g carb. (34g sugars, 2g fiber), 1g pro.

READER RAVE

"This is a great dessert when camping. I've made it numerous times using different fillings (especially cherry)."
—ANNIMEL, TASTEOFHOME.COM

CARROT DUMP CAKE

Our family loves carrot cake. I experimented to find an easier way to make it so we could enjoy it more often. This super moist version guarantees smiles all around the table.
—*Bonnie Hawkins, Elkhorn, WI*

Prep: 10 min. • **Bake:** 25 min. + cooling
Makes: 12 servings

1	can (8 oz.) crushed pineapple
1	cup shredded carrots (2 medium carrots)
1	cup finely chopped walnuts
1	pkg. spice cake mix (regular size)
¾	cup unsalted butter, melted
	Whipped cream, optional

1. Preheat oven to 350°. Mix pineapple, carrots and walnuts; spread into a greased 11x7-in. baking dish. Sprinkle with cake mix; drizzle with butter.
2. Bake until golden brown, 25-30 minutes. Cool on a wire rack. If desired, serve with whipped cream.
1 piece: 339 cal., 21g fat (9g sat. fat), 31mg chol., 263mg sod., 37g carb. (20g sugars, 1g fiber), 4g pro.

CRANBERRY-CHERRY NUT PIE

This delightful and stress-free pie using refrigerated crust combines cranberries with convenient cherry pie filling for a fresh, fun flavor.
—Taste of Home *Test Kitchen*

Prep: 20 min. • **Bake:** 40 min. + cooling
Makes: 8 servings

- 1 **can (21 oz.) cherry pie filling**
- 2 **cups fresh or frozen cranberries, thawed**
- ¾ **cup sugar**
- ½ **cup chopped walnuts**
- 2 **Tbsp. cornstarch**
- 1 **tsp. vanilla extract**
- ½ **tsp. ground cinnamon**
- ⅛ **tsp. ground allspice**
- 2 **sheets refrigerated pie crust**
- 2 **Tbsp. butter**
- 1 **tsp. 2% milk**
- 1 **Tbsp. coarse sugar**

1. Preheat oven to 375°. For filling, mix first eight ingredients. Unroll one crust into a 9-in. pie plate. Add filling; dot with butter.
2. Unroll the remaining crust onto a work surface; make cutout vents using small cookie cutters. Place top crust over filling; seal and flute edge. Decorate top with cutouts. Brush with milk; sprinkle with coarse sugar.
3. Bake pie on a lower oven rack until the crust is golden brown and the filling is bubbly, 40-45 minutes. If desired, cover edge with foil during the last 30 minutes to prevent crust from overbrowning. Cool on a wire rack.
1 piece: 498 cal., 22g fat (8g sat. fat), 18mg chol., 235mg sod., 73g carb. (41g sugars, 2g fiber), 4g pro.

CAN'T LEAVE ALONE BARS

I bring these quick-and-easy treats to church meetings, potlucks and housewarming parties. I often make a double batch so we can enjoy some at home.
—*Kimberly Biel, Java, SD*

- -

Prep: 20 min. • **Bake:** 20 min. + cooling
Makes: 3 dozen

- 1 **pkg. white cake mix (regular size)**
- 2 **large eggs, room temperature**
- ⅓ **cup canola oil**
- 1 **can (14 oz.) sweetened condensed milk**
- 1 **cup semisweet chocolate chips**
- ¼ **cup butter, cubed**

1. Preheat oven to 350°. In a large bowl, combine the cake mix, eggs and oil. Press two-thirds of the mixture into a greased 13x9-in. baking pan. Set remaining cake mixture aside.

2. In a microwave-safe bowl, combine the milk, chocolate chips and butter. Microwave, uncovered, until chips and butter are melted; stir until smooth. Pour over crust.

3. Drop teaspoonfuls of the remaining cake mixture over top. Bake until lightly browned, 20-25 minutes. Cool before cutting.

1 serving: 152 cal., 7g fat (3g sat. fat), 19mg chol., 122mg sod., 20g carb. (15g sugars, 0 fiber), 2g pro.

BIRTHDAY CAKE FREEZER POPS

On my quest to find birthday cake ice cream—my favorite flavor—I came up with these easy ice pops. Now, instead of going to the store whenever a craving hits, I just head to my freezer.

—*Dawn Lopez, Westerly, RI*

- -

Prep: 25 min. + freezing • **Makes:** 1½ dozen

- ⅔ **cup sprinkles, divided**
- 18 **disposable plastic or paper cups (3 oz. each)**
- 2 **cups cold 2% milk**
- 1 **pkg. (3.4 oz.) instant vanilla pudding mix**
- 1 **carton (8 oz.) frozen whipped topping, thawed**
- 2 **cups crushed vanilla wafers (about 60 wafers)**
- 18 **wooden pop sticks**

1. Spoon 1 tsp. sprinkles into each cup.

2. In a large bowl, whisk milk and pudding mix 2 minutes. Let stand until soft-set, about 2 minutes. Stir in whipped topping, crushed wafers and remaining sprinkles.

3. Cut a 1-in. hole in the tip of a pastry bag or in a corner of a food-safe plastic bag; fill bag with pudding mixture. Pipe into prepared cups. Top cups with foil and insert pop sticks through foil.

4. Freeze until firm, about 4 hours. Let stand at room temperature 5 minutes before gently removing pops.

1 pop: 161 cal., 7g fat (3g sat. fat), 4mg chol., 96mg sod., 23g carb. (15g sugars, 0 fiber), 1g pro. **Diabetic exchanges:** 1½ starch, 1½ fat.

EASY PUMPKIN SPICE PUDDING PIE

Caramel, pumpkin, ginger, nuts and cream cheese—these classic fall flavors combine in a no-bake pie that couldn't be easier or more delicious.

—*Cynthia Brabon, Mattawan, MI*

Prep: 20 min. + chilling • **Makes:** 8 servings

⅓ cup hot caramel ice cream topping, warmed
1 9-in. graham cracker crust (about 6 oz.)
⅓ cup chopped walnuts
3 Tbsp. chopped pecans

FILLING

1 cup cold whole milk
¼ cup refrigerated Italian sweet cream nondairy creamer
1 pkg. (3.4 oz.) instant pumpkin spice pudding mix
½ cup Philadelphia ready-to-serve cheesecake filling
½ tsp. pumpkin pie spice
¼ tsp. ground ginger

TOPPINGS

1 carton (8 oz.) frozen whipped topping, thawed
1 Tbsp. hot caramel ice cream topping
1 Tbsp. coarsely chopped walnuts
1 Tbsp. coarsely chopped pecans

1. Spread caramel topping over bottom of crust. Sprinkle with nuts.

2. For filling, whisk milk, creamer and pudding mix 2 minutes. Stir in cheesecake filling and spices until blended. Pour over nut mixture. Let stand 10 minutes.

3. Spread whipped topping over filling. Refrigerate until set, 4 hours or overnight. Before serving, drizzle with 1 Tbsp. caramel topping; sprinkle with walnuts and pecans.

1 piece: 397 cal., 21g fat (8g sat. fat), 13mg chol., 403mg sod., 46g carb. (41g sugars, 1g fiber), 4g pro.

ROOT BEER FLOAT PIE

This is the kind of recipe your kids will cherish. And you don't even need to use an oven.

—*Cindy Reams, Philipsburg, PA*

Prep: 15 min. + chilling • **Makes:** 8 servings

- 1 **carton (8 oz.) frozen reduced-fat whipped topping, thawed, divided**
- ¾ **cup cold diet root beer**
- ½ **cup fat-free milk**
- 1 **pkg. (1 oz.) sugar-free instant vanilla pudding mix**
- 1 **graham cracker crust (9 in.) Maraschino cherries, optional**

1. Set aside and refrigerate ½ cup whipped topping for garnish. In a large bowl, whisk the root beer, milk and vanilla pudding mix for 2 minutes. Fold in half of the remaining whipped topping. Spread mixture into the graham cracker crust.

2. Spread remaining whipped topping over pie. Freeze for at least 8 hours or overnight.

3. Dollop reserved whipped topping over each serving; top with a maraschino cherry if desired.

1 piece: 185 cal., 8g fat (4g sat. fat), 0 chol., 275mg sod., 27g carb. (14g sugars, 0 fiber), 1g pro. **Diabetic exchanges:** 2 starch, 1 fat.

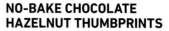

NO-BAKE CHOCOLATE HAZELNUT THUMBPRINTS

Years ago, a friend gave me a recipe for no-bake chocolate peanut treats. I thought it was a quick and clever way to whip up a batch of sweets without heating up the kitchen, and I started making different variations. This one includes luscious chocolate-hazelnut spread and crunchy hazelnuts. Yum!

—*Lisa Speer, Palm Beach, FL*

Prep: 30 min. + chilling
Makes: about 3½ dozen

- 1 **carton (8 oz.) spreadable cream cheese**
- 1 **cup (6 oz.) semisweet chocolate chips, melted**
- ½ **cup Nutella**
- 2¼ **cups graham cracker crumbs**
- 1 **cup finely chopped hazelnuts, toasted**
- 1 **cup whole hazelnuts, toasted**

1. Beat the cream cheese, melted chocolate chips and Nutella until blended. Stir in cracker crumbs. Refrigerate until firm enough to roll, about 30 minutes.

2. Shape mixture into 1-in. balls; roll in the chopped hazelnuts. Make an indentation in the center of each with the end of a wooden spoon handle. Fill with a hazelnut. Store between layers of waxed paper in an airtight container in the refrigerator.

Note: To toast nuts, bake in a shallow pan in a 350° oven for 5-10 minutes or cook in a skillet over low heat until nuts are lightly browned, stirring occasionally.

1 cookie: 111 cal., 8g fat (2g sat. fat), 3mg chol., 46mg sod., 10g carb. (6g sugars, 1g fiber), 2g pro.

SPICED CAPPUCCINO KISS COOKIES

This recipe combines two of my favorite flavors: coffee and cinnamon. You can always find these cookies on my holiday treat trays.
—*Cynthia Messenger, Mount Pleasant, SC*

Prep: 30 min. + chilling • **Bake:** 10 min./batch
Makes: 2 dozen

- ½ cup unsalted butter, softened
- ¼ cup packed brown sugar
- ¾ cup sugar, divided
- 1 large egg, room temperature
- 1½ tsp. instant espresso powder
- 1 tsp. vanilla extract
- 1¼ cups all-purpose flour
- ¼ tsp. baking soda
- ¼ tsp. salt
- 2 tsp. ground cinnamon
- 24 striped chocolate kisses

1. Beat butter, brown sugar and ¼ cup sugar until light and fluffy. Beat in egg, espresso powder and vanilla. In another bowl, whisk together flour, baking soda and salt; gradually beat into the creamed mixture. Refrigerate, covered, until firm enough to shape, about 1 hour.

2. Preheat oven to 350°. Mix cinnamon and remaining sugar. Shape dough into twenty-four 1-in. balls; roll in cinnamon sugar. Place 2 in. apart on ungreased baking sheets.

3. Bake until lightly browned, 10-12 minutes. Immediately top cookies with the chocolate kisses, pressing lightly. Cool slightly on pans before removing to wire racks to cool.

1 cookie: 117 cal., 5g fat (3g sat. fat), 19mg chol., 46mg sod., 17g carb. (11g sugars, 0 fiber), 1g pro.

TEST KITCHEN TIP

These cookies taste like a snickerdoodle with a hint of espresso. Add the espresso powder with the egg and vanilla instead of the flour mixture to ensure that it dissolves.

COOKIE SWIRL COBBLER

An extra-rich, chocolate chip cookie dough and crescent roll topping provide a tasty twist on a classic cherry cobbler. Serve it with a scoop of vanilla ice cream.
—Jeanne Holt, Mendota Heights, MN

Prep: 20 min. • **Bake:** 25 min. + cooling
Makes: 12 servings

- 1 cup (about 8 oz.) refrigerated chocolate chip cookie dough, softened
- 2 Tbsp. brown sugar
- ⅓ cup white baking chips
- ¼ cup plus 2 Tbsp. toasted sliced almonds, divided
- 1 can (21 oz.) cherry pie filling
- ½ tsp. almond extract, divided
- 2 cups fresh or frozen unsweetened raspberries
- 1 tube (8 oz.) refrigerated crescent rolls
- ¾ cup confectioners' sugar
- 3 to 4 tsp. 2% milk
  Vanilla ice cream, optional

1. Preheat oven to 350°. Combine cookie dough, brown sugar, baking chips and ¼ cup almonds. Set aside. In a large saucepan, heat the cherry pie filling over medium heat until bubbly. Remove from the heat; stir in ¼ tsp. almond extract. Fold in raspberries. Transfer to a greased 13x9-in. baking dish.

2. Unroll the crescent dough into one long rectangle; press perforations to seal. Drop small spoonfuls of cookie dough mixture over top; spread gently to cover. Roll up jelly-roll style, starting with a long side; pinch seam to seal. Cut crosswise into 12 slices; arrange cut side up on cherry mixture.

3. Bake until golden brown, 25-30 minutes. Cool 10 minutes. Meanwhile, combine the confectioners' sugar, the remaining almond extract and enough milk to make a medium-thick glaze. Drizzle rolls with glaze; sprinkle with remaining toasted almonds. Serve warm, with ice cream if desired.

1 serving: 308 cal., 11g fat (4g sat. fat), 2mg chol., 224mg sod., 49g carb. (22g sugars, 2g fiber), 3g pro.

EASY PECAN PIE BARS

I'm always searching for fast and easy recipes to take to the teachers' lounge. The staff goes nuts for these shortcut pecan pie bars.
—Kathro Yoder, Defiance, OH

Prep: 10 min. • **Bake:** 40 min. + cooling
Makes: 2 dozen

- 1 pkg. yellow cake mix (regular size)
- ⅓ cup butter, softened
- 1 large egg, room temperature
FILLING
- 1½ cups corn syrup
- ½ cup packed brown sugar
- 1 tsp. vanilla extract
- 3 large eggs, room temperature
- 1 cup chopped pecans

1. Preheat oven to 350°. Line a 13x9-in. baking pan with foil; grease foil.

2. Reserve ⅔ cup cake mix; set aside. Combine remaining cake mix, butter and 1 egg; beat on low speed until blended. Press onto bottom of prepared pan. Bake 15 minutes. Cool on a wire rack.

3. For filling, beat corn syrup, brown sugar, vanilla and reserved cake mix until blended. Add eggs; beat on low speed just until combined. Pour over warm crust; sprinkle with pecans.

4. Bake until center is set, 25-30 minutes longer. Cool completely in pan on a wire rack. To serve, refrigerate at least 15 minutes. Lift out of pan; discard foil, then cut into bars.

1 bar: 223 cal., 8g fat (3g sat. fat), 38mg chol., 174mg sod., 38g carb. (30g sugars, 0 fiber), 2g pro.

TEST KITCHEN TIP

Lightly spritz the inside of the measuring cup with cooking spray when measuring corn syrup. It will slide right out, ensuring you get every last drop in your recipe.

EASY MOCHA CREAM PIE

This chocolate crust is excellent with a cool no-bake mocha filling.
—Taste of Home *Test Kitchen*

- -

Prep: 20 min. + chilling
Bake: 15 min. + cooling • **Makes:** 8 servings

2¾ cups chocolate bear-shaped crackers
     or chocolate wafer crumbs, crushed
2   Tbsp. plus ½ cup sugar, divided
½   cup butter, melted
¼   cup cold water
1   tsp. instant coffee granules
1   envelope unflavored gelatin
½   cup semisweet chocolate chips
1½ cups heavy whipping cream, divided
2   pkg. (8 oz. each) cream
     cheese, softened
     Caramel sundae syrup, optional
     Chocolate syrup, optional

1. Preheat oven to 350°. Combine crushed crackers and 2 Tbsp. sugar with melted butter. Using the bottom of a glass, press cracker mixture onto bottom and up the sides of a greased 9-in. deep-dish pie plate. Bake until set, 12-15 minutes. Cool completely on a wire rack.
2. Meanwhile, mix cold water and instant coffee granules until blended. Sprinkle gelatin over coffee mixture; let stand for 5 minutes. Microwave chocolate chips and ¼ cup cream on high until the chips are melted; stir until smooth. Stir gelatin into chocolate mixture until smooth. Cool slightly. Beat the cream cheese and remaining sugar until smooth. Gradually beat in remaining cream. Beat in chocolate mixture until blended. Transfer filling to crust. Refrigerate, covered, until set, about 2 hours.
3. If desired, drizzle with caramel and chocolate syrups.
1 piece: 699 cal., 54g fat (31g sat. fat), 139mg chol., 400mg sod., 49g carb (33g sugars, 3g fiber), 8g pro.

5 INGREDIENTS

BLUEBERRY ICE CREAM TART

Absolutely no one will believe how easy this beautiful treat is to make! The quick crust boasts just a hint of cinnamon. It's a simply wonderful, cool summer dessert.
—*Shirley Foltz, Dexter, KS*

- -

Prep: 15 min. + freezing • **Makes:** 12 servings

1½ cups crushed vanilla wafers
    (about 45 wafers)
1   tsp. ground cinnamon
⅓   cup butter, melted
1   qt. vanilla ice cream, softened
1   can (21 oz.) blueberry pie filling

1. In a small bowl, combine wafer crumbs and cinnamon; stir in the butter. Press onto the bottom of a greased 9-in. springform pan; set aside.

2. Place ice cream in a large bowl; gently fold in pie filling. Spread over crust. Cover and freeze until firm. Remove from the freezer 10 minutes before serving. Remove sides of pan and cut tart into wedges.

1 slice: 316 cal., 13g fat (7g sat. fat), 36mg chol., 143mg sod., 48g carb. (34g sugars, 2g fiber), 2g pro.

READER RAVE

"My kids love this and request that I make it every year when our blueberries come in. I just make my own blueberry pie filling and use that instead of canned. Simple!"
—ELF69, TASTEOFHOME.COM

FAST FIX

GRILLED BANANA BROWNIE SUNDAES

My niece Amanda Jean and I have a lot of fun in the kitchen creating different dishes. One of us will start with recipe idea and it just grows from there—and so does the mess! That's exactly what happened with this luscious grilled dessert.
—*Carol Farnsworth, Greenwood, IN*

Takes: 15 min. • **Makes:** 8 servings

- 2 medium bananas, unpeeled
- 4 oz. cream cheese, softened
- ¼ cup packed brown sugar
- 3 Tbsp. creamy peanut butter
- 8 prepared brownies (2-in. squares)
- 4 cups vanilla ice cream
- ½ cup hot fudge ice cream topping, warmed
- ½ cup chopped salted peanuts

1. Cut unpeeled bananas crosswise in half, then lengthwise in half. Place quartered bananas on an oiled grill rack, cut side down. Grill, covered, over medium-high heat on each side until lightly browned, 2-3 minutes. Cool slightly.

2. In a small bowl, beat cream cheese, brown sugar and peanut butter until smooth.

3. To serve, remove bananas from peel; place over the brownies. Top with cream cheese mixture, ice cream, fudge topping and peanuts.

1 serving: 505 cal., 28g fat (11g sat. fat), 62mg chol., 277mg sod., 57g carb. (33g sugars, 3g fiber), 10g pro.

TEST KITCHEN TIP

Homemade brownies are divine. But when time is tight, speed things up by preparing a boxed brownie mix. Not sure which brand of brownie mix to buy? Visit www.tasteofhome.com/article/best-brownie-mix-brand to see the brands our editors and the *Taste of Home* Test Kitchen recommend.

FRESH RASPBERRY ICEBOX CAKE

Layered icebox cakes are so fun because they look impressive but couldn't be easier. Fresh raspberries make this one really special. Use Anna's Ginger Thins if you like the look of scalloped edges. Regular gingersnaps work just as well if those are not available.
—*Elisabeth Larsen, Pleasant Grove, UT*

Prep: 25 min. + chilling • **Makes:** 12 servings

- 1 carton (8 oz.) **mascarpone cheese**
- 3 cups cold **heavy whipping cream**
- 2 Tbsp. **sugar**
- 2 Tbsp. **grated lemon zest** (about 2 lemons)
- 2 pkg. (5¼ oz. each) **thin ginger cookies**
- 5 cups **fresh raspberries** (about 20 oz.), divided

1. Stir mascarpone cheese; let stand at room temperature 30 minutes. Meanwhile, beat cream until it begins to thicken. Add sugar; beat until soft peaks form. Reserve ½ cup cream; cover and refrigerate. Add the lemon zest and mascarpone to the remaining whipped cream; beat until stiff peaks form, 30-60 seconds.

2. On a serving plate, spread ½ cup of the cream mixture in a 7-in.-diameter circle. Arrange six cookies in a circle on top of the cream, placing a seventh cookie in the center. Gently fold 4 cups of raspberries into the remaining cream mixture. Spoon about 1 cup raspberry cream mixture over the cookies. Repeat layers six times, ending with cookies (there will be eight cookie layers in all). Spread the reserved whipped cream over cookies; top with remaining raspberries. Refrigerate, covered, overnight.

Note: This recipe was tested with Anna's Ginger Thins Swedish cookies.

1 slice: 421 cal., 35g fat (21g sat. fat), 91mg chol., 132mg sod., 25g carb. (13g sugars, 3g fiber), 4g pro.

CHERRY-PEACH DUMPLINGS

You can make this fruity dessert on your stovetop, but if you really want impress your guests, simmer it in an electric skillet right at the dinner table. They'll hardly be able to wait to dig in!
—*Patricia Frerk, Syracuse, NY*

Prep: 15 min. • **Cook:** 20 min.
Makes: 6 servings

1   **can (21 oz.) cherry pie filling**
½   **cup water**
2   **Tbsp. lemon juice**
½   **tsp. ground cinnamon**
¼   **tsp. ground cloves**
1   **can (15¼ oz.) sliced peaches, drained**
1   **large egg, room temperature**
    Whole milk
1½ **cups biscuit/baking mix**
    Additional cinnamon and whipped cream, optional

In a 10-in. skillet, combine the first five ingredients. Add peaches; bring to a boil. Place egg in a 1-cup measuring cup; add enough milk to measure ½ cup and stir until combined. Place biscuit mix in a bowl; stir in milk mixture with a fork just until moistened. Drop by six spoonfuls over top of boiling fruit. Simmer, uncovered, for 10 minutes; cover and simmer until a toothpick inserted in a dumpling comes out clean, about 10 minutes longer. Sprinkle with cinnamon if desired. Serve warm, with whipped cream if desired.
1 serving: 286 cal., 4g fat (1g sat. fat), 32mg chol., 349mg sod., 58g carb. (10g sugars, 2g fiber), 4g pro.

BERRY TARTLETS

Berry lovers won't be able to get enough of these delectable miniature tarts. Raspberries and blueberries work well with the whipped cream and lemon curd mixture, but feel free to use whatever berries suit your tastes. You can make the pie pastry from scratch or use a store-bought crust to keep prep easy.
—*Mary Walters, Westerville, OH*

Prep: 25 min. • **Bake:** 25 min. + cooling
Makes: 1 dozen

    Pastry for double-crust pie (9 in.)
2 Tbsp. sugar
1 Tbsp. cornstarch
1 pkg. (12 oz.) frozen unsweetened mixed berries, thawed
1 Tbsp. lemon juice
TOPPING
⅓ cup heavy whipping cream
¼ cup lemon curd
1 tsp. sugar
¼ tsp. vanilla extract
    Fresh berries, optional

1. Preheat oven to 400°. On a lightly floured surface, roll dough to ⅛-in. thickness. Using a 4-in. round cookie cutter, cut 12 circles, rerolling scraps as necessary. Press circles onto bottoms and up sides of ungreased muffin cups.
2. Mix sugar and cornstarch; toss with berries and lemon juice. Spoon 2 Tbsp. filling into each cup. Bake on a lower oven rack until pastry is golden brown and filling is bubbly, 24-26 minutes. Cool tartlets 10 minutes before removing from pan to a wire rack; cool completely.
3. For topping, beat cream until soft peaks form. In another bowl, mix lemon curd, sugar, vanilla and 1 Tbsp. whipped cream; fold in remaining whipped cream. Spoon over filling. If desired, top with fresh berries. Refrigerate until serving.
Pastry for double-crust pie (9 in.): Combine 2½ cups all-purpose flour and ½ tsp. salt; cut in 1 cup cold butter until crumbly. Gradually add ⅓ to ⅔ cup ice water, tossing with a fork until dough holds together when pressed. Divide dough in half. Shape each into a disk; cover and refrigerate 1 hour or overnight.
1 tartlet: 241 cal., 14g fat (9g sat. fat), 42mg chol., 160mg sod., 26g carb. (9g sugars, 1g fiber), 2g pro.

TOFFEE BROWNIE TRIFLE

This decadent combination of pantry items is a terrific way to dress up a brownie mix. Try it with other flavors of pudding or substitute your favorite candy bar. It tastes great with low-fat and sugar-free products, too.
—*Wendy Bennett, Sioux Falls, SD*

Prep: 20 min. • **Bake:** 25 min. + cooling
Makes: 16 servings

1 pkg. fudge brownie mix (13x9-in. pan size)
2½ cups cold whole milk
1 pkg. (3.4 oz.) instant cheesecake or vanilla pudding mix
1 pkg. (3.3 oz.) instant white chocolate pudding mix
1 carton (8 oz.) frozen whipped topping, thawed
2 to 3 Heath candy bars (1.4 oz. each), chopped

1. Prepare and bake brownies according to package directions for cake-like brownies, using a greased 13x9-in. baking pan. Cool completely on a wire rack.
2. In a large bowl, beat the milk and pudding mixes on low speed for 2 minutes. Let stand for 2 minutes or until soft-set. Fold in the whipped topping.
3. Cut the brownies into 1-in. cubes; place half in a 3-qt. glass trifle bowl or serving dish. Cover with half of the pudding. Repeat layers. Sprinkle trifle with the chopped candy bars. Refrigerate leftovers.
1 serving: 265 cal., 8g fat (4g sat. fat), 7mg chol., 329mg sod., 45g carb. (31g sugars, 1g fiber), 3g pro.

PISTACHIO BROWNIE TOFFEE BARS

These brownie bars have a homespun appeal and the surprise of pistachios. Fudge brownie mix makes them easy to prepare.
—*Matt Shaw, Warrenton, OR*

- -

Prep: 20 min. • **Bake:** 30 min. + cooling
Makes: 3 dozen

- ¾ cup butter, softened
- ¾ cup packed brown sugar
- 1 large egg yolk, room temperature
- ¾ tsp. vanilla extract
- 1½ cups all-purpose flour

FILLING

- 1 pkg. fudge brownie mix (13x9-in. pan size)
- ⅓ cup water
- ⅓ cup canola oil
- 1 large egg, room temperature

TOPPING

- 1 pkg. (11½ oz.) milk chocolate chips, melted
- ¾ cup chopped salted roasted pistachios

1. Preheat oven to 350°. In a large bowl, cream butter and brown sugar until light and fluffy. Beat in egg yolk and vanilla. Gradually beat in flour, mixing well. Press onto bottom of a greased 15x10x1-in. baking pan.

2. Bake until golden brown, 12-14 minutes. Meanwhile, in a large bowl, combine brownie mix, water, oil and egg until blended.

3. Spread brownie batter over hot crust. Bake until center is set, 14-16 minutes. Cool completely in pan on a wire rack.

4. Spread melted chocolate over top; sprinkle with pistachios. Let stand until set. Cut into 36 bars.

1 bar: 219 cal., 12g fat (5g sat. fat), 23mg chol., 112mg sod., 27g carb. (17g sugars, 1g fiber), 3g pro.

PUMPKIN PIE CUPCAKES WITH WHIPPED CREAM

I combined my two loves, cupcakes and pie, into one amazing fall treat. These pumpkin cupcakes have a pie crust bottom and a snow white topping.
—*Julie Herrera-Lemler, Rochester, MN*

- -

Prep: 45 min. • **Bake:** 20 min. + cooling
Makes: 2 dozen

- 1 sheet refrigerated pie crust
- 1 can (15 oz.) solid-pack pumpkin
- 4 large eggs, room temperature
- ½ cup canola oil
- ½ cup water
- 2 tsp. vanilla extract
- 3 cups all-purpose flour
- 2 cups sugar
- 1 Tbsp. cornstarch
- 2 tsp. baking powder
- 1 tsp. baking soda
- 1 tsp. pumpkin pie spice
- ½ tsp. salt

WHIPPED CREAM

- 2 cups heavy whipping cream
- ½ cup confectioners' sugar
  Ground cinnamon

1. Preheat oven to 350°. Line 24 muffin cups with foil liners.

2. On a work surface, unroll crust. Cut 24 circles with a floured 2¼-in. round cookie cutter, rerolling scraps as necessary. Press one crust circle into each liner. Bake until lightly browned, 10-12 minutes. Cool on wire racks.

3. In a large bowl, beat the pumpkin, eggs, oil, water and vanilla until well blended. In another bowl, whisk flour, sugar, cornstarch, baking powder, baking soda, pie spice and salt; gradually beat into pumpkin mixture. Pour ¼ cup batter into each prepared cup.

4. Bake until a toothpick inserted in center comes out clean, 20-25 minutes, rotating pans halfway through baking. Cool in pans 10 minutes before removing to wire racks to cool completely.

5. For whipped cream, in a large bowl, beat the cream until it begins to thicken. Add the confectioners' sugar; beat until soft peaks form. To serve, dollop cream over cupcakes; sprinkle with cinnamon.

1 cupcake: 297 cal., 15g fat (6g sat. fat), 60mg chol., 185mg sod., 37g carb. (21g sugars, 1g fiber), 4g pro.

CHERRY UPSIDE-DOWN BREAD PUDDING

I love warm bread pudding and enjoy fixing this for my family on a chilly day. You could use a different flavor of pie filling and omit the chocolate chips to make a completely different dessert. The creative possibilities are endless!

—*Ronna Farley, Rockville, MD*

Prep: 20 min. + cooling • **Cook:** 2¾ hours
Makes: 12 servings

- 1 loaf (16 oz.) sliced white bread
- 1 can (21 oz.) cherry pie filling
- ½ cup butter, softened
- 1 cup sugar
- 5 large eggs, room temperature
- 2 cups 2% milk
- 1 tsp. ground cinnamon
- 1 tsp. vanilla extract
- ¾ cup semisweet chocolate chips
  Sweetened whipped cream, optional

1. Place bread on ungreased baking sheets. Broil each pan 3-4 in. from heat until golden brown, 1-2 minutes on each side; let cool. Cut into 1-in. pieces; set aside.

2. Spoon pie filling into a greased 5- or 6-qt. slow cooker. In a large bowl cream butter and sugar until crumbly. Add eggs, one at a time, beating well after each addition. Beat in milk, cinnamon and vanilla (mixture may appear curdled). Gently stir in the chocolate chips and reserved bread cubes; let stand until bread is softened, about 10 minutes. Transfer to slow cooker.

3. Cook, covered, on low until set and a knife inserted near the center comes out clean, 2¾-3¼ hours. Serve warm, with whipped cream if desired.

¾ cup: 393 cal., 15g fat (8g sat. fat), 101mg chol., 305mg sod., 58g carb. (27g sugars, 2g fiber), 8g pro.

LAYERED CANDY CANE DESSERT

This fabulous dessert has the magical flavor of candy canes, plus the bonus of a rich and chocolaty Oreo cookie crust. And it looks like a winter wonderland.

—Dawn Kreuser, Green Bay, WI

- -

Prep: 25 min. + chilling • **Makes:** 24 servings

- 1 pkg. (14.3 oz.) Oreo cookies
- 6 Tbsp. butter, melted
- 1 pkg. (8 oz.) cream cheese, softened
- ¼ cup sugar
- 2 Tbsp. 2% milk
- 1 carton (12 oz.) frozen whipped topping, thawed, divided
- ¾ cup crushed candy canes (about 7 regular size), divided
- 2 pkg. (3.3 oz. each) instant white chocolate pudding mix
- 2¾ cups cold 2% milk

1. Pulse cookies in a food processor until fine crumbs form. Add melted butter; pulse just until combined. Press onto bottom of a 13x9-in. dish. Refrigerate while preparing the filling.

2. Beat cream cheese, sugar and milk until smooth. Fold in 1 cup whipped topping and ½ cup crushed candies. Spread over crust.

3. Whisk pudding mix and milk 2 minutes; spread over cream cheese layer. Spread with remaining whipped topping. Refrigerate, covered, 4 hours. Sprinkle with remaining candies just before serving.

1 piece: 251 cal., 13g fat (7g sat. fat), 20mg chol., 250mg sod., 32g carb. (25g sugars, 1g fiber), 2g pro.

DOWN SOUTH SWEET TEA CAKE

This recipe combines two of the best and most famous ingredients from the South: sweet tea and pecans. A cake mix simplifies prep and helps ease the holiday time crunch.
—*Melissa Millwood, Lyman, SC*

Prep: 20 min. • **Bake:** 45 min. + cooling
Makes: 12 servings

- 1 pkg. yellow cake mix (regular size)
- 1 pkg. (3.4 oz.) instant vanilla pudding mix
- 1 cup strong brewed tea, cooled, divided
- 4 large eggs, room temperature
- ¾ cup canola oil
- 1 tsp. vanilla extract
- ½ tsp. lemon extract
- 1 cup chopped pecans, toasted
- 2 cups confectioners' sugar
- ⅓ cup unsalted butter, melted

1. Preheat oven to 350°. Grease and flour a 10-in. fluted tube pan. In a large bowl, combine cake mix, pudding mix, ¾ cup tea, eggs, oil, vanilla and lemon extract; beat on low speed for 30 seconds. Beat on medium for 2 minutes. Stir in the pecans. Transfer to prepared pan. Bake until a toothpick inserted in center comes out clean, 45-50 minutes.
2. Cool in pan 10 minutes before removing to a wire rack to cool completely. In a small bowl, mix confectioners' sugar, butter and enough remaining tea to reach desired consistency. Pour glaze over top of cake, allowing some to flow over sides.
1 slice: 511 cal., 29g fat (6g sat. fat), 76mg chol., 357mg sod., 62g carb. (44g sugars, 2g fiber), 4g pro.

COCONUT POPPY SEED CAKE

I'm known for my coconut cake and it is definitely one of my most-requested desserts. You can change it up by using different cake mixes and pudding flavors.
—*Gail Cayce, Wautoma, WI*

Prep: 15 min. • **Bake:** 20 min. + cooling
Makes: 24 servings

- 1 pkg. white cake mix (regular size)
- ½ cup sweetened shredded coconut
- ¼ cup poppy seeds
- 3½ cups cold whole milk
- 1 tsp. coconut extract
- 2 pkg. (3.4 oz. each) instant vanilla pudding mix
- 1 carton (8 oz.) frozen whipped topping, thawed
- ⅓ cup sweetened shredded coconut, toasted, optional

1. Prepare cake according to the package directions, adding coconut and poppy seeds to batter.
2. Pour into a greased 13x9-in. baking pan. Bake at 350° until a toothpick inserted in the center comes out clean, 20-25 minutes. Cool cake completely.
3. In a large bowl, whisk the milk, extract and pudding mixes for 2 minutes. Let stand for 2 minutes or until soft-set. Spread over the cake. Spread with whipped topping. Sprinkle with toasted coconut if desired.
1 piece: 211 cal., 9g fat (4g sat. fat), 27mg chol., 231mg sod., 30g carb. (20g sugars, 1g fiber), 3g pro.

CREAM-FILLED CUPCAKES

These decadent chocolate cupcakes have a fun filling and shiny chocolate frosting that make them extra special. They always disappear in a flash!
—*Kathy Kittell, Lenexa, KS*

Prep: 20 min. • **Bake:** 15 min. + cooling
Makes: 2 dozen

- 1 pkg. devil's food cake mix (regular size)
- 2 tsp. hot water
- ¼ tsp. salt
- 1 jar (7 oz.) marshmallow creme
- ½ cup shortening
- ⅓ cup confectioners' sugar
- ½ tsp. vanilla extract

GANACHE FROSTING
- 1 cup semisweet chocolate chips
- ¾ cup heavy whipping cream

1. Prepare and bake cake batter according to package directions, using paper-lined muffin cups. Cool for 5 minutes before removing from pans to wire racks to cool completely.
2. For filling, in a small bowl, combine water and salt until salt is dissolved. Cool. In a small bowl, beat the marshmallow creme, shortening, confectioners' sugar and vanilla until light and fluffy; beat in the salt mixture.
3. Cut a small hole in the corner of a pastry or plastic bag; insert round pastry tip. Fill the bag with cream filling. Push the tip through the bottom of paper liner to fill each cupcake.
4. Place chocolate chips in a small bowl. In a small saucepan, bring cream just to a boil. Pour over chocolate; whisk until smooth. Cool mixture, stirring occasionally, to room temperature or until ganache reaches a dipping consistency.
5. Dip cupcake tops in ganache; chill for 20 minutes or until set. Store cupcakes in the refrigerator.

1 cupcake: 262 cal., 15g fat (5g sat. fat), 32mg chol., 223mg sod., 29g carb. (20g sugars, 1g fiber), 2g pro.

BANANA CREAM PIE WITH CAKE MIX CRUST

I added something special to the classic banana cream pie: A crunchy peanut-buttery streusel tops it off.
—*Matthew Hass, Ellison Bay, WI*

Prep: 15 min. • **Bake:** 30 min. + chilling
Makes: 10 servings

- 1 pkg. yellow cake mix (regular size), divided
- 1 large egg, room temperature, lightly beaten
- 3 Tbsp. butter, softened and divided
- 1 cup cold 2% milk
- 1 pkg. (3.4 oz.) instant banana cream pudding mix
- 1 medium banana, sliced
- 1 carton (8 oz.) frozen whipped topping, thawed and divided
- ⅓ cup creamy peanut butter
  Additional sliced ripe banana

1. Preheat oven to 350°. Grease a 9-in. pie plate. Stir together 1¾ cups cake mix, egg and 1 Tbsp. butter until combined. Turn onto a floured surface; knead until a smooth dough forms. Roll dough to fit prepared pie plate. Flute edge. Prick bottom several times with a fork. Bake until golden brown, 12-15 minutes. Cool crust in pan on a wire rack.
2. Whisk milk and pudding mix 2 minutes. Fold in banana and 1 cup whipped topping. Transfer to cooled crust. Top with remaining whipped topping. Refrigerate at least 3 hours.
3. Meanwhile, mix remaining cake mix, peanut butter and remaining butter until crumbly. Transfer to a parchment-lined rimmed baking pan. Bake until golden brown, 14-18 minutes, stirring once. Cool completely.
4. Top pie with additional sliced banana and some of the crumb topping (save additional crumb topping for another use).

1 piece: 394 cal., 16g fat (8g sat. fat), 30mg chol., 526mg sod., 55g carb. (35g sugars, 1g fiber), 6g pro.

BLACK FOREST TART

Cherry pie filling and a melted chocolate drizzle top this rich, fudgy tart.

—Taste of Home *Test Kitchen*

- -

Prep: 35 min. + chilling
Bake: 25 min. + cooling • **Makes:** 12 servings

- 1¼ **cups chocolate wafer crumbs**
- ¼ **cup sugar**
- ¼ **cup butter, melted**

FILLING

- ½ **cup butter**
- 6 **oz. semisweet chocolate, chopped**
- 3 **large eggs, room temperature**
- ⅔ **cup sugar**
- 1 **tsp. vanilla extract**
- ¼ **tsp. salt**
- ⅔ **cup all-purpose flour**

TOPPING

- 1 **can (21 oz.) cherry pie filling**
- 2 **oz. semisweet chocolate, chopped**
- 1 **Tbsp. heavy whipping cream**

1. In a small bowl, combine wafer crumbs and sugar; stir in the butter. Press onto the bottom and up the sides of a lightly greased 11-in. fluted tart pan with removable bottom.
2. Place pan on a baking sheet. Bake at 350° until lightly browned, 8-10 minutes. Cool on a wire rack.
3. In a microwave, melt butter and chocolate; stir until smooth. Cool for 10 minutes. In a large bowl, beat the eggs, sugar, vanilla and salt until thickened, about 4 minutes. Blend in chocolate mixture. Stir in flour and mix well.
4. Pour into the crust; spread evenly. Bake at 350° until a toothpick inserted in the center comes out clean, 25-30 minutes. Cool tart completely on a wire rack. Spread pie filling over the top.
5. In a microwave, melt chocolate and cream; stir until smooth. Cool for 5 minutes, stirring occasionally. Drizzle over tart. Chill until set.
Note: This tart is best served the day it is prepared.
1 slice: 411 cal., 21g fat (12g sat. fat), 86mg chol., 258mg sod., 54g carb. (36g sugars, 2g fiber), 5g pro.

start WITH **YELLOW CAKE MIX**

LEMON CHEESECAKE TARTS

To make these cute tarts even quicker, add the filling to store-bought phyllo tart shells.
—*Sarah Gilbert, Aloha, OR*

Prep: 30 min. • **Bake:** 10 min. + cooling
Makes: 2 dozen

- 2 sheets refrigerated pie crust
FILLING
- 1 pkg. (8 oz.) cream cheese, softened
- 1 tsp. vanilla extract
- 1 jar (10 oz.) lemon curd, divided
- 1 container (8 oz.) frozen whipped topping, thawed
- 1 cup fresh blueberries
  Confectioners' sugar, optional

1. Preheat oven to 450°. On a work surface, unroll crusts. Cut 24 circles with a floured 3-in. scalloped round cookie cutter, rerolling scraps as necessary. Press circles onto the bottoms and partway up sides of ungreased muffin cups, smoothing edges. Prick bottoms generously with a fork.
2. Bake until light golden brown, 5-7 minutes. Remove crusts from pans to wire racks to cool completely.

3. In a large bowl, beat cream cheese and vanilla until blended; beat in ¼ cup lemon curd. Fold in a third of the whipped topping, then fold in remaining topping.
4. Spoon 2 Tbsp. cream cheese mixture into each tart shell; top each with 1 tsp. lemon curd. Top with the blueberries; refrigerate until serving. Dust with confectioners' sugar if desired.

1 tart: 166 cal., 9g fat (5g sat. fat), 22mg chol., 95mg sod., 18g carb. (10g sugars, 0 fiber), 1g pro.

STRAWBERRY SHORTCAKE PUFFS

When my friend Kelly brought me a pint of strawberries, I decided to make strawberry shortcake with my own elegant spin. These light and airy puff pastry stacks let the sweet fruit shine.
—*Jenny Dubinsky, Inwood, WV*

Prep: 25 min. • **Bake:** 15 min. + cooling
Makes: 12 servings

- 1 sheet frozen puff pastry, thawed
- 4 cups fresh strawberries, sliced
- ¼ cup plus 3 Tbsp. sugar, divided
- 1½ cups heavy whipping cream
- ½ tsp. vanilla extract

1. Preheat oven to 400°. On a lightly floured surface, roll puff pastry to a 10-in. square; cut into 12 rectangles (approx. 3x2½-in.). Place on ungreased baking sheets. Bake pastry until golden brown, 12-15 minutes. Remove to wire racks; cool completely.
2. In a large bowl, toss strawberries with ¼ cup sugar. Let stand 30 minutes, stirring occasionally. In another bowl, beat cream until it begins to thicken. Add vanilla and remaining sugar; beat until stiff peaks form.
3. To serve, split pastries horizontally in half. Top each bottom half with 2 Tbsp. whipped cream and 1 Tbsp. strawberries; replace top half. Top with the remaining whipped cream and strawberries.

1 serving: 246 cal., 16g fat (8g sat. fat), 34mg chol., 76mg sod., 23g carb. (11g sugars, 2g fiber), 3g pro.

EASY NUTELLA CHEESECAKE

A creamy chocolate-hazelnut spread tops a crust made of crushed Oreo cookies to make this irresistible baked cheesecake.
—*Nick Iverson, Denver, CO*

Prep: 35 min. • **Bake:** 1¼ hour + chilling
Makes: 16 servings

- 2½ cups lightly crushed Oreo cookies (about 24 cookies)
- ¼ cup sugar
- ¼ cup butter, melted
FILLING
- 4 pkg. (8 oz. each) cream cheese, softened
- ½ cup sugar
- 2 jars (26½ oz. each) Nutella
- 1 cup heavy whipping cream
- 1 tsp. salt
- 4 large eggs, room temperature, lightly beaten
- ½ cup chopped hazelnuts, toasted

1. Preheat oven to 325°. Pulse cookies and sugar in a food processor until fine crumbs form. Continue processing while gradually adding butter in a steady stream. Press mixture onto bottom of a greased 10x3-in. springform pan. Securely wrap bottom and sides of springform in a double thickness of heavy-duty foil (about 18 in. square).
2. For filling, beat cream cheese and sugar until smooth. Beat in Nutella, cream and salt. Add eggs; beat on low speed just until blended. Pour over crust.
3. Bake until a thermometer inserted in center reads 160°, about 1¼ hours. Cool 1¼ hours on a wire rack. Refrigerate the cheesecake overnight, covering when completely cooled.
4. Gently loosen sides from pan with a knife; remove rim. Top cheesecake with chopped toasted hazelnuts.

1 slice: 900 cal., 62g fat (22g sat. fat), 129mg chol., 478mg sod., 84g carb. (71g sugars, 4g fiber), 12g pro.

SLOW-COOKER BLUEBERRY COBBLER

I love blueberries, and this easy cake-mix cobbler showcases them beautifully. Serve it warm with a big scoop of French vanilla ice cream or a dollop of whipped cream.
—Teri Rasey, Cadillac, MI

Prep: 15 min. • **Cook:** 3 hours
Makes: 12 servings

- 4 cups fresh or frozen blueberries
- 1 cup sugar
- 1 Tbsp. cornstarch
- 2 tsp. vanilla extract
- 1 pkg. French vanilla cake mix (regular size)
- ½ cup butter, melted
- ⅓ cup chopped pecans
  Vanilla ice cream, optional

In a greased 5-qt. slow cooker, combine blueberries, sugar and cornstarch; stir in vanilla. In a large bowl combine cake mix and melted butter. Crumble over blueberries. Top with pecans. Cover slow cooker with a double layer of white paper towels; place lid securely over towels. Cook, covered, on low until the topping is set, 3-4 hours. If desired, serve with ice cream.

½ cup: 331 cal., 11g fat (6g sat. fat), 20mg chol., 343mg sod., 58g carb. (39g sugars, 2g fiber), 2g pro.

TEST KITCHEN TIP

Placing paper towels under the lid of the slow cooker will catch condensation and keep it from dripping on the cobbler topping.

ROCKY ROAD COOKIE CUPS

Traditional rocky road ice cream is chock-full of nuts, marshmallows and chocolate. Using prepared chocolate chip cookie dough makes it easy to enjoy those same flavors in these fast, kid-friendly cups.
—*Charlotte McDaniel, Jacksonville, AL*

Prep: 20 min. • **Bake:** 15 min. + cooling
Makes: 2 dozen

- 1 tube (16½ oz.) refrigerated chocolate chip cookie dough
- ¾ cup miniature marshmallows
- 2 Tbsp. miniature semisweet chocolate chips
- ¼ cup sliced almonds, toasted

1. Preheat oven to 350°. Shape dough into 1¼-in. balls; press evenly onto bottom and up sides of 24 greased mini-muffin cups.
2. Bake until edges are golden, 10-12 minutes. Using the back of a measuring teaspoon, make an indentation in each cup. Immediately place 3 marshmallows and ¼ teaspoon chocolate chips in each cup; sprinkle with almonds. Return to oven; bake 1 minute longer. Cool completely in pans on wire racks.
Note: To toast nuts, spread in a 15x10x1-in. baking pan. Bake at 350° until lightly browned, 5-10 minutes, stirring occasionally. Or place in a dry nonstick skillet and heat over low heat until lightly browned, stirring occasionally.
1 cookie: 103 cal., 5g fat (2g sat. fat), 1mg chol., 64mg sod., 14g carb. (9g sugars, 0 fiber), 1g pro.

LEMON SLICE SUGAR COOKIES

Here's a refreshing variation of my grandma's sugar cookie recipe. Lemon pudding mix and a lemon-tinged icing add a subtle tartness that tingles your taste buds.
—*Melissa Turkington, Camano Island, WA*

Prep: 15 min. + chilling
Bake: 10 min./batch + cooling
Makes: about 2 dozen

- ½ cup unsalted butter, softened
- 1 pkg. (3.4 oz.) instant lemon pudding mix
- ½ cup sugar
- 1 large egg, room temperature
- 2 Tbsp. 2% milk
- 1½ cups all-purpose flour
- 1 tsp. baking powder
- ¼ tsp. salt

ICING
- ⅔ cup confectioners' sugar
- 2 to 4 tsp. lemon juice

1. In a large bowl, cream butter, pudding mix and sugar until light and fluffy. Beat in egg and milk. In another bowl, whisk the flour, baking powder and salt; gradually beat into creamed mixture.
2. Divide dough in half. On a lightly floured surface, shape each into a 6-in.-long roll. Wrap in plastic; refrigerate until firm, about 3 hours.
3. Preheat oven to 375°. Unwrap and cut dough crosswise into ½-in. slices. Place 1 in. apart on ungreased baking sheets. Bake until the edges are light brown, 8-10 minutes. Cool on pans 2 minutes. Remove to wire racks to cool completely.
4. In a small bowl, mix confectioners' sugar and enough lemon juice to reach a drizzling consistency. Drizzle over cookies. Let stand until set.
Freeze option: Place wrapped dough logs in a freezer container and freeze. To use, unwrap frozen logs and cut into slices. Bake as directed, increasing time by 1-2 minutes.
1 cookie: 110 cal., 4g fat (2g sat. fat), 18mg chol., 99mg sod., 17g carb. (11g sugars, 0 fiber), 1g pro.

A

ABC Soup 123
Andouille Sausage Hash 22
Antipasto Bake 75
Antipasto Platter 102
Apple Cinnamon Cake. 268
Apple-Gouda Pigs in a Blanket. 89
Apple Pie a la Mode. 270
Arborio Rice & White Bean Soup 121
Artichoke & Spinach Dip Pizza 88
Asian Chicken Crunch Wraps 241
Asian Pulled Pork Sandwiches 60
Asparagus Nicoise Salad. 236
Asparagus with Horseradish Dip. 96
Aunt Marion's Fruit Salad Dessert 170

B

Bacon Cheeseburger Balls 62
Bacon-Encased Water Chestnuts 82
Bacon Swiss Squares. 49
Bacon-Tomato Salad. 183
Baked Onion Dip. 66
Banana Chip Pancakes. 12
Banana Cream Chocolate Truffles 287
Banana Cream Pie with Cake Mix Crust . . . 312
Barbecued Meatballs 64
BBQ Chicken & Apple Bread Pudding. . . . 235
Berry Breakfast Parfaits 19
Berry Dream Cake. 272
Berry, Lemon & Doughnut Hole Trifle. . . . 280
Berry Smoothie Bowl 52
Berry Tartlets 305
Birthday Cake Freezer Pops 294
Birthday Cake Waffles. 27
Black Forest Tart 313
Blackened Catfish with
    Mango Avocado Salsa 229
Blue Cheese Potato Chips 75
Blueberry Crunch Breakfast Bake. 51
Blueberry Ice Cream Tart. 301
Blueberry Oatmeal 16
Breaded Pork Tenderloin. 220
Breadstick Pizza. 82
Breakfast Relleno. 48
Breakfast Spuds. 43

Broccoli-Chicken Rice Soup 132
Brunch Pizza Squares 12
Buffalo Chicken Deviled Eggs. 104
Buffalo Macaroni & Cheese Bites. 70

C

Cake & Berry Campfire Cobbler. 290
Calzone Pinwheels 68
Camper's Breakfast Hash 36
Campfire Pancakes with
    Peanut Maple Syrup. 47
Can't Leave Alone Bars. 293
Caramel Fudge Cheesecake 282
Caribbean Bread Pudding 273
Carrot Dump Cake 290
Cashew-Chicken Rotini Salad. 175
Cheddar Corn Dog Muffins 160
Cheese & Garlic Biscuits 156
Cheese & Sausage Breakfast Pizza 33
Cheese Broccoli Soup 158
Cheese-Filled Garlic Rolls 132
Cheeseburger Skillet Dinner. 221
Cheesy Bacon Ranch Potato Stuffing 207
Cheesy BBQ Beef Dip. 61
Cheesy Beef Taco Dip 96
Cheesy Cream of Asparagus Soup 150
Cheesy Pizza Rolls. 138
Cheesy Potato Egg Bake. 32
Cheesy Summer Squash Flatbreads 222
Cherry-Almond Tea Mix 64
Cherry-Peach Dumplings 304
Cherry Upside-Down Bread Pudding 308
Chicken & Broccoli Rabe Soup
    with Tortellini 128
Chicken & Waffles 243
Chicken, Asparagus & Corn Chowder. . . . 117
Chicken Chile Rellenos Casserole 222
Chicken Gnocchi Pesto Soup. 135
Chicken Parmesan Slider Bake 92
Chicken Potpie Galette
    with Cheddar-Thyme Crust 227
Chicken Zucchini Casserole. 237
Chile Rellenos Souffle. 9
Chili & Cheese Crustless Quiche 14
Chili Cornbread Salad. 194

Chilled Fruit Cups. 175
Chocolate Mocha Dusted Almonds 66
Chocolate Peanut Butter Chip Cookies. . . 271
Christmas Pizza Squares. 66
Chunky Creamy Chicken Soup 147
Coconut Poppy Seed Cake. 311
Coffee Ice Cream Cookie Cups 286
Collard Greens & Pulled Pork Egg Rolls . . . 87
Colorful Spiral Pasta Salad 164
Confetti Cornbread. 153
Connie's Tortellini Salad. 191
Cookie Swirl Cobbler. 298
Corn & Broccoli in Cheese Sauce. 200
Corn Cakes with Poached Eggs 25
Corn Chowder with Potatoes 142
Corn Spoon Bread 176
Cranberry-Cherry Nut Pie 292
Cranberry Cocktail. 72
Cranberry Pineapple Salad. 207
Cranberry Salad. 212
Cream-Filled Cupcakes 312
Creamy Blueberry Gelatin Salad 184
Creamy Caramel Dip 96
Creamy Carrot Casserole. 172
Creamy Coleslaw 192
Creamy Pineapple Fluff Salad 177
Creamy Ranchified Potatoes. 197
Crunchy Asian Chicken Salad. 249
Crunchy Ramen Salad 167
Crunchy Spinach Casserole 193
Cucumber Shell Salad 213

D

Dad's Favorite Barbecue Meat Loaves. . . 254
Day After Thanksgiving Cookies 277
Deluxe Hash Brown Casserole. 202
Dill Chicken Soup 135
Dilly Cheese Ball. 69
Dilly Veggie Pizza 76
Down South Sweet Tea Cake 311

E

Easy Cheddar Chicken Potpie. 258
Easy Chicken Tamale Pie 257
Easy Four-Layer Chocolate Dessert 278

Easy Irish Cream 106
Easy Meatball Stroganoff.............. 219
Easy Mocha Cream Pie................. 300
Easy Nutella Cheesecake.............. 314
Easy Parmesan Biscuits............... 132
Easy Pecan Pie Bars 298
Easy Pumpkin Spice Pudding Pie 295
Easy Tortellini Spinach Soup 147
Egg Baskets Benedict 39
Egg-Topped Wilted Salad 57

F

Farmhouse Ham Chowder 118
Favorite Cheesy Potatoes 210
Festive Apple Dip 80
Fluffy Green Grape Salad.............. 205
Freezer Strawberry Shortbread
    Dessert 269
French Lentil & Carrot Soup 149
Fresh Raspberry Icebox Cake.......... 303
Fried Chicken & Pulled Pork
    Cornbread Poppers 97
Frozen Peanut Butter & Chocolate
    Terrine 288
Fruity Croissant Puff 42
Fruity Frappe......................... 17
Fruity Waffle Parfaits 45

G

Garlic Knots.......................... 120
Garlic Salmon Linguine 241
Garlic Spaghetti Squash
    with Meat Sauce 250
Garlic Tilapia with Mushroom Risotto ... 227
Grandmother's Toad in a Hole 14
Green Chili Chops with Sweet Potatoes ... 260
Green Onion Rolls 115
Green Pea Casserole.................. 170
Grilled Banana Brownie Sundaes 302
Grilled Sausage-Basil Pizzas 262
Gumbo in a Jiffy 121

H

Ham & Broccoli Cornbread 140
Ham & Cheese Biscuit Stacks........... 62
Ham & Cheese Puffs 101
Hash Brown Pancakes with
    Smoked Salmon & Dill Cream......... 26
Hawaiian Ham Strata 11

Hazelnut Cake Squares 282
Hearty Homemade Chicken Noodle Soup 142
Hearty Mac & Cheese 250
Hearty Vegetable Soup................ 159
Herbed Bread Twists................. 123
Herbed Parmesan Bread.............. 116
Herbed Rice Pilaf 180
Holiday Brussels Sprouts 181
Honey Buffalo Meatball Sliders 81
Honey Chicken Stir-Fry................ 228
Honey-Squash Dinner Rolls 150

I

Italian Chicken Meatball & Bean Soup ... 126
Italian Crumb-Crusted Beef Roast...... 231
Italian Herb & Cheese Breadsticks 131
Italian Meatball Buns.................. 103
Italian Wedding Soup Supper 246

J

Jerk Chicken with Tropical Couscous.... 230

K

Kids' Favorite Chili 137

L

Lasagna Cups 246
Layered Candy Cane Dessert 309
Layered Cornbread Salad 189
Lemon Berry Dump Cake.............. 274
Lemon-Berry Ice Cream Pie 289
Lemon Cheesecake Tarts.............. 314
Lemon Slice Sugar Cookies............ 317
Lemonade Icebox Pie 270
Lemony Tortellini Bacon Salad.......... 244
Loaded Chicken Carbonara Cups....... 238
Loaded Pulled Pork Cups.............. 109
Loaded Tater Tot Bake 28
Luscious Lime Slush................... 82

M

Macaroni Coleslaw.................... 188
Make-Ahead Biscuits & Gravy Bake 34
Makeover Swiss Chicken Supreme...... 238
Mango & Grilled Chicken Salad 242
Marshmallow Fruit Dip................ 65
Mediterranean Artichoke & Red Pepper
    Roll-Ups........................... 78
Mediterranean Bulgur Bowl 233

Mexican Deviled Eggs.................. 72
Mexican Fondue 108
Mexican Street Corn Bake 178
Mini Grilled Cheese 104
Mini Ham Quiches 35
Mini Mac & Cheese Dogs 101
Mini Sausage Pies 232
Mini Sausage Quiches................. 46
Minty Pineapple Fruit Salad 199
Mississippi Mud Pie.................. 284
Mom's Chocolate Bread 134
Monkey Bread Biscuits................ 126
Muffin-Tin Tamale Cakes 136
Mushroom Cheese Bread 112
Mushroom Tortellini Soup 124
Mushrooms & Peas Rice Pilaf.......... 199

N

Navy Bean Vegetable Soup 123
Nectarine & Beet Salad................ 169
9-Layer Greek Dip 93
No-Bake Chocolate Hazelnut
    Thumbprints 296
Nutella Hand Pies..................... 279
Nutty Broccoli Slaw 204

O

Old-Fashioned Oatmeal Raisin
    Cookies 284
One-Skillet Pork Chop Supper 253
Orange Dream Pull-Apart Bread 31
Orange-Glazed Meatballs 63
Orange Marmalade Breakfast Bake 37

P

Peanut Butter Rocky Road
    Cheesecake 274
Pesto Pasta & Potatoes 185
Pesto Pull-Apart Bread................ 148
Pina Colada Carrot Salad.............. 213
Pina Colada Fruit Dip................. 61
Pistachio Brownie Toffee Bars 306
Pizza Macaroni & Cheese.............. 218
Pizza Rolls 73
Polenta Parmigiana................... 75
Pork Edamame Soup 145
Poutine 208
Pressure-Cooker Black Bean
    Chicken Nachos..................... 84

Pressure-Cooker Ham & Cheddar
   Breakfast Casserole.................. 20
Prosciutto Pinwheels 90
Puff Pastry Danishes.................... 19
Pulled Pork Grilled Cheese 224
Pumpkin-Chocolate Chip Pancakes 21
Pumpkin Pie Cupcakes
   with Whipped Cream 306

Q

Quick & Easy Baklava Squares.......... 85
Quick Barbecued Beans 186
Quick Chicken & Wild Rice Soup........ 118
Quick Focaccia Bread 161
Quick Tacos al Pastor 227

R

Ramen Noodle Salad................... 201
Ramen Sliders 94
Ranch Potato Salad.................... 178
Ravioli Lasagna 245
Red Velvet Cinnamon Rolls 40
Reuben Rounds........................ 79
Reuben Waffle Potato Appetizers 102
Rich & Creamy Mashed Potatoes........ 183
Roasted Red Pepper Triangles........... 77
Roasted Tomato Quiche 54
Roasted Vegetable & Goat Cheese
   Quiche 51
Roasted Veggie Strudel 251
Rocky Road Cookie Cups 317
Root Beer Float Pie 296
Rosemary Cheddar Muffins 155

S

Salmon & Artichoke Quiche Squares 39
Salmon Party Spread 95
Salmon Sweet Potato Soup............. 133
Salsa Rice............................ 168
Saucy Chicken & Tortellini............. 217
Sausage & Apple Cornbread Bake 53
Sausage & Spinach Calzones 265
Sausage Bacon Bites................... 13
Sausage Cheese Biscuits............... 31
Sausage Dressing 191
Sausage, Egg & Cheddar Farmer's
   Breakfast........................... 40
Sausage Spinach Bake................. 24
Savory Biscuit-Breadsticks 129

Scalloped Potatoes & Ham 165
Shortcut Coconut-Pecan Chocolate
   Tassies............................. 282
Shrimp Egg Drop Soup................. 139
Shrimp Lover Squares 87
Simple Iced Coffee 22
Skinny Cobb Salad.................... 261
Slow-Cooked Beef Vegetable Soup...... 113
Slow-Cooked Meatball Soup........... 158
Slow-Cooked Mexican Beef Soup 126
Slow-Cooked Wild Rice................ 173
Slow-Cooker Blueberry Cobbler 316
Slow-Cooker Cherry Buckle 285
Slow-Cooker Chorizo Breakfast
   Casserole 45
Slow-Cooker Ham & Eggs 22
Slow-Cooker Italian Mushrooms 209
Slow-Cooker Sausage & Waffle Bake..... 56
Slow-Cooker Spicy Pork Chili 125
Slow-Cooker Spinach & Artichoke Dip.... 98
S'mores Monkey Bread Muffins........ 118
So-Easy Snack Mix 69
Southwest-Style Shepherd's Pie 254
Southwestern Fish Tacos.............. 235
Spiced Cappuccino Kiss Cookies 297
Spicy Peanut Chicken Chili 141
Spicy Rice Casserole.................. 240
Spicy Shredded Beef Sandwiches....... 248
Spinach & Tortellini Soup.............. 152
Spinach Dip in a Bread Bowl........... 78
Spinach-Egg Breakfast Pizzas.......... 29
Spinach Feta Strata 17
Spinach Feta Turnovers 256
Strawberry-Banana Pudding Cake...... 276
Strawberry-Chicken Salad
   with Buttered Pecans................ 196
Strawberry Shortcake Puffs............ 314
Stromboli Sandwich 90
Sweet Pea Pesto Crostini.............. 71
Swiss & Caraway Flatbreads 144

T

Tandoori Chicken Panini............... 242
Tangy Bacon Green Beans............. 167
Tasty Turkey Skillet 264
Taylor's Jalapeno Poppers 104
Teriyaki Salmon Bundles............... 98
Tex-Mex Breakfast Haystacks 10
Toffee Brownie Trifle.................. 305

Tortellini Bake........................ 262
Tropical Cranberry Cobbler............ 281
Turkey & Cornbread Stuffing Rellenos... 216
Turkey & Dumpling Soup 161
Turkey Chili 115
Turkey Lo Mein 252
Turkey Ramen Noodle Salad........... 186
Turkey Salsa Bowls
   with Tortilla Wedges................. 259
Turkey Sausage, Butternut Squash &
   Kale Soup 131

V

Veggie Cheese Soup 131
Very Vanilla French Toast.................8

W

Warm Broccoli Cheese Dip 107
Weekday Beef Stew.................... 225
Weeknight Taco Soup 139
Weeknight Turkey Tortilla Soup 116
White Bean & Chicken Enchilada Soup ... 157

Z

Zesty Garbanzo Sausage Soup 155